INTERCOUNTRY ADOPTION

INTERCOUNTRY ADOPTION

A Multinational Perspective

Edited by
Howard Altstein and Rita J. Simon

New York
Westport, Connecticut
London

Library of Congress Cataloging-in-Publication Data

Intercountry adoption : a multinational perspective / edited by Howard
   Altstein and Rita J. Simon.
      p. cm.
   Includes bibliographical references and index.
   ISBN 0-275-93287-7
   1. Intercountry adoption—History.   2. Intercountry adoption—Case
studies.   I. Altstein, Howard.   II. Simon, Rita James.
   HV875.5.I54   1991
   362.7′34—dc20   90-7380

Library of Congress Catalog Card Number: 90-7380
ISBN: 0-275-93287-7

First published in 1991

Praeger Publishers, One Madison Avenue, New York, NY 10010
An imprint of Greenwood Publishing Group, Inc.

Printed in the United States of America

The paper used in this book complies with the
Permanent Paper Standard issued by the National
Information Standards Organization (Z39.48-1984).

10 9 8 7 6 5 4 3 2 1

To Sam and Rachel;

To David, Judith & Daniel; and

To Children Everywhere.

CONTENTS

Part III: THE MIDDLE EAST

TABLES AND FIGURES

Tables

ACRONYMS

ACS   adopted child syndrome
BAP   British Adoption Project
FACE   Families Adopting Children Everywhere
ICA   intercountry adoption
INS   Immigration and Naturalization Service (United States)
LAPA   Latin America Parents Association
ROK   Republic of Korea
SOD   Stars of David

1

Introduction

HOWARD ALTSTEIN
RITA J. SIMON

This book describes the experiences of foreign-born adoptees and their families in seven societies spread across three continents. It also provides a brief history of intercountry adoption (ICA), specifies the rules and procedures for ICA in different societies, and evaluates the pros and cons, the successes and failures of ICA in each of the seven nations.

ICA began primarily as a North American philanthropic response to the devastation of Europe in World War II that resulted in thousands of orphaned children. When the European continent was rebuilt and its economy stabilized, the problem of orphaned children was basically solved. But a revitalized economy, coupled with a reduction in Europe's male population (again a result of World War II), led to an increased rate of childlessness. Western societies then turned to Third-World countries with high birth rates for a solution to the dearth of healthy infants in the West.

Western interest in ICA in the 1980s, however, is a far cry from its interest following World War II. In the mid-1940s, Western countries were interested in ICA as a solution to the problem of parentless children. By the 1980s, their interest was sparked primarily by the needs of childless couples. The increase in the number of childless Western couples is the result of a combination of factors, including a declining birth rate, a rise in the level of infertility, and the widespread use of readily available contraceptives.

HISTORICAL PERSPECTIVE

Most writers date the popularization of adoption with the Pharaoh's daughter snatching Moses from the bulrushes of the Nile, although some would argue that Moses was actually a foster child in that he lived with the Pharaoh's daughter but was nursed by and eventually returned to his birth mother. History, however, has rarely viewed adoption from the perspective of a child's security. Rather, adoption was usually considered a way to consolidate property, assure inheritance, or guarantee accession to power. An example of the last case is the five "good emperors of Rome." Nerva reigned from A.D. 96–98 and adopted Trajan as his successor. Trajan then ruled from A.D. 98–117 and, in turn, adopted Hadrian to be his successor. Hadrian, who ruled from A.D. 117–138, adopted Antoninus Pius. The latter ruled from A.D. 138–161 and adopted Marcus Aurelius, insuring his succession. Marcus Aurelius reigned as emperor for 19 years (A.D. 161–180), but he broke the adoption series by elevating his birth son, Commodus, as heir, and Commodus proved to be a disaster.[1]

Collecting information in preparation for writing this volume, we became sensitized to the "two-camp explanation" for the ICA movement, and we believe it important to present both views as objectively as possible. Since the 1960s, Third-World countries have had a surplus of healthy infants; thus, they offered an easy solution to the problem of childlessness in Western societies. What could be more humane, Westerners reasoned, than to remove seemingly unwanted, even discarded, children from what appeared to be lives of misery and poverty and transplant them into an environment where material comfort and social opportunity abounded? All would benefit: the childless couple would be fulfilled, and the adopted children would be given unprecedented opportunities.[2]

But what the West has generally viewed as charitable, humane—even noble—behavior, developing countries have come to define as imperialistic, self-serving, and a return to a form of colonialism in which whites exploit and steal natural resources.[3] In the 1970s and 1980s, children were the natural resource being exploited and out of which developing nations were being cheated.

Sending and receiving countries agree that the following three factors are usually present when large-scale ICA takes place: a civil or international war, an imbalance in socioeconomic conditions between sending and receiving countries, and cooperative links between the social and child welfare agencies of the countries in question. In most cases of large-scale ICA, all three of these factors have been present, although there are some notable exceptions. For example, as of 1989, the 14-year fratricidal Lebanese civil war had not produced a significant number of ICAs from Lebanon into the West, even though France maintains close social, economic, and political ties with that country. Between 1979 and 1987, only 126 Lebanese children were adopted by American families. Some attempts to facilitate ICA from Lebanon have been made by the Antiochian Christian Orthodox Archdiocese of North America through its Children's Relief Fund, but these efforts have not produced appreciable results. Costs per adoption are estimated to be between $15,000 and $20,000—extremely high by any standard.[4]

Nigeria provides a second exception. Even though the Nigerian civil war of the 1960s resulted in thousands of children being made orphans, Nigeria spurned all foreign adoption offers. African countries have not generally sanctioned the adoption of their children by foreigners. For example, only 137 African children were adopted by U.S. citizens between 1979 and 1987. In 1989, a small adoption agency was established in the United States exclusively for ICA into the United States of African-born children.[5] Known as Americans for African Adoptions, the agency is active in Ethiopia, West Africa, and Mali. No adoption figures are yet available, but the numbers are probably rather small.

NUMBERS OF CHILDREN INVOLVED

Agency-sponsored ICA began at the end of World War II when European orphans, particularly from Germany and Greece, were adopted by American families.[6] As a result of the Displaced Persons Act of 1948—the first legislative provision pertaining to orphan immigrants (among other categories of refugees)—4,065 "orphans" entered the United States.[7] Combined with the number of orphans entering the United States under the Refugee Acts of 1953,[8] this figure increased to 5,814. Almost one-third of these children (1,806) were born in Greece, and they comprised the neediest group of orphaned European children—primarily as a result of World War II, but also as a function of the Greek civil war that had begun in 1946. During the same period, 2,418 Asian-born children were brought to the United States through ICAs, and two-thirds (1,602) of these were Japanese. The post–World War II period turned out to be the first and shortest era of ICA, lasting only about five years, from 1948 to 1953.

The second phase of ICA, the one that now appears to be slowly waning, began in the mid-1950s, again as a Western response to children made parentless by an international conflict—the Korean War. The adoption of Korean-born children by Westerners presaged an era in child placement different from the era of adopting racially and culturally similar children after World War II. For the first time in history, relatively large numbers of Western couples, mostly in the United States, were adopting children who were racially and culturally different from themselves. Between 1953 and 1962, approximately 15,000 foreign-born children were adopted by American families.[9] In the ten years ending in 1976, approximately 32,000 additional foreign-born children were adopted by U.S. citizens, and about 65 percent of these children came from Asia, primarily from the Republic of Korea (ROK). To illustrate how much ICA has increased in popularity among Americans, during the four years between 1984 and 1987 almost 38,000 foreign-born children, 60 percent from ROK, were adopted by American families.[10]

Between 1966 and 1976, some 60 percent of the West European children adopted by Americans were born in West Germany or Italy.[11] It is interesting to note that, although Western European families adopted many non-European-born children, West Germany continued to export orphans until as recently as 1981. From 1976 to 1981, 304 West German-born children were adopted by Americans. One explanation holds that many of these were racially mixed children fathered by black U.S. servicemen stationed in Germany, children who might have a difficult time being fully accepted into mainstream German society.

American couples adopted 77,908 foreign-born children between 1977 and 1987. In 1987 alone, 10,097 foreign-born children were adopted in the United States, 50 percent more than in 1974. It is worth noting, however, that although ICA involves thousands of children, these numbers are still comparatively small when placed into the perspective of national adoption figures.[12] (There are an estimated 140,000–160,000 adoptions in the United States every year.) The rate of increased ICAs into the United States appears to be matched in Western Europe. It is estimated that about 10,000 intercountry adoptees enter Western Europe each year, a figure that approximates one percent of all European "new births."

Recent developments in the ROK and other countries that previously sanctioned almost unrestricted adoption of their children by Westerners indicate that the number of children available for adoption will soon be reduced.[13] Ecuador, Brazil, and the Philippines have already curtailed or eliminated the practice of allowing children to leave their respective countries for adoption purposes. In most cases, the reasons these countries give for deciding to curb the practice are "irregularities," usually defined as the selling of children.[14] Less explicitly stated is a nationalistic resentment against the practice developing in these countries.

KOREAN AND OTHER ASIAN ADOPTIONS

From the 1950s until the early 1970s, the ROK was the main provider of healthy infants to the United States and Western Europe. For 30 years, the ROK allowed almost unrestricted adoption of its orphaned and abandoned children by foreigners. Although no exact figures exist, it is estimated that in the 30 years between the early 1950s and the 1980s, more than 100,000 Korean children were adopted by Western families.[15] But for a number of reasons—including the end of the Vietnam War, an overall improvement in the economies of Asian countries, and the development of domestic child welfare programs that encouraged domestic adoptions—the 1970s saw changes in the pattern of ICA from Asia. Another important factor that reduced the numbers of Korean children adopted by Westerners was 1980 legislation liberalizing the availability of abortion in ROK.

The occupation of South Vietnam by the North Vietnamese brought with it a new attitude toward allowing children to leave Vietnam for adoption, especially by Americans. North Vietnam halted the former government's almost unrestricted policy of allowing Vietnamese children to be adopted by foreigners, especially Americans. In 1975, when Vietnam was ruled by a government friendly to the United States, 655 Vietnamese children had been adopted by Americans; in 1980, however, practically no children were available for adoption. The widespread and embarrassing publicity surrounding the U.S. government's involvement in "Operation Baby Lift" contributed to the policies enacted by the new government in Saigon.[16] While Vietnamese authorities were halting foreign adoptions of their country's children, they were also struggling with the problem of how to treat children born to Vietnamese mothers but fathered by American citizens. The much politicized "Amerasian" issue, however, should not be confused with ICA. In the vast majority of cases, ICA deals with non-blood-related child custody, whereas the Amerasian issue is concerned with family reunification.

Although Asia remained a prime source of adoptees for Western couples, the relationship between sending and receiving countries— particularly from the Asian perspective—was never a totally comfortable one. Asia's reliability as a permanent source of children was therefore questionable, and for good reasons.[17]

Recent statements by ROK government officials demonstrate why Western fears of ROK's reliability as a "sender" nation appear justified. In a front-page story in the *Washington Post*, the head of the ROK's Ministry of Health and Social Affairs' adoption unit was quoted as saying that "foreign adoptions in the not-too-distant future will decrease to a negligible number."[18] The *New York Times* reported that by the beginning of 1990, the ROK would be "phasing out its program of sending babies from its orphanages overseas for adoption." In 1989, 3,552 Korean-born children were adopted by Americans. The figure for 1986 was 6,188.[19]

In 1988, Americans who watched the Olympic Games being telecast from the ROK viewed a short segment on ICA from Korea. The NBC commentator described how some Koreans thought the adoption of Korean children by foreigners was a "national shame" and an "embarrassment."[20] Korean officials had asked leading adoption agencies in Korea to temporarily suspend all ICAs from Korea during the Olympics because they did not want international attention focused on the practice.[21]

Because of these events—and in response to North Korea's continual goading that the ROK was selling its children to the West—by mid-1989, the ROK was communicating to the West that it was rethinking its policy of almost unrestricted exportation of its orphans. By 1989, the four ROK adoption agencies (Eastern Child Welfare, Korean Social Services, Social Welfare Society, and Holt International) contracting with U.S. agencies to place Korean children with American families had begun to reduce the number of children allowed to leave the country for adoption purposes. Perhaps taking the lead from the ROK, India, the Philippines, and Hong Kong have also reexamined their administrative and legal procedures concerning ICAs, and waiting periods for children from these countries have consequently grown much longer.

LATIN AMERICAN ADOPTIONS

The events in the ROK have directed American interest closer to U.S. borders, toward Latin American countries experiencing civil wars and economic instability. The number of children adopted into the United States from Latin America increased almost threefold—from 332 to 977— between 1973 and 1975.[22] Although this figure represents only 17 percent of total ICAs into the United States in 1975, it demonstrates a substantial increase since 1973, when only 8 percent of all intercountry adoptees were from Latin America.[23] By 1987, Latin America accounted for 23 percent of all children entering the United States for adoption, an increase of 15 percent since 1973 (compared with a 4 percent increase in ICAs from ROK during the same period).

As shown in the following chart, the seven-year interval between 1980 and 1987 saw a 51 percent increase in all ICAs into the United States— from 5,122 children in 1980 to almost 10,095 in 1987. Interestingly, although the number of intercountry adoptees into the United States from Latin America increased by 798 children during that period, the percentage of total adoptees from Latin America actually declined—from 29 percent in 1980 to 23 percent in 1987.

ICA: Total Numbers and Numbers from Latin America

	1973	1975	1980	1987
Total	4,015	5,633	5,122	10,095
Latin America	332	977	1,498	2,296

Note: Table is a compilation of data found in Resnick in Philip Bean (ed.), *Adoption: Essays in Social Policy, Law, and Sociology* (London: Tavistock, 1984) and *Beunas Noticias*, p. 11.

Because supplying countries are primarily developing nations—where gender usually plays an important part in ascribed status—one might expect to find more female than male orphans leaving their respective birth countries for foreign adoption. As shown in the following chart, however, this assumption is not entirely borne out. In 1986, for example, although more females than males were released for adoption by the ROK and India, there was no difference in the gender of the children released by countries in Latin America.

Children Released to ICA by Gender, 1986 (%)

	Male	Female
Korea	40	60
India	40	60
Latin America	50	50

EVALUATIONS OF THE ICA EXPERIENCE

Several studies concerning ICA policy issues were conducted in the 1970s and 1980s.[24] The medical literature covered a broad range of issues—from relatively minor maladies such as sleeping problems among intercountry adoptees to the possibility that adoptees might be carriers of such infectious diseases as hepatitis B and tuberculosis. In some cases, particularly if a child was known to be born to a mother who was HIV-positive or who had a history of hemophilia, AIDS screening was recommended (especially for children born in Brazil, Venezuela, Haiti, and Honduras).

When empirical pieces appeared, they were usually very limited examinations in scope and size and most often involved case-study designs.[25] Several studies, however, did have large enough samples to be of scientific interest. In 1980, Bagley and Young reported a follow-up study of approximately 100 abandoned Hong Kong–born girls adopted by British families. By ages 12–18, regardless of the emphasis placed on Chinese attitudes in their adoptive homes, these children were "Anglicized," had high self-esteem, and had only intellectual (as opposed to emotional) interest in Hong Kong. Interestingly, parents reported "patronizing attitudes" on the part of extended family members toward these children.[26]

In 1985, 1986, and 1987, three studies were published that examined the psychosocial adjustment of intercountry adoptees living in Europe. The first two were empirical investigations using samples large enough for scientific interest, and the third was an edited book that reported worldwide policies and programs relating to ICA. In the 1985 study, Kühl had a sample of 145 teenage intercountry adoptees in Germany.[27] In the 1986[28] and 1987[29] studies, Hoksbergen concluded that, for the most part, intercountry adoptees in the Netherlands had made positive psychosocial adjustments—with themselves, their families, and the larger community.

In October 1987, the *Open Door Society News* reported a study by Edward Suh that involved an unstated number of families in Iowa who had adopted a total of 172 Korean-born children.[30] The parents reported that their main areas of difficulty lay in their children's language development, physical ailments, and disciplinary problems.

In 1988, Estela Andujo[31] reported on the ethnic identities of 60 native Mexican children adopted by Hispanic and white American parents. Although Andujo found many similarities between the two groups, children adopted by white parents tended to identify themselves as Americans, whereas those adopted by Hispanics identified themselves as Mexican-Americans. Differences were also found using color as a self-descriptor. Cross-ethnically adopted children were almost three times more likely than in-ethnically adopted children to use color as an identifying characteristic.

Another study in 1988 described language development in 70 foreign-born adults who had been adopted as children in Sweden.[32] Substantively, this report did not reveal important psychosocial findings, but interesting methodological comments were made. The study's translator stated: "[I]t is extremely difficult to find a group of internationally adopted persons who represent anything else but themselves. The number of background variables makes it evident that you must have an enormously large sample if you want to generalize from your results."

WHY SO FEW NATIVE-BORN U.S. ADOPTEES?

Pressure continues to mount from childless couples in the United States and Western European countries for additional sources of healthy orphans. In the United States alone, two million couples and one million single individuals wanted to adopt in 1989.[33] This pressure stems from a number of factors: a steadily declining birth rate in the industrialized world coupled with population increases in the developing world, growing infertility among certain age groups in the West (seemingly tied to later-age marriages), and the availability of reliable methods of voluntarily terminating pregnancy, specifically abortion. Each of these factors plays an important role in the pent-up Western demand for adoptable children.

Birth Rates

While birth rates in the West have been falling for about 200 years, developing nations have been experiencing consistently higher birth rates and lower infant mortality.[34] For example, from 1980 to 1985, the average numbers of births per 1,000 people in the United States and Holland were 15.7 and 12.2, respectively. By contrast, Colombia and Brazil (two countries supplying orphans to the West) had birth rates twice as high—31 and 20.6 per 1,000 people, respectively.[35] In 1986, the United States recorded its lowest birth rate since records have been kept, 64.9 live births per 1,000 women aged 15–44.[36] Overall, it is estimated that developing countries will continue to outpace the West in population growth, doubling to eight billion people in the next three decades.[37]

Excluding Japan, this population imbalance is primarily a white/non-white issue that has influenced the West's looking toward the vast pool of non-Western-born children as potential adoptees. Many of these children are born into societies that are having difficulty sustaining their populations or are beset by internal and external conflicts. It is easy to see how charges of racism, racial arrogance, and exploitation can be leveled at the West for assuming that developing societies may not be able to care for their infants and thus may view ICA as a means of dealing with their increasing populations.

Infertility

One factor affecting U.S. birth rates is the apparently strong correlation between age at first marriage and subsequent infertility.[38] One of every six American couples between the ages of 15 and 44 is estimated to have some type of infertility problem.[39] Even though the overall infertility rate for American couples was almost 6 percent in 1982[40] (up from 2.3 percent in 1965), the rate for women 30–34 years old was 14 percent, and for women 35 to 39 it was 25 percent.[41] Should any of these infertile couples want to adopt American-born infants, only one in 40 would be successful.[42] In fact, the overall ratio of available U.S.-born adoptees to potential adopters could be as high as 100 to one.[43]

Abortion

The increasing Western abortion rate is another factor that seems to skew the imbalance between couples who want to adopt and the availability of adoptable children in the United States. The abortion factor presents something of an oversimplified cause and effect analogy: namely, that increased abortions cause a reduction in the number of adoptable children. A few figures might help place this perception in some type of perspective. The following chart shows that, in 1975, a reported 1.034 million abortions were performed in the United States. By 1985, this number had climbed to 1.588 million.[44]

Number of U.S. Abortions (in Millions), 1975–1985

	1975	1982	1984	1985
Abortions	1.034	1.573	1.577	1.588

During the decade ending in 1989, a reported three of every 100 American women between the ages of 15 and 44 had abortions.[45] Of the one million American teenagers who became pregnant in 1988 (and every year for the past five years), 400,000 had abortions.[46]

The following charts further define who is having the 1.588 million known abortions annually.[47]

Abortions per 1,000 Women by Age

Age	Number of Abortions
15–17	32.2
18–19	62.4
20–24	54.6
25–29	33.0
30–34	17.9
35–39	9.8
>40	3.4

Abortions per 1,000 Women by Annual Income ($)

Income	Abortion Rates
<11,000	62.5
11,000–24,900	32.5
>25,000	16.5

These figures show that, for the most part, women having abortions are between the ages of 15 and 29. Almost one-third of pregnant American females between the ages of 15 and 17 abort their pregnancies, as do two-thirds of 18- to 19-year-olds. Of women between 20 and 24, 55 percent also voluntarily terminate their pregnancies. Slightly more than half of these pregnant women are nonwhite, and almost two-thirds have annual incomes of less than $11,000. More than 5 percent of all nonwhite

American women have abortions annually, whereas only 2 to 3 percent of white women do. The profile that emerges from these data is the classic image of the underclass in American society: young, poor, and nonwhite. Most likely, low levels of education and a lack of marketable job skills also characterize these women; education and occupation are not only closely tied, but they are also highly associated with race and income.

Some observers see an inverse relationship between the high abortion rate and the low number of children available for adoption. Their argument holds that many of the aborted fetuses, if allowed to go full term, would be surrendered by their mothers for adoption. According to this hypothesis, abortion rates are a powerful factor linked to the dwindling supply of U.S.-born potential adoptees. The argument rests on the assumption that many women unable to abort would voluntarily surrender their newborns for adoption, but data suggest that this assumption is erroneous. For example, even though the percentage of first-born children born to or conceived by unwed American women between 1985 and 1988 rose to 40 percent, only 4–6 percent of women aged 15–44 surrendered their infants for adoption. This leaves the overwhelming majority of unwed mothers attempting to raise their children alone.[48]

Of children born to teenagers (15 to 19 years old), the percentage placed for adoption (8 percent) is slightly higher than the national average. However, less than one percent of black teenage women place their children for adoption—even though 79 percent of all first-time black births or conceptions from 1985 to 1988 occurred in unwed black women under 30 years old.[49] According to William Pierce, President of the National Committee for Adoption, 90 percent of white unwed mothers and 99 percent of black unwed mothers opt to keep their children rather than place them for adoption.[50] Even when unwed motherhood was more stigmatized than it is today, only 30 percent of single mothers surrendered their children for adoption.[51] It should also be noted that about 20 percent of all abortions are performed on married women, who rarely relinquish their children for adoption.

It appears then that two of the three factors discussed at the beginning of this section—a declining Western birth rate coupled with an expanding Third-World population, and increasing rates of Western infertility—have lowered the number of children available for adoption in the West. They also explain why Western couples continue to look toward the Third World for a solution to their childlessness.

ADOPTED CHILD SYNDROME

A controversial term has recently been coined for describing adopted children—*adopted child syndrome* or *ACS*. Broadly defined, ACS refers to a set of deviant behaviors typical of some adoptees. We have chosen to include a general discussion of ACS in this chapter because of its timeliness and significance to the field. It should be noted, however, that ACS is not recognized as a diagnostic category by the American Psychiatric Association in its manual of mental disorders.[52] We also want to emphasize that the vast majority of all types of adoptions (relative and nonrelative, transracial, and ICA)—some say as many as 95 percent—are highly successful arrangements requiring no intervention by mental health practitioners.[53] And an overwhelming number of adoptions involving children beyond the age of five, perhaps even older than nine, turn out to be successful.[54] In fact, a well-designed 1985 study found that, not only are adoptees much more confident in their judgments than non-adoptees, but they also tend to view their adoptive parents as more helpful, predictable, and comforting than nonadoptees do their birth parents.[55] A 1982 investigation involving more than 5,000 people concluded that "the majority of adoptions can justly be characterized as successes."[56]

Most adoption investigators agree, however, that adoptees are more likely than non-adoptees to receive mental health services.[57] If, as it is estimated, the nonrelative adoptions account for about 1 or 2 percent of all children in the United States, then the approximate 4.6 percent of all nonrelative adoptees referred for help with emotional difficulties does make them somewhat overrepresented on the rolls of human service providers.[58] Some figures suggest that adoptees constitute 5 percent of all children referred for outpatient services and 10 percent of children in inpatient facilities.[59] But these comparative figures reveal little if anything beyond numerical indicators. We do not know the conditions under which these children were referred, whether the events precipitating referral were chronic or acute; nor do we know the diagnoses and prognoses.

David Kirschner, the originator of the term ACS, estimates that about 10 percent of all adoptees manifest behaviors that could fall into the category broadly defined as ACS. Speaking at the 1987 American Adoption Congress,[60] Kirschner described such behaviors as pathological lying, shallow or manipulative relationships, truancy, stealing, promiscuity, setting fires, educational difficulties, and so on. He also indicated that these adoptees may demonstrate low frustration tolerances, low self-images, and several other negative behavior patterns.[61]

An important question that should be answered before this syndrome becomes accepted is the extent to which all adolescents engage in the acting-out behaviors described by Kirschner and experience low self-image and low tolerance for frustration. Developmentally, certain "normatively deviant" (i.e., expected) behaviors are attached to specific developmental stages, particularly adolescence. When these behaviors are seen through the perspective of a child's being adopted, they may be attributed to the adoptive status itself—a process known as "labeling."

Kirschner also indicated that the results of a survey he conducted of Long Island–area mental health professionals suggest that adoptees may be more apt to experience emotional difficulties than nonadoptees. Although it is generally recognized that adoptees are more likely than nonadoptees to be in clinical treatment, the explanations for this set the stage for controversy. Are adoptees in treatment because they are experiencing greater difficulties in daily living, or are they proportionally overrepresented because of nonpsychiatric factors? For example, what role do inherited genetic determinants and prenatal experiences play? Are women who are intent upon surrendering their infants for adoption more prone to drug and alcohol abuse during pregnancy and not as medically responsible as other women? What effect do preadoption social experiences (e.g., quality of preadoption placements, and prior physical or sexual abuse or neglect) have on these children? What is the impact of being a member of a family that is aware of and sensitive to available mental health resources—a family "acculturated" into the help-seeking mode by its preadoption experiences with social services (e.g., home and personal investigation) and financially able to afford such services? Could these factors help explain why adoptees (and their families) have a greater proclivity to seek professional emotional support, or do adoptees in fact have more emotional problems (or fewer coping skills) than nonadoptees? Few data exist to conclusively answer these questions.

One can only speculate on what relationship, if any, exists between ICA and ACS. No large, long-term study has been conducted that addresses any possible connection. One might assume that intercountry adoptees experience both grief and abandonment at being simultaneously relinquished by their birth parents and removed from their cultural and ethnic roots. However, it is not known whether this would impact upon developing ACS or increase the likelihood of requiring psychotherapy.

APPENDIX
Children Adopted Abroad by U.S. Parents, 1948–1987

1948-1962

Korea	4,162	22%
Greece	3,116	16%
Japan	2,987	13%
Germany	1,845	10%
Austria	744	4%
Other countries	6,376	
TOTAL	19,230	

1963

Korea	370	25%
Italy	259	17%
Greece	177	12%
Japan	168	11%
Other Asian	84	6%
Hong Kong	77	5%
Other countries	346	
TOTAL	1,481	

1964

Korea	520	31%
Italy	208	12%
Japan	179	11%
Greece	139	8%
Hong Kong	106	6%
China (Taiwan)	71	4%
Other coutries	457	
TOTAL	1,680	

1965

Korea	466	32%
Italy	169	12%
Greece	116	8%
Japan	116	8%
Germany	87	6%
Hong Kong	66	5%
Other countries	437	
TOTAL	1,457	

1966

Korea	436	26%
Germany	320	19%
Italy	148	9%
Japan	127	8%
Greece	112	7%
China (Taiwan)	77	5%
Other countries	466	
TOTAL	1,686	

1967

Germany	563	30%
Korea	478	25%
Italy	134	7%
Japan	91	5%
England	81	4%
Philippines	72	4%
Other countries	486	
TOTAL	1,905	

1968

Korea	515	32%
Germany	349	22%
Philippines	98	6%
Japan	95	6%
Italy	80	5%
Vietnam	67	4%
Other countries	408	
TOTAL	1,612	

1969

Korea	746	36%
Germany	290	14%
Canada	257	12%
Japan	91	4%
England	90	4%
China (Taiwan)	75	4%
Other countries	531	
TOTAL	2,080	

1970

Korea	845	35%
Canada	339	14%
Germany	307	13%
Philippines	141	6%
England	94	4%
Japan	92	4%
Other countries	591	
TOTAL	2,409	

1971

Korea	1,174	43%
Canada	345	13%
Germany	195	11%
Philippines	153	6%
Vietnam	89	3%
Japan	88	3%
Other countries	680	
TOTAL	2,724	

1972		
Korea	1,585	52%
Canada	355	12%
Germany	204	7%
Philippines	136	4%
Vietnam	119	4%
Japan	88	3%
Other countries	536	
TOTAL	**3,023**	

1973		
Korea	2,183	54%
Vietnam	324	8%
Canada	289	7%
Philippines	205	5%
Germany	197	5%
Colombia	107	3%
Other countries	710	
TOTAL	**4,015**	

1974		
Korea	2,453	51%
Vietnam	561	12%
Colombia	245	5%
Philippines	223	5%
Canada	188	4%
Germany	177	4%
Other countries	923	
TOTAL	**4,770**	

1975		
Korea	2,913	52%
Vietnam	655	12%
Colombia	379	7%
Philippines	244	4%
Mexico	162	3%
Thailand	139	2%
Other countries	1,171	
TOTAL	**5,663**	

1976		
Korea	3,859	59%
Colombia	554	8%
Vietnam	424	6%
Philippines	323	5%
Thailand	180	3%
Mexico	127	2%
Other countries	1,026	
TOTAL	**6,493**	

1977		
Korea	3,858	59%
Colombia	575	9%
Vietnam	327	5%
Philippines	325	5%
Mexico	156	2%
El Salvador	98	2%
Other countries	1,154	
TOTAL	**6,493**	

1978		
Korea	3,945	57%
Colombia	599	11%
Philippines	287	5%
Mexico	152	3%
India	149	3%
El Salvador	98	2%
Other countries	85	
TOTAL	**5,315**	

1979		
Korea	2,406	49%
Colombia	626	13%
Philippines	297	6%
India	231	5%
El Salvador	139	3%
Mexico	139	3%
Other countries	1,026	
TOTAL	**4,864**	

1980		
Korea	2,683	52%
Colombia	653	12%
India	319	6%
Philippines	253	3%
El Salvador	179	3%
Mexico	144	3%
Other countries	908	
TOTAL	**5,139**	

1981		
Korea	2,444	50%
Colombia	628	13%
India	314	6%
Philippines	278	6%
El Salvador	224	5%
Mexico	116	2%
Other countries	864	
TOTAL	**4,868**	

1982		
Korea	3,254	57%
Colombia	534	9%
India	409	7%
Philippines	345	6%
El Salvador	199	3%
Chile	113	2%
Other countries	895	
TOTAL	5,749	

1985		
Korea	5,694	61%
Philippines	515	5%
India	496	4%
El Salvador	310	3%
Honduras	181	2%
Guatamala	175	2%
Other countries	1,914	
TOTAL	9,285	

1983		
Korea	4,412	61%
Colombia	608	8%
India	409	6%
Philippines	302	4%
El Salvador	240	3%
Chile	172	2%
Other countries	984	
TOTAL	7,127	

1986		
Korea	6,188	62%
Philippines	634	10%
India	588	9%
Guatamala	228	4%
El Salvador	147	2%
Mexico	143	2%
Other countries	2,017	
TOTAL	9,945	

1984		
Korea	5,157	62%
Colombia	595	7%
India	468	6%
El Salvador	364	4%
Mexico	168	2%
Other countries	1,575	
TOTAL	8,327	

1987		
Korea	5,910	58%
India	807	8%
Philippines	593	6%
Guatamala	291	3%
Mexico	178	2%
El Salvador	135	1%
Other countries	2,183	
TOTAL	10,097	

1948-1987 Total   137,437

NOTES

1. Letter from Professor Louis H. Feldstein, Yeshiva University, Department of Classics, New York, November 6, 1988. We would like to thank Mr. Martin Schutz for Professor Feldstein's address.

2. Not everyone shared that view, however. At a conference on ICA in 1988, adoption researcher John Triseliotis termed ICA a "contemporary type of slavery" in which developing countries sell their children to the West. Triseliotis believes that Western families cannot shield their intercountry adoptees from racism and that, no matter how hard these families try, their foreign-born children will have difficulty developing healthy cultural identities. International Conference on Adoption and Permanent Care: Permanence in Country, Culture and Family, Melbourne, 27 November–1 December 1988.

3. Helen Miller, "Recent Developments in Korean Services for Children," *Children* (January–February 1971): 36; William Montalbo, "Colombia Has The Babies If You Have The Money," *Philadelphia Inquirer*, 14 July 1977.

4. "Update on Agencies," *Face Facts* 13, no. 2 (March–April 1989): 42.

5. "Update on Agencies," *Face Facts* 13, no. 3 (May–June 1989): 41.

6. The figures cited on ICA in this chapter are based on the best available primary (governmental) and secondary sources. However, gaps exist due to incomplete and fragmentary reporting, particularly in the early years of data collection.

7. Richard H. Weil, "International Adoptions: The Quiet Migration," *International Migration Review*, 18(2) (1984): 276.

8. Ibid; Richard H. Weil and Gerald Adcock, *Intercountry Adoptions: Where Do They Go From Here?* (Michigan: Bouldin-Haigh-Irwin, 1979).

9. Helen Miller, "Korea's International Children," *Lutheran Social Welfare* (Summer 1971): 12–23.

10. Ibid; Weil and Adcock, *Intercountry Adoptions*.

11. Weil and Adcock, *Intercountry Adoptions*; Miller, "Korea's International Children."

12. Diane Cole, "The Cost of Entering the Baby Chase," *New York Times*, 28 April 1988: C8; Lynne McTaggart, *The Baby Brokers: The Marketing of White Babies in America*, (New York: Dial Press, 1980).

13. Peter Maass, "Orphans: Korea's Disquieting Problem," *Washington Post*, 14 December 1988: 1.

14. "Ecuador Restricts Adoptions After Kidnap Ring is Cracked," *New York Times*, 22 January 1989: 8. Confidential discussion with major adoption organization executive, 19 January 1989.

15. Maass, "Orphans."

16. For a more thorough presentation of these events, see: Rita James Simon and Howard Altstein, *Transracial Adoption: A Follow-up*, (Lexington, MA: Lexington Books, 1981), Chapter 6; Rita James Simon and Howard Altstein, *Transracial Adoptees and Their Families: A Study of Identity and Commitment*, (New York: Praeger, 1987), Chapter 11.

17. T. Melone, "Adoption and Crisis in the Third World: Thoughts on the Future," *International Child Welfare Review* 29 (June 1976): 20–25.

18. Maass, "Orphans."

19. Tamar Lewin, "South Korea Slows Export of Babies for Adoption," *New York Times*, 12 February 1990: B10.

20. NBC (19 September 1988), 10:45 P.M.

21. Maass, "Orphans."

22. Rosa Perla Resnick, "Latin American Children in Intercountry Adoption," in *Adoption Essays in Social Policy, Law and Sociology*, edited by Philip Bean, (New York: Tavistock Publications, 1984), 1273.

23. Ibid.

24. Barbara Joe, "In Defense of Intercountry Adoption," *Social Service Review* 52 (March 1978): 1–20. For legal aspects, see: Eugenie Hochfield, "Across National Boundaries," *Juvenile Court Judge Journal* 14 (October 1963); Burton Sokoloff, et al., "A Five Year Follow-up of Vietnamese Refugee Children," *Clinical Pediatrics* 23 (October 1984): 565. For behavioral and medical reactions of intercountry-adopted children, see: S. P. Kim, "Behavioral Symptoms in 3 Transracially Adopted Asian Children: Diagnosis Dilemma," *Child Welfare* 59, no. 4 (1980): 213–24; Jerri Ann Jenista, and Daniel Chapman, "Medical Problems of Foreign Born Adopted Children," *American Journal of Diseases of Children* 141 (March 1987): 298–302.

25. D. C. Kim, "How They Fared in American Homes: A Follow-up Study of Adopted Korean Children in the US," *Children Today* 6, no. 2 (1977): 2–6; "Issues in Transracial and Transcultural Adoption," *Social Casework* 59, no. 8 (1978): 477–86; C. Pilton, "Post Adoption Support," *Adoption and Fostering* 88, no. 2 (1977): 21; S. P. Kim, et al., "Adoption of Korean Children by New York Area Couples: A Preliminary Study," *Child Welfare* 58, no. 7 (1979): 419–27; Glenda French, "ICA: Helping a Young Child Deal with Loss," *Child Welfare* (May/June 1989): 272; Hei Sook Park Wilkinson, *Birth Is More Than Once: The Inner World of Adopted Korean Children*, (Bloomfield, MI: Sunrise Ventures, 1985).

26. C. Bagley and L. Young, "The Long Term Adjustment and Identity of a Sample of Intercountry Adopted Children," *International Social Work* 23 (1980): 16–22.

27. W. Kühl, *When Adopted Children of Foreign Origin Grow Up*, (Osnabrück: Terre Des Hommes Germany V, 1985).

28. R. A. C. Hoksbergen, *Adoption in World Wide Perspective*, (Berwyn: Swets North America, 1986).

29. R. A. C. Hoksbergen, *Adopted Children at Home and At School*, (Lisse, Holland: Swets & Zeitlinger, 1987).

30. Edward Suh, "Life Adjustment Problems Among Adopted Korean Children," *Open Door Society News* 3 (October 1987): 3.

31. Estela Andujo, "Ethnic Identity of Transethnically Adopted Hispanic Adolescents," *Social Work* 33, no. 6 (November–December 1988): 531; "Children Adopted across Ethnic Lines Lack Sense of Heritage, Study Finds," *Psychiatric News* XXI/13 (4 July 1986): 25–26.

32. *Adoption Researchers' Newsletter* 9 (17 October 1988): 4.

33. "Red Tape and Expense Slows Adoption," *New York Times*, 28 April 1988: C8.

34. Philip Shabecoff, "Warning on Births Provokes Dissent," *New York Times*, 23 August 1987: 25.

35. Merlise Simons, "Abortion across Latin America Rising Despite Illegality and Risk," *New York Times*, 26 November 1988: 6.

36. "U.S. Fertility at Low and Life Expectancy at High," *New York Times*, 8 September 1987: 18.

37. "World Is Growing by 90 Million People Each Year," *Baltimore Sun*, 24 May 1989: 10.

38. Robert Lindsey, "Adoption Market: Big Demand, Tight Supply," *New York Times*, 5 April 1987: 1. The accuracy of data concerning infertility rates is sometimes questionable: writers citing similar sources report widely differing figures. Ben Wattenberg, "No Curse on the Career Woman," *Baltimore Sun*, 16 April 1987: 15A; Susan Faludi, "Infertility and the Career Woman: An Epidemic of Hype," *Baltimore Sun*, 4 May 1989: 5E.

39. Diane Cole, "The Cost of Entering the Baby Chase," *New York Times*, 9 August 1987, Business section: 9.

40. *Ms.*, (January–February 1989): 148. (Quoting a 1982 Congressional Office of Technology study.)

41. Wattenberg, "No Curse on the Career Woman."

42. "Adoption v. Abortion," *Newsweek*, 28 April 1986: 39.

43. William R. Greer, "The Adoption Market: A Variety of Options," *New York Times*, 26 June 1986: C1.

44. Ibid. S. K. Henshaw, J. D. Forrest, and J. Van Vort, "Adoption Services in the United States, 1984 and 1985," *Family Planning Perspectives* (March/April 1987).

45. Gina Kolata, "Studies Find Abortion Rate Staying Constant," *New York Times*, 6 October 1988: A24; "The Battle Over Abortion," *Newsweek*, 1 May 1989: 28. (Quoting a survey conducted by the Alan Guttmacher Institute.)

46. Lena Williams, "Teen Age Sex: New Codes Amid the Old Anxiety," *New York Times*, 27 February 1989: 1.

47. "The Future of Abortion," *Newsweek* (International Edition), 17 July 1989: 32.

48. Richard L. Berke, "Late Childbirth is Found on Rise," *New York Times*, 22 June 1989: 16; "Adoption Seldom Chosen by Pregnant Teenagers," *The Roundtable* 3, (1 November 1988): 5; Jacqueline H. Plumez, "Adoption's Grim Alternatives," *New York Times*, 18 November 1988: A35; and "Adopt/Abort," *Time*, 2 November 1987: 60; Christine Bachrach, "Adoption Plans, Adopted Children, and Adoptive Mothers," *Journal of Marriage and the Family* (May 1986): 243–253.

49. Berke, "Late Childbirth on Rise"; Sandra Hofferth and Cheryl Hayes, "Risking the Future: Adolescent Sexuality, Pregnancy and Childbearing," *Fact Sheet* (Governor's Council on Adolescent Pregnancy, State of Maryland) 1, no. 4 (November–December 1988). Based on data from the National Research Council, Washington, DC, 1987.

50. Jane Gross, "Homes For Unwed Mothers Undergo Revival," *New York Times*, 23 July 1989: 1.

51. Plumez, "Adoption's Grim Alternatives."

52. American Psychiatric Association, *Diagnostic and Statistical Manual of Mental Disorders*, rev. ed., (Washington, DC: APA, 1987). *DSM-III-R*.

53. For a thorough review of the literature, see: Alfred Kadushin and Judith A.

Martin, *Child Welfare Services*, 4th ed., (New York: Macmillan Publishing Co., 1988).

54. Kadushin and Martin, *Child Welfare Services*.

55. Kathlyn S. Marquis and Richard A. Detweiler, "Does Adopted Mean Different? An Attributional Analysis," *Journal of Personality and Social Psychology* 48, no. 4 (1985): 1054.

56. Paul and Evelyn Brinich, "Adoption and Adaptation," *Journal of Nervous and Mental Disease* 170, no. 8 (1982): 489–493. The studies of David Brodzinsky have been particularly insightful in examining the adjustment patterns of adoptees. See: David Brodzinsky and Marshall D. Schelter, *The Psychology of Adoption*, (New York: Oxford University Press, 1990).

57. For an excellent review of the literature on this topic, see: Marquis and Detweiler, "Does Adopted Mean Different?"

58. Kadushin and Martin, *Child Welfare Services*, 622; Robin Marantz Henig, "Chosen and Given," *New York Times Magazine*, 11 September 1988: 70.

59. Henig, "Chosen and Given."

60. Boston, 30 May 1987.

61. Ibid.

I

NORTH AMERICA

2

Intercountry Adoptions: Experiences of Families in the United States

RITA J. SIMON
HOWARD ALTSTEIN

Within the large numbers of volumes on the subject of adoption are warnings and expressions of doubt about the wisdom of the decision to adopt. ACS, discussed in the introduction, is the most recent expression of those warnings. Concerns focus primarily on the child's emotional and mental health and on the fear that the parents and child will not bond and develop the love and loyalty that family members ideally feel toward one another. On the face of them, certain adoptions seem more problematic, more emotionally complicated, and more demanding than others. Transracial adoptions and ICAs fit that description. They not only bring together non–blood-related individuals, but also people of different races, ethnicities, and cultures—in the hope that, out of these differences, a loving, intimate family will be forged.

For almost 20 years, we have studied families with adopted children who were racially and culturally different from their parents.[1] In each of our three volumes describing various phases in the chronology of adoptive families, we have tried to capture the quality of life in these families: the children's feelings about being adopted, the parents' reflections on the wisdom of their decision, details about both biological and adopted children's relationships with each other, the children's performance in school, their friendships, their racial and ethnic identities, their interest in locating their birth parents, and the parents' expectations about the strength of the ties and commitments they and their children are likely to have after the children grow up and leave home.

The study as a whole describes happy and satisfying experiences. Some of the families had easier times than others, and the early childhood years presented fewer problems than the adolescent years. In our second volume we reported that, during early adolescence, adopted children in one out of five families stole items from the home—a sister's stereo, a brother's bicycle, money from mother's purse. These children had no other record of delinquency. A few years later, when we contacted the families for the third survey, all of the parents reported that the stealing had stopped. Along the way, there were other problems as well—drinking, drugs, staying out late, and lack of interest in school. Except for the stealing, however, most parents reported the same behaviors for children who had been born to them as they did for their adopted children.

Almost all of the children spoke of their adopted families as the only ones they had known or wanted to know. Some expressed curiosity about their birth parents: "So I'd know what I'll look like when I'm grown up." On measures of family integration and self-esteem, there were no differences between the scores of adopted and biological children.

This chapter describes yet another set of experiences with a special type of adoption. It reports the experiences of families who adopted children primarily from outside the United States. The parents in these families belong to one of two organizations—the Stars of David (SOD) or Families Adopting Children Everywhere (FACE). SOD is a Boston-based, nationwide adoptive parent group comprised of Jewish (or intermarried) couples whose avowed purpose is to rear their adopted children as Americans and Jews, but with a knowledge and respect for the cultures of their birth. Thus, a Korean boy adopted into an SOD family is likely to receive a Hebrew name, undergo ritual circumcision, and have a bar mitzvah, a ceremony marking the religious transition from childhood to adulthood. A Colombian girl will also participate in a naming ceremony and may have a bat mitzvah. Both will learn about their birth cultures through language, books, food, travel, and observance of ceremonies and rituals. Both will be American children—legally and socially—as a function of their adoptions, their environments, and their lifestyles. Since its founding in the early 1980s, SOD has grown from 35 families in the Boston area to more than 700 families across the country.

Families Adopting Children Everywhere (FACE) is an adoptive parent group comprised largely of Christian families in the Baltimore-Washington area. Families in both groups adopt foreign-born children as well as black and white American children.

The research presented in this chapter is the first of its kind in that it is an objective attempt to assess the interactive effects of ICA on the psychosocial adjustment of adoptees and their adoptive parents and siblings. We assessed adoptees' relationships with their siblings and parents, as well as their school performance, friendship patterns, social activities, and future ambitions. We also asked the families to interpret the reactions of their communities and religious congregations to their adopted child(ren). We had the families describe their religious practices, as well as the types of activities and ceremonies they engaged in that commemorated their children's birth cultures.[2]

Before turning to the experiences of the SOD and FACE families, however, a brief account of the general procedures that American families must go through to adopt overseas children is in order.

THE ICA PROCESS

It is important to emphasize that procedures (regulations, forms, affidavits, fees, etc.) vary not only from country to country, but also from agency to agency—both within the United States and within the adoptee's birth country. Some agencies, for example, have open intake periods that allow potential adopters to file at any time; others have periodic intake with limited filing periods. Whether the ICA is agency-sponsored or private is yet another major difference. In reality, however, practically all U.S. legal procedures involved with ICAs are variations on a theme because all must comply with U.S. federal and state laws and Immigration and Naturalization Service (INS) procedures.

The birth countries of potential adoptees often have complex statutes, procedures, behavioral assumptions, and general paperwork that can make ICA a web of forms, certificates, stamps of approval, letters of reference, and so on. Some countries do not allow proxy adoptions, but insist instead that prospective adopters spend time (and money) in their countries before adoption can take place. An adopting couple may be required to stay in a foreign country for as little as one to seven days or as long as eight weeks. On the other hand, some countries allow adoptees to be escorted into the United States by adults other than the potential parents. Still others require that orphans be adopted through their local courts. Countries may place considerable importance—or no importance at all—on an adopter's religion, age, marital status, and income. On the whole, American families have found it easier (less bureaucratically cumbersome) to adopt orphans from Korea than from Latin America. In general, however, an ICA usually takes between 18 and 24 months—from the time the adoption process begins until the orphan is placed with the adoptive family.

Steps in ICA

We include here a series of general steps in the ICA process usually followed by adoption agencies in the United States. They are presented neither as a model nor a progression. These steps—Inquiry, Orientation, Preliminary Application, Formal Application/Homestudy, INS Forms, and Post-placement Follow-up—represent the American side of the ICA process. As will be seen, however, many important agency policies are in fact restrictions imposed directly by the birth countries of adoptees.

Inquiry

When a couple initially telephones an adoption agency for information about an ICA, the agency's requirements are usually described to them, and then they are referred to a local adoptive-parent support group. (See the following section, Orientation.) Potential adopters are also sent several application forms that ask for basic information. Subjects typically discussed in the initial call include:

Marital status. Agencies and individual countries often have regulations requiring that couples be married for a given length of time. Some accept applications from single individuals and gay couples; others do not.

Age. Although adoption agencies themselves may have age limitations, more often it is the birth country that determines the ages of adopters. For example, potential parents of a Korean-born child must be between 25 and 40 years old. India has a similar age limit of 40. Thailand and certain Latin-American countries require that parents be older than 30. Age maximums vary—from 45 for the Philippines, Thailand, and some other Asian countries, to 50 or higher for Latin-American countries.

Prior children. Agencies sometimes have provisions to prevent adoptees from being placed in families with children under a certain age, usually two years old. On the other hand, some countries will not place their orphaned nationals in families where they will be third children (this rule is usually not enforced if the adoptee is a special needs child). Practically all countries allow their children to be placed into families where they will be first or second children.

Parental handicap. American agencies do not generally place any physical preconditions on potential adopters. Certain countries, however (most notably Thailand), will not place a child in a family where one or both potential parents are physically handicapped.

Income. Practically all agencies and most countries require that potential adopters have a minimum annual income, generally $20,000. This rule is usually waived for members of the U.S. military, whose benefits and allowances by and large compensate for lower salaries.

Maternal/paternal leave. Some agencies require parents to take maternal/paternal leave from their jobs and remain at home with an adoptee for a length of time determined by the child's age.

Fertility. Agency policies regarding fertility vary. Policies may be developed by agencies themselves or dictated by the birth countries of adoptees. In any case, some agencies accept applications only from couples who can medically document their infertility. Others may not accept couples undergoing fertility treatment at the time of application. Some agencies have no regulations regarding infertility.

Orientation

Adoption agencies usually require interested couples to attend "orientation to adoption" courses offered by adoptive-parent support groups or local community colleges. In addition to providing an introduction to the adoption experience, parent support groups such as FACE and Latin America Parents Association (LAPA) assist potential adopters examine their motivations for adoption. They also discuss potential difficulties with intercountry adoptees and postadoption adjustment. It is not uncommon for a couple to reconsider its decision to adopt a child from outside the United States after attending one of these classes. Although there is no time requirement for these sessions, they usually average 6–12 hours.

Preliminary Application

At this point, potential adopters are asked to address in writing the issues discussed during the initial call to the agency and provide an autobiographical statement. A fee is generally requested with the submission of the application.

Formal Application/Homestudy

The formal application/homestudy, the heart of the ICA process, is usually conducted after preliminary forms have been submitted and an adoption course has been satisfactorily completed. The homestudy is required by both the INS and state laws. Although there are variations in the way a homestudy might be conducted, in most cases it will determine whether a couple's application to adopt is accepted by the agency. Homestudies are almost always conducted by state-licensed social workers.

During a homestudy, the social worker explores with the prospective adopters their reasons for wanting to adopt a foreign-born child, their personal values, and their childrearing practices. Home visits are arranged, and in-office interviews are conducted—usually with the couple both together and separate. Many agencies also conduct group interviews. The social worker then evaluates the couple's readiness to assume the responsibilities of parenthood of a foreign-born child.

The formal application process requires prospective adopters to submit a wide variety of certificates, affidavits, forms, and so on. These documents include:

Formal application (including age, marital history, education, etc.)
Criminal background check, certified by state police

Photographs of all nuclear family members

Marriage certificate

Birth certificates

Medical forms for parents and any other children living with them

Employment letter

Most recent Internal Revenue Service Form 1040

Financial statement (e.g., market value of home, and/or other assets)

Written assurance from health-care provider that there will be immediate medical coverage upon the adoptee's arrival into the family, and that no waiting period exists for pre-existent conditions

Several personal letters of reference, at least one or two from "respected community members" (e.g., clergy). (Some states ask the adoption agency to interview one of the references by telephone and one in person.)

State clearance that neither parent has ever been involved in cases involving child abuse and/or neglect

Latin American countries may require a mental health certificate consisting of a psychiatrist's evaluation of prospective adopters.

INS Forms

Competent attorneys specializing in ICA are usually needed both in the United States and in the adoptee's birth country to negotiate the legal procedures involved with this type of adoption. Although the number and types of documents needed for foreign-born children to enter the United States may vary, all are required to have visas. All adoptions must be finalized in the United States (usually after six months) even if a child was legally adopted in the birth country. After finalization, parents must apply for U.S. citizenship for the adopted child.

Most of the following INS forms are good for one year. After that, they must be resubmitted.

I-600a: Application for Advance Processing of Orphan Petition. This form, intended to expedite the adoption process, is submitted before the actual adoption. It allows the INS to approve the couple for adoption before delivery of an orphan.

I-600: Petition to Classify Orphan as an Immediate Relative. This form is completed only after all information about the orphan to be adopted is known to the adopting parents.

FD-258: Finger Print Check. This form establishes whether either of the adopting parents has ever been arrested and/or convicted of an offense.

I-171: Notice of Approval of Relative Immigration Visa Petition. When a couple's application is approved by the INS, they are sent form I-171 authorizing the issuance of a visa to the adoptee.

Post-placement Follow-up

As part of the homestudy process, almost all adoption agencies offer post-placement service that lasts for about six months after a child has entered the United States. This service usually consists of periodic meetings with the social worker in the adoption agency offices, the adopter's home, or both. Issues discussed include childrearing practices and the effect the child is having on the adopters' marital relationship (and other nuclear- and extended-family relationships).

STARS OF DAVID (SOD)[3]

The parents in SOD ranged in age from 30 to 60, with a median age of 40 for mothers and 43 for fathers. All of the mothers and 95 percent of the fathers had completed four years of college, and more than 75 percent of the parents had post-graduate degrees. The fathers worked as professionals, mainly as engineers, accountants, and professors. Even though almost all of the mothers had earned at least a bachelor's degree, approximately one-third described themselves as full-time homemakers. The other two-thirds worked mainly as teachers and social workers. The median annual family income was $69,600. At least 60 percent of the families lived in all-white or mostly white neighborhoods, and about one-third lived in largely Jewish neighborhoods.

The following chart describes the number of children adopted by the 59 SOD families.

Numbers of Children Adopted by SOD Families

Number of Children Adopted	Number of Families	Number of Children
1	36	36
2	17	34
3	4	12
4	1	4
8	1	8

Note: The 59 SOD families adopted a total of 94 children. The average number of children per family was 1.6.

Thirty-three families did not have any children born to them. Twenty had one child, four had two children, and two had three children. Together, the 59 families had a total of 128 children—94 adopted and 34 born to them. We interviewed 37 of the 94 adopted children and 23 of the 34 biological children. We were able to interview a higher percentage of the children born into the families because more of them were at least six years old at the time of the study. In 15 families, the adopted child was the only child. In 21 families, the adopted child was the oldest. And in 18 families, he or she was the youngest child. In the remaining five families, the adopted child was somewhere between the youngest and the oldest. Altogether, the families adopted 39 boys and 55 girls.

The ages of first adoptees at the time of adoption ranged from less than one month (thirteen families) to nine years (one family). Forty-six families adopted children less than one year old, four families adopted children between one and two years old, four families adopted children between two and four years old, four families adopted children between four and eight years old, and one family adopted a child older than eight. Families who adopted more than one child were a little more likely to adopt older children: Of the 23 families who adopted a second time, seven adopted children between two and eight years old.

The following chart describes the racial, ethnic, and national characteristics of the children adopted by the SOD families.

Racial, Ethnic, and National Characteristics of SOD Adoptees

	1st Adoptee	2nd Adoptee	3rd or Later Adoptee	Combined
Korean	23	9	4	36
Hispanic	15	6	1	22
Other Asian	4	2	3	9
American Black	3	2	4	9
American Indian	2	–	–	2
American White	12	4	–	16
Total	59	23	12	94

The length of time couples were married before first adoptions ranged from one to more than ten years. The median was 6.5 years. Thirty-four families chose to adopt because they could not bear children, and ten because they could not bear any more children. Nine families opted to adopt because they did not want to bear children, citing overpopulation and the number of needy children in the world as their reasons. Six families cited other reasons. The reason most often cited for a family's adopting the child it had was that it was the child most readily available.

Jewish Practices and Ties to Community

Thirty-five percent of the SOD families were synagogue members at the time they adopted their first child, and most of them discussed their plans with a rabbi before adopting. With two exceptions, the families reported a positive response from their rabbis, and fellow congregation members were almost unanimous in their positive and supportive reactions.

Fewer than ten percent of the families attended synagogue on a weekly basis. Most attended only on the High Holidays of Rosh Hashana and Yom Kippur. Among families who attended, Boston respondents were more likely to go to a Reform temple. The Washington and New York families were more likely to attend a Conservative synagogue and were more observant of rituals such as dietary laws (33 percent vs. 16 percent for the Boston families) and lighting Sabbath candles. Three out of five Washington families observed rituals on a regular basis, compared to less than one in three Boston families. The practices that at least 75 percent of all the families engaged in included making or attending a seder on Passover, lighting candles on Hanukkah, attending synagogue on the High Holidays, and having mezzuzahs on their doorposts.

Although only 35 percent of the families claimed membership in a synagogue, four out of five Boston families reported belonging to at least one Jewish organization (not including SOD).

Although highly educated in the secular realm, three-quarters of the parents reported that they had received little in the way of a Jewish education when they were growing up. Only three of the mothers and five of the fathers had attended Jewish day schools. At least two-thirds of the fathers had attended Hebrew school in the afternoons, as had 40 percent of the mothers.

Three out of four families had their adopted children undergo formal conversion ceremonies. With two exceptions, families with birth sons had brits (ritual circumcisions) for them, but only two out of three of the adopted sons participated in such ceremonies. None of the Boston families expected either their biological or their adopted children to attend Jewish day school, compared to 40 percent of the Washington and New York families. Half of the Boston families planned to send both their adopted and biological children to after-school Hebrew programs; the others expected to do nothing in the way of formal Jewish education. Only two of the Washington families do not anticipate providing their children with any type of formal Jewish education. All but ten of the families plan for their children to have bar or bat mitzvahs. None of the families differentiate between adopted and biological children in their plans for Jewish education and rites of passage ceremonies.

The parents were asked whether it was "very important," "somewhat important," or "not important" that their children observe, engage in, or identify with the following aspects of Jewish life. The following chart shows the percentage of parents who answered "very important."

Importance to SOD Parents of Children's Participation in Jewish Life

Observance	Percent*
Be educated about Jewish history/culture	88
Marry a Jew	26
Observe Jewish holidays	57
Participate in Jewish community life	34
Contribute to Jewish charities	43
Have mostly Jewish friends	4
Observe Jewish rituals and customs	41
Taking pride in being a Jew	93

*Percent represents parents who said it was "very important" that their children participate in these aspects of Jewish life.

The responses suggest an odd approach to Jewish identity in that the parents seemed to focus more on individual behavior than on family and community ties. Note, for example, the small percentages who believed it was very important that their children marry Jews, have mostly Jewish friends, and participate in Jewish community life. A higher percentage indicated that contributing to Jewish charities and observing Jewish holidays and rituals were important. And nearly all believed it was very important that their children be educated in Jewish history and culture and take pride in the fact that they were Jewish.

Three out of four parents reported that they had spent time learning about their adopted child's birth culture and that the family engaged in ceremonies and rituals stemming from that culture. The ethnic experiences these families described included preparing special foods, having cultural artifacts and books in the home, attending classes on the child's birth culture, belonging to ethnic organizations, establishing ties with other families who have children of that culture, and learning the language of the child's birth culture. Indeed, only two families said they did not engage in any such activities because they felt that it was the Jewish identity and heritage that the children should live with and inherit.

Parents' Account of Children's Performance in School and of Familial Relationships

At the time of our study, 22 birth children and 31 adopted children were old enough to be in elementary or high school. The following chart compares the average grades reported by parents in the preceding school year for their first- and second-born and first- and second-adopted children.

School Grades of SOD Children by Order of Birth and Adoption

		Grades		
Status	A	B	C	D
Birth				
First child	12	4	2	–
Second child	3	1		
Adopted				
First child	6	7	5	1
Second child	4	6	2	

Parents reported higher grades for their birth children than they did for their adopted children. However, when we controlled for age of adoption and compared the grades of the 15 children adopted before they were one year old with those of birth children, the differences all but disappeared.

School Grades of SOD Children by Age at Adoption

	Grades			
Status	A	B	C	D
Birth	15	5	2	–
Less than one year when adopted	10	5		

Using a four-point scale, we asked the parents to characterize their relationship with each of their children. Positions on the scale were: (1) "positive and good"; (2) "positive outweighs negative"; (3) "negative outweighs positive"; and (4) "negative." If parents checked a category other than "positive and good," we asked them to explain the problems they were having with a given child. Only one family used "negative outweighs positive" to describe the relationship with a birth child. An additional three families said that there were some problems but—all things considered—they used "positive outweighs negative" to describe their relationships with their birth children. Those three families described their problems as emotional and personality ones. The one family who checked "negative outweighs positive," described drugs, drinking, and parent-directed anger.

The picture is somewhat more complicated for the adopted children. For first adoptees, ten families indicated that there were problems but checked "positive outweighs negative." Six parents chose "negative outweighs positive," and nine chose "negative," to describe their relationships with first-adopted children. Of the 23 families with more than one adopted child, none checked "negative" or "negative outweighs positive." Six said that there were problems, but positive factors outweighed negative ones. Most frequently described were disobedience, anger, and emotional and personality problems. Three families mentioned drugs and drinking.

Looking at the responses another way, 83 percent of the parents chose "positive and good" to characterize their relationships with all of their birth children (34 total), and 68 percent chose "positive and good" to characterize their relationships with all of their adopted children (94 total). There were not enough birth children to compare, but 58 percent of the parents rated their relationships with first adoptees "positive and good," and 74 percent rated their relationships with second adoptees "positive and good."

Using the same four-point scale, parents were asked to characterize their adopted and birth children's relationships with each other. Only one of the 26 families with both birth and adopted children described these relationships as "negative." One family chose "negative outweighs positive," and two said there were problems but chose "positive outweighs negative." The four families who described problems talked about sibling rivalry and jealousy. A total of 22 families (85 percent) evaluated the relationships between birth and adopted siblings as "positive and good." There were not enough families with more than one birth child to make a comparison among birth siblings worthwhile. Among the 23 families with more than one adopted child, however, two sets of parents used "negative outweighs positive" to describe their adopted children's relationships with each other; five checked "positive outweighs negative." A total of 16 families (70 percent) evaluated the relationships among their adopted children as "positive and good." The ratings of adopted siblings' relationships with one another are not quite as high as those for relationships between adopted and birth children, but they are high enough to indicate generally positive relationships.

Finally, we asked the parents what advice they would offer families like themselves who were considering adoption. Sixty-two percent urged it unequivocally. Another 25 percent urged adoption but only after a couple had thought long and hard about it and was sure of their motivations. Nine percent said only that a family should think long and hard before doing anything, and four percent (2 families) advocated against adoption.

The Children

We turn now to what the children in these SOD families had to say about their experiences. We interviewed a total of 60 children—23 birth and 37 adopted. The racial and ethnic breakdown of the adopted children old enough to be interviewed was as follows: 13 Korean, 3 other Asian, 11 Hispanic, 9 American black, and 1 American white.[4] Birth children's ages ranged from 6 to 23, and adoptees' ages ranged from 6 to 21. The median age for birth interviewees was 11.4; for adoptees, it was 9.8. The grade level of birth children ranged from second grade to college, and for adoptees from kindergarten to college. The median school year was eighth grade for birth children and fourth grade for adoptees. Forty-five percent of both the birth and adopted children were boys. Three out of five birth interviewees were the oldest child in a family, and one out of three of adoptees was the oldest.

Fourteen percent of birth children and 22 percent of adoptees were attending Jewish day schools. Three out of five birth children in the appropriate age categories were attending after-school Hebrew classes, compared to two out of five adoptees (but more adoptees were attending Jewish day schools). Altogether, 14 of the 21 birth children in the appropriate age range were attending either Jewish day schools or after-school Hebrew classes, compared to 15 of the 29 adoptees in the appropriate age range. These percentages (for both birth and adopted children) are high compared to a cross-section of the Jewish community in those cities. Forty-three percent of the adoptees said they speak, read, and/or write Hebrew, as did 30 percent of the birth children. Only two of the adopted children speak, read, and write Spanish; another two speak but do not read or write Spanish. Four birth children also speak Spanish. None of the children speak, read, or write Korean. These responses clearly indicate that the adoptees were not retaining or learning the languages of their birth cultures.

The following chart describes the Jewish ritual and ceremonial observances that the families engage in on a regular basis, as reported by the children. The chart reveals little difference between the two groups: Most of the children reported observance of major holidays but not daily or weekly activities such as dietary laws and the Sabbath.

Observance of Jewish Rituals as Reported by SOD Children

Observance	Percent Engage in Regularly	
	Birth	Adopted
Observe Dietary Laws	21.7	17.7
Light Sabbath Candles	39.1	38.2
Attend Synagogue on Rosh Hashana	91.3	90.6
Fast part or all of Yom Kippur	70.0	62.0
Light candles on Hanukkah	95.6	97.2
Attend a Seder on Passover	91.3	94.1
Dress up for Purim	56.5	59.4
Help build or sit in a Sukkah	69.6	79.6

Like their parents, only a small number (two birth children and six adoptees) reported that they and their families attended temple or synagogue on a regular basis. By contrast, 87 percent of the birth children and 80 percent of the adoptees reported having (or planning to have) a bar or bat mitzvah. Forty-two percent of the birth children and 27 percent of the adopted children reported having read at least one book about Jewish history or culture in the preceding year. Three of the adopted children also reported reading a book about their birth culture. Looking toward the future, we asked the children whether they expected to participate in Jewish community life when they were adults and on their own: 64 percent of the birth children and 57 percent of the adopted children responded yes. Most of them mentioned joining a temple or synagogue.

When asked whether it bothered them that they looked different from their parents, two-thirds of the adopted children said it was not a source of difficulty and it caused them no problems. The responses of ICAs and other adopted children (most of whom were American black) were similar. Three of the ten children who mentioned specific problems said they were uncomfortable at extended-family or Jewish functions. Twenty-two of the adopted children also recalled problems during the preceding three years involving children calling them names and making fun of them because of their racial backgrounds. Two-thirds ignored the incidents, but half later told their parents or a teacher about what had happened.

When asked how they would describe themselves to a stranger, none of the birth children mentioned physical characteristics or religion; they all mentioned personality characteristics. In contrast, 37 percent of the adopted children mentioned race, religion, and the fact that they were adopted. This distribution (approximately one-third mentioning racial, religious, and adoptive status characteristics as opposed to personality traits) was similar among ICAs and other (non-ICA) adoptees.

The Self-Esteem Scale developed by Morris Rosenberg and Roberta Simmons in 1968 remains one of the most frequently used and reliable measures of this concept to date. It has been used in countless studies, including the most recent contact we had with a cohort of transracial adoptees we began to study in 1972. We also used the Self-Esteem Scale in this study, and the results are shown in Table 2.1.

On five of the nine items, birth children were more likely than adoptees to take a positive attitude about themselves, to believe they had a number of good qualities, and to feel well-satisfied with themselves. But the adopted children were less likely to feel that they were "no good," "a failure," or that they didn't have much to be proud about. It is interesting that the adopted children scored higher when responding against a negative image, whereas the birth children made more direct, positive assessments of themselves. In other words, the adopted children were more likely to assert their self-esteem in response to negative assessments such as "I feel I do not have much to be proud of" or "I think I'm no good."

There were no differences in the relationships the birth and adopted children had with their grandparents, aunts and uncles, and other relatives. For almost all the children, these ties were positive; for a few, however, relatives lived far away and visits were infrequent.

Table 2.2 demonstrates that we found no significant differences in the preferences expressed by birth and adopted children when we asked them, "Who knows best who you are?" The same was true when we asked them to whom they would be most likely to go if they were "happy about something," "worried about something," and "accused of stealing." Parents and siblings were the most likely confidants of both birth and adopted children. Among adopted children, there were no differences between ICAs and the others. For example, 59 percent of the ICAs named a family member when asked, "Who knows best who you are?"

The extent to which adopted and birth children believed themselves integral parts of their families can also be observed by comparing their

Table 2.1
Self-Esteem Scores of SOD Children

Items	Percent Showing High Self Esteem*	
	Adopted	Birth
1. I take a positive attitude toward myself (Strongly Agree)	32.1	47.6
2. I wish I could have more respect for myself (Strongly Disagree)	16.7	15.0
3. I certainly feel useless at times (Strongly Disagree)	4.2	15.8
4. I feel I have a number of good qualities (Strongly Agree)	37.0	52.4
5. All in all, I am inclined to feel that I am a failure (Strongly Disagree)	64.3	50.0
6. I am able to do things as well as most other people (Strongly Agree)	21.4	33.3
7. I feel I do not have much to be proud of (Strongly Disagree)	48.0	31.1
8. On the whole, I am well satisfied with myself (Strongly Agree)	28.0	55.0
9. At times I think I am no good (Strongly Disagree)	20.0	9.5

*As measured by "strongly agree" or "strongly disagree" responses depending on which is appropriate for determining high self-esteem.

scores on the "family integration scale" used in the British Adoption Project (BAP). The children's responses to family integration items are listed in Table 2.3.

On three of the eight items—"trust," "similar treatment," and "parents stick by me"—the adoptees' responses indicated that they had less of a sense of family integration than did the birth children. On the other five items, the differences were negligible. Comparing the responses of ICAs to those of other adoptees, we found that there were no differences between the two groups. For example, on the three items for which adoptees' responses differed from those of birth children, ICAs and other adoptees were almost identical. To the statement, "People in our family trust one another," 22.2 of the ICAs answered "strongly agree,"

Table 2.2
Most Likely Confidants of SOD Children (%)

	Birth		Adopted	
	Parent and Siblings	Non-Family*	Parent and Siblings	Non-Family
Who knows best who you are	52.2	47.8	57.6	42.4
Happy about something	64.2	35.8	64.5	35.5
Worried about something	57.1	42.9	68.2	31.8
Wrongly accused of stealing	66.6	33.4	63.0	37.0

*Includes friends, teachers, police, store owner.

and 66.4 percent answered "agree." On the trouble item ("If I am in trouble, I know my parents will stick by me"), 30.7 percent of the ICAs answered "strongly agree," and 53.8 percent answered "agree." To the statement that they are treated in the same way as their siblings, 20 percent of the ICAs responded "disagree," and 8 percent said "strongly disagree."

These responses, however, were the first indications we had from the adopted children that they felt less comfortable with or less integrated into their families than the birth children. And these responses were not inconsistent with those of the parents regarding their relationships with their adopted children. We did note that the children who checked responses indicating that they felt greater distance from their parents were the ones who were three years or older at the time of their adoptions.

When we probed further and asked about the ties they expected to have to their parents in the future, 74 percent of the birth children versus 43 percent of the adopted children responded with "very close." The remaining 26 percent of the birth children answered "close," as did 50 percent of the adopted children. Seven percent of the adopted children said "fairly close." Among ICAs, 36 percent expected "very close" ties, 56 percent "close," and 8 percent "fairly close." Again, we found no real differences between ICAs and other adoptees. The responses of the birth children, however, did exhibit a greater sense of integration and commitment than those of the adopted children. Although we asked about the ties that birth and adopted children expected to have to each other in the

Table 2.3
SOD Children's Responses to BAP Family Integration Items (%)

Family Integration Items	Categories of Children	
	Birth	Adopted
I enjoy family life.		
Strongly agree	54.6	45.2
Agree	45.4	51.6
Disagree	–	3.2
Strongly disagree	–	–
I would like to leave home as soon as possible when I am able to*		
Strongly disagree	–	7.7
Disagree	33.3	30.8
Agree	50.0	46.2
Strongly agree	16.7	15.4
People in our family trust one another.		
Strongly agree	45.5	23.3
Agree	54.5	60.0
Disagree	–	10.0
Strongly disagree	–	6.7
Most families are happier than ours.		
Strongly disagree	27.8	29.6
Disagree	72.2	63.0
Agree	–	7.4
Strongly Agree	–	–
I am treated in the same way as my brothers and sisters.		
Strongly agree	18.2	21.4
Agree	40.9	53.6
Disagree	31.8	17.9
Strongly disagree	9.1	7.1
Most children are closer to their parents than I am.		
Strongly disagree	42.9	25.0
Disagree	42.9	66.7
Agree	14.3	8.3
Strongly agree	–	–
If I am in trouble, I know my parents will stick by me.		
Strongly agree	52.4	31.0
Agree	47.6	55.2
Disagree	–	10.3
Strongly disagree	–	3.5
My parents know what I am really like as a person.		
Strongly agree	42.9	27.6
Agree	47.6	65.5
Disagree	9.5	6.9
Strongly disagree	–	–

*The numbers for this item were smaller: 12 birth children and 13 adopted. We included the item because the distributions were similar to those in which the numbers ranged from 18 to 31.

future, the numbers were unfortunately too small to make the responses worth comparing.

FAMILIES ADOPTING CHILDREN EVERYWHERE (FACE)

The FACE respondents were obtained by placing a notice in their monthly newsletter describing our study and asking interested families to contact us. The families' locations limited the size of our sample: we were able to interview only 21 families of the more than 30 who contacted us. The procedure for interviewing FACE families was the same one employed for the SOD families—personal interviews in the home with the parents and the children. Among the 21 FACE families, we interviewed 36 children—5 born to the parents and 31 adopted. All of the adopted children had been born overseas. These 36 children represented 68 percent of the total number of children in the FACE families at the time of our study. The other 17 were either too young to be interviewed or were adults who no longer lived in their parents' homes.

Parents' ages ranged from 26 to 54 years, with a median age of 37 for the mothers and 40 for the fathers. Among the mothers, 53 percent had completed at least four years of college, as had 67 percent of the fathers. Most of the fathers worked as professionals, mainly in the fields of accounting, physics, and social work; the others were in business. All of the FACE mothers worked outside the home except for two who were attending school. The mothers were teachers, nurses, and white- and pink-collar clerical and business workers. The median annual family income was $57,600. Seventy percent of the families lived in all-white or largely white neighborhoods.

The following chart describes the number of children adopted by the FACE families.

Numbers of Children Adopted by FACE Families*

Number of Children Adopted	Number of Families	Number of Children
1	3	3
2	15	30
3	3	9
4	–	–
5 & more	–	–

*The 21 FACE families adopted a total of 42 children (with an average of 2).

Of the 21 FACE families, 14 did not have any children born to them. Three had one child, and four had two children. We interviewed 31 of the 42 adopted children and 5 of the 11 children born into the families. Three of the children born into the families were not interviewed because they were more than 25 years old and no longer lived at home; the other three were too young. The 11 adopted children we did not interview were all too young.[5] The adopted child was the only child in 81 percent of the families. He or she was the oldest in 5 percent, and the youngest in 14 percent. The families had 26 adopted girls and 16 adopted boys, with ages ranging from six weeks to fourteen years. Four families had adopted children who were less than three months old at the time of adoption. Seven were between four and twelve months old, and the other ten families adopted children between one and ten years old.

The following chart describes the racial, ethnic, and national characteristics of the adopted children.

Racial, Ethnic, and National Characteristics of FACE Adoptees

	1st Adoptee	2nd Adoptee	3rd or Later Adoptee	Combined
Korean	13	13	3	29
Other Asian	2	1		3
Hispanic	6	4		10
Total	21	18	3	42

The length of time couples were married before their first adoptions ranged from one to more than ten years. The median number was 6.5 years. Two-thirds of the families chose to adopt because they could not bear children. The reason most often cited for a family's adopting the child it had was that it was the child most readily available.

Five of the fathers and seven of the mothers were Catholic; the rest belonged to a variety of Protestant congregations. Sixty-seven percent of the parents reported attending church on at least a weekly basis. Except for three families, all were church members.

Sixteen of the families engaged in ethnic activities that they believed enhance their children's identification with their birth cultures. They seek out friendships with other families from those countries, display artifacts in their homes, prepare ethnic foods, and celebrate ethnic festivals.

Five of the families did not engage in any such activities because the child was too young, because they wanted the child to identify with

American culture, or because the child was not interested and the families did not believe they knew enough about the culture to push it.

Of the 31 adopted children, 26 were old enough to attend school past kindergarten: 8 attended Christian day schools, 5 secular private schools, and 13 public schools. Grade levels ranged from kindergarten to the 11th grade. One of the children was in a special education program with no grade levels. The parents reported an average grade of A for eleven children, B for nine, C for four, and D for one.

On the four-point scale, 19 of the families described their relationships with their children as "positive and good." Two families chose "positive outweighs negative" to describe their relationships with at least one child. These families emphasized the child's age as the explanation: he or she was engaged in typical adolescent behavior including sibling rivalry, anger, jealousy, and testing of house rules.

In only nine families could the parents assess their children's relationships to each other. Of those nine, five described the relationship as "positive"; two as "positive outweighs negative" (citing the "usual sibling rivalry"); one as "negative outweighs positive" (describing anger and jealousy on the part of one adopted child toward another); and one as "negative" (reporting that their two separately adopted children had engaged in sexual relations with each other). This last family is reported in more detail in the section called Special Families.

The racial and ethnic breakdown of the 31 adopted children old enough to be interviewed was as follows: 24 Korean, 2 Indian, and 5 Hispanic. Their ages ranged from 5 to 17, with a median age of 9.7. There were 8 boys and 23 girls. Ten of the adoptees were the oldest children in their families, fourteen were the youngest, and seven were middle children.

Eight of the adoptees described themselves as Catholic and 23 as Protestant. Lutheranism was the Protestant denomination named by more of the children than any other. Seventy-one percent of the children reported attending church at least once a week, 88 percent on Christmas Eve, and 75 percent on Easter morning. All of the Catholic children reported going to confession and taking communion. Seventy-seven percent of the children said grace before meals on a regular basis, 30 percent prayed together as a family on a regular basis, and 79 percent had been baptized. Twenty percent of the children said that they had read a book about Christianity during the preceding year, and 23 percent had read at least one book about their birth cultures. Of the 31 adopted children, 9 said that the fact that they looked different from their parents and siblings had caused them some problems. They mentioned personal slurs and innuendoes such as being called "Chinese eyes," being stared at, or being asked questions such as: "Is that really your Mom?"

All of the 28 adopted children whose grandparents were still alive said that they felt close to them. Thirteen reported weekly phone conversations, four monthly visits, and four more visits on holidays. All the adoptees had aunts and uncles, and 28 said they felt close to them.

Asked how they would describe themselves to a stranger, only one of the adopted children mentioned being adopted, and none mentioned race or religious identity. All of them described personality characteristics and used terms such as "nice," "friendly," "smart," and "good at sports."

The FACE adoptees responses to the "trust" items ("Who knows best who you are?" and "To whom would you be most likely to go if you were . . .") are shown in Table 2.4. Their family integration responses were consistent with their trust responses, indicating that the adopted children had strong and positive ties to their families (see Table 2.5). The Self-Esteem Scale revealed the responses listed in Table 2.6. (Note that we omitted two self-esteem items because only nine of the children answered those questions. For each of the other items reported, there were at least 23 responses.)

Looking toward the future, 41 percent of the FACE adoptees expected to have "very close" ties to their parents, 44 percent "close" ties, and 15 percent "fairly close" ties. When asked the same question about their siblings, the adoptees' expectations were not quite as positive: 33 percent answered "very close," 28 percent "close," 28 percent "fairly close," and 11 percent "not close." Given the ages of the children involved, expectations about ties with siblings are probably less reliable predictors of future behavior than are expectations about ties to parents.

The last set of questions involved the type of work the children wanted to do when they grew up and their expectations about how active they

Table 2.4
Most Likely Confidants of FACE Adoptees (%)

	Parents and Siblings	Non-Family Member
Who knows best who you are	69	31
Happy about something	61	39
Worried about something	63	37
Wrongly accused of stealing	79	21

Table 2.5
FACE Adoptees' Responses to BAP Family Integration Items (%)

	Strongly Agree	Agree	Disagree	Strongly Disagree
I enjoy family life	32	61	3	3
I would like to leave home as soon as possible when I am able to *	--	22	55	22
People in our family trust one another	29	61	3	6
Most families are happier than ours	6	13	52	29
I am treated in the same way as my brother and sister	16	39	22	22
Most children are closer to their parents than I am *	3	16	45	35
If I'm in trouble, I know my parents will stick with me *	42	35	10	13
My parents know what I am really like as a person	26	65	6	3

*Based on numbers of less than 20.

would be in church activities. Almost all the children had professional aspirations, expecting to be doctors, dentists, lawyers, teachers, social workers, writers, or scientists. (One said "athletic coach.") Of the ten adoptees who answered the item about future involvement in church affairs, six said that they expected to be active.

At the very end of the interviews, we asked, "Is there anything else you would like to tell us?" Five of the children answered, "My family loves me very much," and one said, "I'm happy."

COMPARING THE SOD AND FACE FAMILIES

How similar were the SOD and FACE families in terms of the dimensions discussed here? Looking at the parents' demographic characteristics, both groups were clearly middle-class, educated, professional families, although the SOD parents were more likely to have post-graduate degrees and higher incomes. Both sets of families lived in predominantly white neighborhoods.

Table 2.6
Self-Esteem Scores of FACE Adoptees (%)

	Strongly Agree	Agree	Disagree	Strongly Disagree
I take a positive attitude toward myself	14	75	11	0
I wish I could have more respect for myself	3	39	54	3
I certainly feel useless at times	8	70	22	0
I feel I have a number of good qualities	36	60	0	4
I feel I do not have much to be proud of	4	16	44	36
On the whole, I am satisfied with myself	20	80	0	0
At times I think I am no good	8	64	28	0

More than 75 percent of the families had decided to adopt because they could not bear any (or any more) children. Fifty-six percent of the SOD families and 67 percent of the FACE families had no birth children. In both groups, parents waited an average of 6.5 years after getting married before they adopted their first child. In both groups, most of the children had been less than one year old at the time of adoption, and Korea was the country from which the largest number of children had been adopted. Unlike the FACE families, the SOD families also adopted American white and black children; FACE families only adopted children from out of the country.

The SOD children ranged in age from 6 to 23 years, and their grade levels in school ranged from kindergarten to college. The age range for FACE children was 5 to 17 years, and their grade levels ranged from kindergarten to eleventh grade. Of the 37 SOD adoptees, 17 were boys, compared to 8 of the 31 FACE adoptees. In both groups, one out of three adoptees was the oldest child in the family.

Almost all of the FACE families were church members and reported attending church on at least a weekly basis. Thirty-five percent of the SOD families reported belonging to a synagogue, and fewer than ten percent reported attending synagogue or temple on a weekly basis. In both groups, 75 percent of the families reported engaging in ceremonies and rituals derived from their adopted children's birth cultures, having books and artifacts in their homes about their children's birth cultures, seeking out Korean and Hispanic friends, or joining ethnic organizations.

There was a difference between how the SOD and FACE parents assessed their relationships with their adopted children. Both sets of parents reported "positive and good" relationships with the children born to them, but 15 of the SOD families (compared to one of the FACE families) reported negative relationships with at least one of their adopted children. All of the "negative" and "negative outweighs positive" assessments described relationships with first adopted children in SOD families. Four of these families' experiences were sufficiently dramatic that we have described them in a separate section, Special Families.

Of the SOD adoptees, 22 percent attended Jewish day schools; the rest attended public schools. Among the FACE children, 25 percent attended Christian day schools, 16 percent attended secular private schools, and the others attended public schools. An additional 27 percent of the SOD children attended afternoon Hebrew school following the regular school day. A comparison of the grades reported for the adopted SOD and FACE children revealed little difference: 32 percent of the SOD families reported A's, compared to 43 percent of the FACE families. Only 3 percent of the SOD families and 4 percent of the FACE families reported D's.

Although 71 percent of the FACE adoptees reported attending church on a regular basis, fewer than 20 percent of the SOD children reported regular synagogue attendance. But the large majority of both groups reported observing other religious practices, especially those revolving around holidays and rites of passage. As noted by weekly church attendance and the saying of grace before meals, the FACE adoptees seemed more involved in religious practices on a regular basis.

When asked to describe themselves, the SOD adoptees were more likely to mention their race, religion, and adopted status than were the FACE adoptees. About the same proportions reported that their looking different from their parents caused them some—but not serious—problems. As examples of the problems they encountered, they mentioned having slurs made against them and being called names. Both sets of adoptees characterized ties with grandparents and aunts and uncles as "close" and "positive."

Among the seven items on the Self-Esteem Scale in which the numbers were large enough to make comparisons, the SOD children showed somewhat higher self-esteem on five; there were no differences on the remaining two items. Responses to the family integration items showed little difference between the two groups.

On the "who knows best" and "to whom would you go if" items, FACE adoptees were more likely to think that their parents knew best who they were, and they would be more likely to turn to their parents if accused of stealing. Remember, however, that the FACE adoptees were slightly younger than the SOD adoptees, and that age factor might be the major explanatory variable.

About 40 percent of both SOD and FACE adoptees said that they expected to have "very close" ties with their parents, and almost all of the others expected to have "close" ties. It is interesting that the children's responses on the family integration items matched their responses on the "expected closeness" items. In other words, children who seemed less committed and integrated into their families also indicated that they expected to have less-close ties to their parents in the future.

Special Families

Three SOD families and one FACE family described serious problems with at least one of their adopted children, and this section describes these problems in some detail. One of the families adopted four siblings from a Caribbean island, one adopted a boy from a Central American country, one adopted a girl from Korea, and one adopted both a boy and a girl from Korea.

A Son from Central America

The parents in the first special family—both of whom were university-educated, successful business executives—had adopted two children because they could not bear any. In considering adoption, their major criterion was that the child be healthy; they did not believe they could cope with a handicapped child. They had wanted a daughter for their first child, but when they learned that N was available, they decided to adopt him. A few years later, when they were told that a girl was available, they also adopted A.

N was not quite six years old when he came from Central America to live with his adoptive parents. For the first nearly six years of his life, N lived in what his adoptive parents described as a war zone. He saw a lot of people killed, and he and his adoptive parents did not know if his birth mother was dead or alive. N's parents believed that he had a guilt complex about having escaped when so many others were killed or forced to remain. They compared N's feelings to those of Jews lucky enough to escape Nazi Germany, many of whom suffered strong feelings of guilt about being alive.

N had been seeing a psychiatrist for the three years preceding our study. His parents described him as hyperactive, experiencing extreme mood swings, and immature. He had also been abusive to his younger sister. In his parents' view, a major difficulty of N's adjustment was that he had been forced to be an adult in his birth country; now, in his adoptive country, he had to learn to be a child. N had very negative feelings about his birth country and wanted to be identified as 100 percent American. He also felt very strongly about his Jewish identity. On the day our interviewers arrived at N's home, he had had a fight with another child at school and had been sent home facing possible suspension. He was too upset, his parents felt, to be interviewed. The parents were critical of N's school, claiming that his teachers had been insensitive to his problems.

N's younger sister (also from a Central American country) was adopted when she was six and presented no special problems. This family's advice to prospective adoptive parents was to recognize that a child's age is crucial: the younger, the better. A child's birth country and personal background may be important factors, but they gain in importance with the age of the child. These parents believed they were lucky with their second adopted child: even though she was six, she seemed emotionally and physically healthy.

A Daughter from Korea

The next family's story involves a Korean foundling whom the adoptive parents found "starving in an orphanage" when she was one year old. At the time of our interview, H was 16 years old. The other child in the family, a birth son, was 17 years old. According to the parents, H had problems from the very beginning. She exhibited rage when she was only one year old, was hyperactive, and had trouble bonding. Within weeks after she was adopted, H had thrown herself against a closed door leading to a room she wished to enter. She had been on dexadrene from the time she was five until she was eleven. At 13, H had been sent to a residential school in another state—a school for severely disturbed children where the teachers were also therapists. H's parents believed that her behavior was destroying their marriage and their family. The father had been increasingly removing himself from the family by doing a great deal of traveling. The brother was tired of being the "good child," the "shining light," and wanted H out of the house. H had tried to attack members of her family with knives, and just before being sent away, she had pulled a knife on a child in school. Every room in the house had a lock on it because H had been stealing from family members. The family pediatrician blamed the adoptive mother for much of H's behavior.

For a time, H denied that she was Korean. In the year preceding our interview, H's parents had noticed improvements in her behavior. On her last visit home, she and her brother had been able to spend "good" time together for the first time (by going to a movie, for example). H has one more year of school.

At the time we interviewed them, the parents were guardedly optimistic that H might be able to come home and become part of the family.

They were bitter at the public school system for not providing them with a "better support system." They had tried to have H placed in a "special program," but school authorities had refused to treat her any differently from the other children until she pulled the knife on a classmate.

H's parents' advice to prospective adoptive parents is much like the advice N's parents gave: race, ethnic background, and country of birth are not important, but age is crucial. H's parents advised adopting *at birth*. They reported that they and the child's therapist believed that the trauma H experienced during her first year of life was at the root of her problems.

Four Siblings from an Island in the Caribbean

As soon as they were married, R and C very much wanted to start a family, but C was 39 years old and had difficulty conceiving. After about a year, they felt they had to make a choice: they could continue going from doctor to doctor, or they could spend their time and money trying to adopt. They opted for the latter and decided on an ICA because (like many other families in our study) they thought it would take less time.

Through contact with a Latin American group, they traveled to a Caribbean island and were introduced to a family of four children, three of whom were living in the same children's home. When they arrived at the home to meet the four-year-old twin girls and their five-year-old brother, the couple was told that another sibling—a brother, nine years old—was living in another institution on the Island. If they wanted to adopt any of the children, they were told, they would have to take all four. Having made the initial investment in the trip to the Island, and feeling that they eventually would like to adopt several children, R and C decided it would make sense to plunge right in and take all four. Thus, three years after they were married, R and C found themselves the adoptive parents of four children.

The oldest brother, B, had been sexually abused, first by his biological father and then by older boys in the children's home. The father, an alcoholic, had abused his wife and children, and the mother disappeared after she either placed the children in the home or they had been taken from her. The twins were 18 months old and the youngest son three when they were placed in the institution. The mother reportedly told officials at the institution that she wanted to start a new life and did not want anything more to do with her children.

A few months after R and C brought the children home, they realized that B, who was then ten, had been sexually assaulting (the parents used the word "raping") his younger sisters and brother almost every day. The couple consulted a therapist who called the Protective Services Department of the county's Social Services Division. The Protective Services Department advocated placing him in a foster home but acknowledged that, in all probability, no foster home would take him. The adoptive parents agreed to keep him, but it changed their lives. The mother, who has a Ph.D. in biology, quit her job so that she could stay home and watch the children. The therapist, the Social Service counselor, and the parents all agreed that B needed constant supervision. The parents believed that, in the two years preceding our interview, B had not engaged in any form of sexual activity.

In addition to being assaultive toward his younger siblings, B was handicapped by severe mental retardation. (He was in an ungraded class at the level designated for severely handicapped children.) At 12 years old, he was unable to read and had difficulty answering many of the questions posed to him during our interview. He showed the interviewer a picture he had drawn and told her, "I don't like to fight. I feel shy and I am very quiet." At the end of the interview, he volunteered that he could remember having many fights with other children in his birth country. He also talked about an older sister who had died several years earlier (each of the other children also mentioned her), about his mother who went somewhere and did not return, and about a father he could not remember.

The other children talked with much sadness about life on the Island. One of the twins (then six years old) said, "I don't have a mommy in _____. The lady was very bad. She used to hit us with a strap." The other twin said, "My mother could not feed us. We don't know if she is dead. Our big sister died; she had no medicine. When we first saw our adoptive parents, we were afraid of them, but then we were happy to come to the U.S."

When asked to describe themselves, one twin said: "I am happy. I play very well with my sister. Other children tell me I'm good." The other said: "I am an Indian. I lived in _____. I play in the playground." None of the three spoke negatively of their older brother. The eight-year-old brother described himself as "eight years old, brown, coming from _____, and I am a Jewish Indian." The three younger children all attended an Orthodox Hebrew day school. This family was more observant than any other in our survey. They observed the Sabbath and attended synagogue regularly. The older son said he would like to learn Hebrew and, when he grew up, "be a good Jewish man."

The parents characterized the children's relationships with each other as very close and very positive. When B spends several weeks with his maternal grandparents in the midwest (none of the grandparents, nor any other relatives or family friends have been told of B's behavior), his siblings write him letters, telling him they miss him and they "can't wait until he comes home."

Toward the end of the interview, as the parents reviewed what had happened over the previous three years, the father said, "We really haven't told you how much fun it is to be with 'our children' and how lucky we feel that only one of these four children has given us problems." The mother acknowledged that she may never work as a professional scientist again.

Asked what advice they would offer other prospective adoptive parents, they said that couples should be "very cognitive" of the costs involved in the country of adoption and of the hassles they are likely to endure. At the first sign of any kind of aberrant behavior, they said, parents should seek professional intervention. They also stressed the importance of finding a pediatrician experienced in treating "poor children," one who could recognize malnutrition, parasites, and other conditions associated with poverty.

A Son from Korea

The fourth family's problems also centered around sexual abuse on the part of one adopted child toward another. The parents were divorced, and the mother (the only parent interviewed) believed that the father had rejected the adopted son, the first of two children the couple had adopted from Korea. The son was four years old when he came to live with his adoptive parents; a daughter was adopted a year later, when she was three. At the time of our interview, the son was 18, living by himself, and had relatively infrequent contacts with his mother. The mother described C as having a sociopathic personality. When C was adopted, he had been a "street child" with no knowledge of or contact with either of his biological parents. According to the mother, C had molested and had sexual intercourse with his adopted sibling for several years, beginning when the sister was nine years old. During those years, both parents worked outside the home, and the housekeeper did not report the boy's behavior. The daughter, who has frontal lobe brain damage that manifests itself in a lack of feeling and generally autistic behavior, attended a special school for learning-disabled children. Her mother described her behavior as more appropriate for a ten-year-old than for the fifteen-year-old that she was. When the mother discovered what was happening, she left her job as an attorney and stayed home full time. After a few months, she arranged for the son to stay with his adopted father, who had left the family home following the parents' divorce. By that time, the son had dropped out of high school where he had been a poor student.

The daughter made no mention of her experiences to the interviewer. The interviewer could, of course, see that she was speaking to an emotionally and cognitively impaired person. Although the mother had close ties with her daughter, she expected little improvement in her relationship with her son. It is worth noting, however, that when the mother was asked if she would do it again—adopt a child from overseas, that is—she said "yes" and recommended it to other families.

CONCLUDING REMARKS

These four families represent the ones with major problems that are clearly a function of children's preadoption experiences. None of these families had considered disrupting the adoption, not even in the case where it seemed clear that the child was destroying the marriage. Instead, the adopted child was sent off to a special school, just as a birth child might have been.

By highlighting these families, we do not mean to suggest that all was sweetness and light in the other 76. For example, in one family, a 14-year-old Korean boy (who was adopted when he was 5½ and had lived in an orphanage for two years before his adoption) was on medication for manic-depression.

In another family, a 16-year-old black son had been attending a military academy for three and a half years because he had been on drugs and was stealing from his parents and siblings.

An eleven-year-old Korean girl, adopted at age seven, had been physically and sexually abused in Korea. She described herself as "stupid" and disliked her Asian appearance. She wanted to look Caucasian. Her 14-year-old adopted Korean brother vowed he would never marry a woman from Korea.

One family adopted a six-year-old boy from the Philippines who had lived in an orphanage almost since birth. He was learning-disabled and somewhat physically handicapped as a result of polio. The parents believed he had been abused at the orphanage, and he had trouble relating to women. He was 16 at the time of our study.

It is clear from these accounts that older children present greater risks to adoptive parents, especially older children who have been abandoned, left on the streets, or institutionalized. They may have scars that will remain with them for a long time, scars that will cause them as well as their adoptive families pain and sorrow. For families who adopt children less than one year old, the future holds promise and security.

NOTES

1. The results of those studies appear in the following volumes: Rita J. Simon and Howard Altstein, *Transracial Adoption*, New York, Wiley, 1977; Rita J. Simon and Howard Altstein, *Transracial Adoption; A Follow Up*, Lexington, Mass., 1981; Rita J. Simon and Howard Altstein, *Transracial Adoptees and Their Families*, New York, Wiley, 1987.

2. We are indebted to Mrs. Sherry Simas, Social Worker, International Children's Services Unit, Associated Catholic Charities of Baltimore, Maryland, and doctoral student, University of Maryland, School of Social Work, for her help with this section.

3. We acknowledge with appreciation the help received from Julie Cowan and

Daniel Simon in collecting the data. Ms. Cowan also worked on the analysis of the data.

4. In later sections of this chapter, we report the responses of the intercountry adoptees separately on specific matters that deal with particularly sensitive "identity" issues. On all topics—for example, those dealing with ceremonial observances, education, and ties to extended family members—there were no differences between the responses of the ICA and other adopted children.

5. Because there were only 5 birth children, we did not compare their responses against those of the 31 adoptees. This section thus describes the responses only of the FACE adoptees.

3

Adoption of Native Children in Canada: A Policy Analysis and a Research Report

CHRISTOPHER BAGLEY

Over the past 150 years, North America's original inhabitants have been subjected to extraordinary ravages of their traditional ways of life—assaults that have threatened their very existence as independent nations. A system of oppression amounting to cultural genocide has resulted in the undermining of the family in many groups of Native people, with a consequent crisis in the care of their children (Morse 1984).

Native or aboriginal peoples in North America are (like the peoples of Europe) a collection of very diverse cultures, ranging from the Inuit in the North to the Pueblo in the South. Devastation by European settlers of the ecological bases of the cultures of many of these aboriginal peoples has led to epidemics of disease, starvation, unemployment, hopelessness, and exploitation (Morrison and Wilson 1986). In the midwest of Canada and the United States, the slaughter of the buffalo by white settlers effectively destroyed a way of life—and with it a nomadic, self-sufficient culture. Native leaders—defeated, demoralized, and facing death from starvation and the guns of the conquering army—signed treaties, the implications of which were not understood (MacDonald 1978). These treaties relegated Native people to tracts of isolated, barren land with no apparent economic value. Only when oil, coal, and natural gas were discovered on these reserves did white administrations again move to dispossess aboriginal populations (Morrison and Wilson 1986).

The mineral and agricultural resources of the lands ceded by aboriginal peoples have provided the basis for acquiring the capital and facilitating the industrial development that have allowed North Americans to attain an average income level higher than anywhere else in the world. Two groups have not, however, shared in that prosperity: the aboriginal people, and the descendants of slaves who were imported from Africa to provide early capital development in agriculture, industry, and trade. The early European settlers also tried to enslave the conquered Amerindian peoples. In slavery, however, aboriginal people retreated into a depressed state; in captivity and servitude, they died in a short time (Buchignani and Engel 1983). Indeed, it would have been convenient for the settlers if all Amerindian people had died out—as happened through systematic policies of genocide on the island that later became Newfoundland. This administratively convenient solution did not occur, however, and "the Indian problem" remains.

THE CANADIAN SITUATION

The international border between Canada and the United States along the 49th parallel is a division that disregards the traditional lands of Native peoples. Many groups view this division as an arbitrary and often humiliating barrier across their national territories. For example, the Blackfoot Nation of southern Alberta—a people who once hunted buffalo over a wide area—is now confined to a small number of reserves. The largest of these reserves is in northern Montana, and the largest in Canada is the Blood reserve near Lethbridge in southern Alberta. Because people from various Blackfoot reserves are linked by kindred and marriage ties, travel across the U.S.-Canadian border is common. For these people, having to submit sacred and ritual objects to customs inspection is a humiliating experience.

The exact number of people of indirect aboriginal descent in Canada is unknown, and census attempts to assess their numbers have been seriously flawed (Bagley 1988a). However, about 4 percent of the Canadian population have direct and major descent from the precolonized aboriginal people. The first group, who make up about half of all aboriginal people, are those who have status under the Indian Act because their forbears signed treaties with the Canadian government (MacDonald 1978). Second are "non-status" aboriginal people (mainly in British Columbia and Alberta), who were remote and "undiscovered" by the colonization process. They did not engage in warfare with the early settlers and did not sign treaties. These groups are still struggling to retain traditional territory; they claim sovereignty over a large part of British Columbia, a land mass the size of Europe. Third are the Metis, originally formed by unions of Native people with early French settlers. Following the final defeat of the French, these people fled to northern areas of what is now Manitoba, Saskatchewan, and Alberta (Buchignani and Engel 1983). Their lot has always been more ambiguous and wretched than that of full-blood Indians. Ever since a revolt by Metis people in the 1880s (following which Metis leaders were hanged), they have been a doubly marginalized group. Because of endogamy over the past century, they are physically indistinguishable from most other aboriginal people. The Inuit (Eskimo) people number about 25,000 today (Johnston 1983).

CURRENT SOCIAL AND HEALTH CONDITIONS
OF ABORIGINAL CHILDREN

Canada is one of the world's richest countries, but the material and health conditions of its aboriginal people are at a level similar to or below that of many Third World countries (CJPH 1982). Native people (including children) are at least five times more likely than whites to suffer serious infections and respiratory diseases, diseases of the central nervous system, and serious injury or death through accidents (Bagley, Wood, and Khumar 1990). Death rates from various causes at a young age are 40 to 90 percent higher than in whites. Many Native people in rural areas have no piped water, indoor plumbing, or sewage disposal (Siggner and Locatelli 1980), and houses are of poor quality and often overcrowded. These conditions are a major cause of the very high tuberculosis rates among Native people (Talbot 1983).

Housing conditions also underlie the extremely high rate of middle-ear infections (and associated hearing loss) in Native children. A similarly high incidence of cerebral palsy among Native children probably reflects the poor prenatal health of Native mothers rather than poor housing conditions as such (Tervo 1983). A Manitoba study has shown that Native children are generally undernourished (Ellestad-Sayed et al. 1981). On most reserves, unemployment rates among Native males range from 80 percent in winter to 50 percent in summer (when seasonal agricultural work at minimum wage can be obtained). Applying for financial assistance from welfare authorities means not only swallowing one's pride, but also having the linguistic and social skills necessary to negotiate what is often a confusing welfare system. It is rare for welfare officials to speak a Native language, and (particularly in northern areas) many Native people speak little or no English. Often the task of applying for a welfare check is left to the woman in a family, and the money obtained is shared with male members of the family.

Our work in southern Alberta indicates that, when welfare checks are denied (or shared with members of the extended family), adults and children alike suffer days and even weeks of what can only be described as semistarvation. Family and kin in Native communities share values, resources, skills, rituals, and food. When food runs out, all suffer— including children.

Because of haphazard or chronic undernutrition, poor perinatal conditions, and poor housing conditions, Native children become ill and die at far greater rates than non-Native children (Evers and Rana 1983; Nuttal

1982; Spady 1982). Some authors have suggested that the health of Native people is no better than that of many Third-World inhabitants and that Canada's overseas relief agencies might do better to concentrate on conditions at home (Young 1983).

In a 1982 editorial, the *Canadian Journal of Public Health* commented that:

> The infant mortality rates in our native people are worse than those of Indonesia or Nigeria. Compared to a child born into a white family in Toronto, the child born into an Indian family in the North-West Territories has only about a third as good a chance of surviving the first year of life; an Inuit child's chances have recently improved to the same level. Diseases of poverty, ignorance, overcrowding and squalor, chronic and acute respiratory disease, and gastroenteritis take a heavy toll among infants, children and young adults. (CJPH 1982: 297)

White social workers in Canada have approached the problems of child neglect and family disorganization (which often occur in a people overburdened by poverty and poor health) with practice models based on individual pathology. The structural aspects of these problems are almost universally ignored. The standard approach to a family in desperate need of adequate housing, income, and health-care support has been to remove children when (in the words of child welfare legislation) the parents are "unable or unwilling to provide the necessities of life." In other words, a family's extreme poverty constitutes valid grounds for removal of a child from his or her family (Government of Alberta 1984).

CHILD WELFARE POLICIES AND INTERVENTIONS

In the twentieth century, Canadian policy toward Native people has been largely paternalistic, attempting to guide Native people into assimilating into Canadian culture. The principle medium of this policy was once the residential schools run by Anglican and Catholic missionaries. Children were forcibly removed from parents and placed in schools that required abandonment (under threat of physical beating) of traditional dress, hairstyles, religion, and language. Although most of these schools were abandoned in the 1960s and 1970s, their effect in terms of cultural genocide is still apparent (Morse 1984). Native people graduated from these schools demoralized, bewildered, and unprepared for any but the most marginal existence. Indeed, with traditional hunting and trapping lifestyles destroyed, chronic unemployment is the norm for 80 percent of adult males.

Under these conditions, it is not difficult to understand why so many Native families have members who are alcoholic or mentally ill. The vast majority of Native families exist in the most desperate poverty.

Native families are subject to the control of provincial Child Welfare

Acts that allow for the "protection" or removal of children when physical and other abuse or neglect is suspected. Because these are civil law statutes, the alleged abuse or neglect does not have to be proved at the stringent level of criminal law proceedings, and judges in family courts who award a provincial government permanent or temporary guardianship over a child usually act as little more than rubber stamps for social workers' decisions (Bagley 1988b).

The effects of provincial child welfare interventions upon Native communities have been documented by Johnston (1983) and Hepworth (1980). Although Native children constitute about 5 percent of the population in the Prairie Provinces (Manitoba, Saskatchewan, and Alberta), in the early 1980s they made up nearly 40 percent of children in residential care. Most of these children had become permanent wards of the Crown not because of abuse, but because of alleged "neglect."

In effect, this means that white social workers perceived the conditions of family life as too far below (or too different from) those of the average white family. In this respect, social work practice in Canada resembled that of an earlier decade in the United States that contributed to "the destruction of the American Indian family" (Unger 1977). According to Hepworth, Johnston, and others, at least one-quarter of *all* Native children are current or past clients of the child welfare system, compared to less than 5 percent of white children.

Although the quality of child care settings to which Native children were removed varied, it was often inferior. Evidence from Alberta (Thomlison 1985) indicates that untrained white foster parents were the main resource used. These well-meaning people were often unequal to the task of caring for bewildered and often disturbed Native children who had been removed from their biological parents—usually for trivial reasons. Often what followed was a classic case of "drift," with a child being moved through a series of foster homes. With each move, the child would become increasingly disturbed, thus decreasing the likelihood of successful placement. By adolescence, the child would usually be too disturbed to live in a family and—after a series of behavioral or psychiatric crises in adolescence—would be permanently institutionalized (Bagley 1986).

Studies of adult prison populations indicate that at least one-third of those incarcerated in the Prairie Provinces are of Native origin (Morse 1984). A significant proportion of Native prisoners are debtors who cannot afford to pay fines imposed for minor crimes.

Case Studies of "Child Protection"

In the past five years, we have collected detailed information on a number of cases involving Native children removed from their parents by child protection workers. Case data were obtained through consultation with a number of Native bands who were attempting to regain children from the legal custody of the Province of Alberta, and through assessments of cases as an expert witness (Bagley 1984).

A single, elaborated account of a case can expose weaknesses in a system of service delivery and provoke the question: Is this an isolated case, or do the identified weaknesses in the delivery and care system apply to many more cases than this one? In Alberta, the case of one Metis child, Richard Cardinal (Bagley 1986), exposed the weaknesses of an entire system.

Richard Cardinal was removed with his three siblings from the care of relatives for reasons of poverty, parental alcoholism, and poor housing. The children went through a series of foster homes. At the age of seven, Richard was separated from his siblings, and another series of second-rate and sometimes abusive foster homes followed. After various emotional crises and suicide attempts, Richard hanged himself at the age of 17. An official inquiry (Thomlison 1985) indicated that the "care" Richard had received was typical of that received by many Native and Metis youth in the child welfare system. In fact, research on 130 cases of youth suicide in Alberta indicated that 11 percent of these children were current or previous wards of the government—compared with an expected frequency in the general population of less than 2 percent. The case of Richard Cardinal was not an isolated one (Bagley 1989a).

Two additional cases illustrate the colonial nature of child welfare administration for Native children. These cases are known to the writer through consultancy with a consortium of Indian bands in northern Alberta who are seeking to gain control of child welfare service delivery systems.

Case A

This girl was removed from her parents at the age of six weeks. She had a respiratory infection, and her parents (both aged 16) were living in an old car in March—in a harsh, northern climate. The child was removed by a social worker acting under authority granted by the Child Welfare Act of Alberta. The child was placed in a temporary foster home. In the following four years, she proceeded through six different foster homes before being stabilized with a farm family in the southern part of the province— nearly 500 miles from her original home. By this time, her biological parents had married and had two other children. Every month, the parents and their two children made a two-day bus trip to a social service office for a visit with their daughter, then they made the bus journey back to their northern reserve. By the age of six, their daughter had bonded to her foster parents and was completely acculturated. When her biological parents came to visit, she fled from them and fought with her younger siblings. Of her biological family, only her mother spoke any English, and the child did not speak her original, native language. The foster parents applied for and were granted an adoption order by the court. Shortly afterward, they moved to another province, and all contact with the child's culture of origin was lost.

Case B

This one-year-old boy was removed by social workers after his mother had moved to the city following the breakdown of her marriage. The mother lived in a miserable apartment and had a drinking problem. The alleged grounds for removal of the child were neglect, and the boy was briefly hospitalized for a respiratory infection. The boy's aunt moved to the city and sought custody of the boy, but this was refused. The boy was instead placed with foster parents and stabilized in his second placement. The aunt, a woman in her fifties who had successfully raised a large family, continued to press for custody. Meanwhile, the foster parents applied for an adoption order on the boy and resisted all attempts by the boy's biological family to visit. A court eventually granted custody of the boy to the aunt—with visitation rights by the foster parents!

In both of these cases (and in many others in Alberta with which I have been involved), social workers have employed ethnocentric models of practice, ignoring both the economic factors that oppress Native people and the cultural patterns of Native families in finding alternative ways to care for children. In particular, social workers have ignored the strengths of the extended family, in which child care is shared by biological parents, aunts, grandparents, and other relatives. The principle cultural value of the extended Native family is that of sharing. Income, food, and resources are shared. Troubles are shared (and solved) within the extended family. And caring for children is shared too.

ADJUSTMENT OF NATIVE CHILDREN ADOPTED BY WHITE PARENTS

Large numbers of Native children in Canada were permanently removed from their biological parents in the 1970s and early 1980s. Social workers rarely considered extended families as sources of permanent care for these children. Through disruptions and varying quality of care, many Native children became emotionally very disturbed; by adolescence, they became unadoptable. Nevertheless, a large number of Native children were placed in white homes before adolescence, without regard to their original ethnicity or their need for cultural support in a society that still holds many negative stereotypes of Native people (Morse 1984). Table 3.1 shows that more than two-thirds of the adopters of Native children have been white. In character, these adoptions are similar to some ICAs: children from very poor families in developing nations are

Table 3.1
Adoption of Indian Children by Indian and Non-Indian Families in Canada

Year	By Indian Families	By Non-Indian Families	Total	% Adopted by Non-Indians
1971	45	235	280	83.9
1972	48	269	317	84.9
1973	100	328	428	76.6
1974	104	261	365	71.5
1975	99	247	346	71.4
1976	114	381	495	77.0
1977	127	385	512	75.1
1978	111	354	465	76.1
1979	156	433	589	73.5
1980	131	435	566	76.5
1981	118	401	519	77.2

Source: Johnston (1983), page 57.

removed by colonial administrations and given to childless couples in a developed country.

What is the long-term adjustment of Native children adopted by white parents in Canada? Surprisingly, there has been no systematic Canadian research on this important subject (Sachdev 1984). Indeed, although there has been much North American study of transcultural and transracial adoptions (Feigelman and Silverman 1983), very little research has been conducted on outcomes for adoptions of Native children by whites. A few recent case studies exist, however, including those in a judicial report on the export of Native children to the United States for purposes of adoption (Kimmelman 1984), and reports of Native children being adopted from Canada to the United States by pedophiles (Campagna and Poffenberger 1988).

Hepworth (1981) had argued that adoptions of Native children were less well-supervised than those of white children, probably reflecting pressures on child welfare authorities by fiscal administrators. Subsequent evidence uncovered in the Kimmelman report on adoptions in Manitoba (1984) has supported this view.

The classic and oft-cited study (there is little else to cite) on Native adoptions is David Fanshel's book, *Far From the Reservation* (1972). Fanshel interviewed 392 sets of parents who had adopted Native children who were zero to 11 years old. The average age at follow-up was 4.5 years. Only data from parental interviews is reported, and the parents were overwhelmingly satisfied with their children's initial adjustment:

Even if the adjustment of the children proves to be somewhat more problematic as they get older—particularly during their adolescence when the factor of racial differences may loom larger—the overall prospect for their futures can be termed "guardedly optimistic." When one contrasts the relative security of their lives with the horrendous growing up experiences endured by their mothers . . . one has to take the position that adoption has saved many of these children from lives of utter ruination. (Fanshel 1972: 339)

One implication of this conclusion (saving the children from "utter ruination") is that adoption of Native children by whites should increase if such children are to be "saved." In this respect, the movement to remove and adopt aboriginal children was part of the movement contributing to what Byler (1977) called "the destruction of the American Indian family." French (1980) called the practices of forced sterilization of Native women and compulsory removal and eventual adoption of their children a "contemporary version of physical and cultural genocide." Although this may be an overstatement of the aims of official policy, it is difficult to escape the view that social work practices in North America have undermined rather than supported the aboriginal family.

Adoption might be in the best interests of an individual child, but the issue becomes more contentious when the child has biological parents and an extended family who both object to the adoption and can offer a home for the child—albeit an economically poor one by North American standards.

We have argued that ICA is an acceptable outcome for orphaned or abandoned children with no possibility of making contact with kin networks (Bagley and Young 1979; 1981). According to a number of follow-up studies, ICAs are rather successful in terms of the long-term psychological outcomes of the children involved (Bagley and Young 1981; Feigelman and Silverman 1983).

In contrast with this rather optimistic picture for Oriental and black children adopted by whites in North America, limited clinical evidence (reviewed by Bagley, Wood, and Khumar 1990) as well as our own clinical experience suggests that disrupted relationships and significant mental health problems are common among Native adolescents adopted by white parents.

A CANADIAN STUDY

We have argued that outcomes for adopted children are best assessed in terms of how adolescents and their parents cope with "identity crises" (Young and Bagley 1982). The results reported here represent the first report of a longitudinal study of adjustment of adopted adolescents from contrasted ethnic groups and family situations. An interview in early adolescence, for example, might identify a temporary adolescent crisis. It is important to review the whole of adolescence, with a review of the growing years by the adoptees themselves when they have reached young adulthood. What might be seen as a troubled adoption at age 13 could appear successful by the time the individual is 18 (Bagley and Young 1981).

Subjects for the present study were obtained from two sources: supplementary questions in a survey of child development in a large, random sample in Calgary (Bagley 1988c) and in two surveys of community mental health (Ramsay and Bagley 1986; Bagley 1989b). These surveys of 1,990 adults yielded 93 families with adopted adolescent children. Of these 93 families, 19 had adopted a child of Native origin, and 7 had adopted a child from overseas. Additional subjects were obtained through random telephone sampling in Calgary. Eventually, a pool of 37 Native and 20 intercountry children aged 13 to 17 was obtained for study.

All subjects were residents of the city of Calgary. From the pool of adopted white children, fairly close matches for the adopted Native children were obtained. Age- and sex-matched, nonadopted, white control groups were obtained from the main sample. The comparability of the samples can be seen in Table 3.2. The term *Native* included children of Native appearance with full or part ancestry. Intercountry adoptees were either Oriental (55 percent) or South American (45 percent). All were classified as nonwhite, as were all of the Native children.

It should be stressed that we were anxious to obtain a randomly selected group of subjects for study, because the use of volunteer subjects introduced a bias. For example, parents having difficulty with adoption might be more likely to volunteer. The overall positive response to the random sampling technique was 84.5 percent. From our initial questioning, we knew the type of child adopted by a couple and whether the child was currently living at home or elsewhere (usually reflecting a breakdown in adoption). The proportion of "adoption breakdowns" was similar between those who agreed to an interview and those who did not. White adoptees (the first comparison group) were sampled for purposes of the present study from a larger pool ($n = 169$) by age and sex, in order to obtain a balanced comparison with the other groups. All of the ICAs identified were included in the comparison samples. The Native adolescents were all residents of reserves in rural areas, and all had at least one sibling who had been removed by social services for alleged neglect. But these children, unlike their siblings, had *never* been removed from a biological parent, and all families had received social service support from their bands to prevent further family problems. At least half of this group, however, had been cared for by a grandmother or aunt for periods ranging from three months to 14.6 years.

Measures of adjustment used were the Coopersmith Self-Esteem inventory, a sensitive and well-validated instrument for measuring adolescent and young adult adjustment (Coopersmith 1987; Bagley 1989c) and a measure of suicidal ideas and behavior (Ramsay and Bagley 1986).

Table 3.2
Comparison of Three Groups of Adopted Adolescents and Nonadopted Controls

Variable	Natives Adoptees (n=37)	White Adoptees (n=42)	Intercountry Adoptees (n=20)	Nonadopted White Adolescents (n=40)	Nonadopted Native Adolescents (n=23)
Mean age adopted (years)	2.4	1.8	3.5	--	--
Educational rank					
Father, % high school+	37.0%	36.0%	60.0%	35.0%	0.0%
Mother, % high school+	32.0%	36.0%	51.0%	30.0%	4.3%
Child's age at interview (years)	14.5	14.2	16.3	14.5	15.2
Maternal age at interview	48.6	50.2	54.8	45.3	38.9
% female	38.0%	40.0%	50.0%	40.0%	52.2%

(continued)

Table 3.2
Continued

Variable	Natives Adoptees ($\underline{n}$=37)	White Adoptees ($\underline{n}$=42)	Intercountry Adoptees ($\underline{n}$=20)	Nonadopted White Adolescents ($\underline{n}$=40)	Nonadopted Native Adolescents ($\underline{n}$=23)
Mother's assessment of child-parent relations:					
No problems	18.9%	50.0%	65.0%	70.0%	56.5%
Some problems	24.3%	26.2%	20.0%	20.0%	26.1%
Many problems	35.2%	11.9%	15.0%	10.0%	17.4%
Profound problems (breakdown of parent-child relations and/or residential care)	21.6%	11.9%	0.0%	0.0%	0.0%
Adoptee's Self-Esteem					
Below 1st quartile of normative group	64.9%	30.9%	25.0%	22.5%	26.1%
Above 3rd quartile of normative group	10.8%	26.2%	35.0%	27.5%	21.7%
Suicidal ideas or deliberate self-harm in past 6 months	40.5%	9.5%	10.0%	12.5%	8.7%

Note: Significance (ANOVA): Significant variation at the 5% level or beyond across all five categories for parental assessment of problems, adoptee's self-esteem, adoptee's suicidal ideas or actions.

Suicidal ideas and acts of deliberate harm are not sufficiently common in adolescence (Bagley 1989a) to be seen as indicators of profound distress or identity crisis. All subjects were interviewed in their own homes. Parents (always the mother, and sometimes the father as well) were interviewed separately from the children.

Results and Discussion

The results shown in Table 3.2 indicate that Native child adoptions are significantly more likely than any other parenting situation to involve problems and difficulties. By the age of 15, one-fifth of the Native adoptees had separated from their adoptive parents. A follow-up two years later indicated that nearly one-half of the Native adoptees—but none of the ICA group—had separated from parents because of behavioral or emotional problems or parent–child conflicts. Follow-up work with remaining groups is continuing.

Overall, the Native adoptees had significantly poorer self-esteem, and they were also more than three times as likely than any other group to have had problems of serious suicidal ideas or committed acts of deliberate self-harm in the previous six months. In contrast, the nonadopted Native adolescents had adjustment profiles not significantly different from those of nonadopted whites. Examination of white and Native adoptees by parental description of adjustment (see Table 3.2) indicates that, even within the group parents describe as having "no or some problems," adopted Native children had significantly poorer levels of self-esteem and higher scores on the suicidal ideation scale than the combined comparison groups.

Multiple regression (Table 3.3) was used to explore the relationships between variables in predicting self-esteem scores. Multiple regression is a technique that, in a series of steps, calculates the amount of variance explained in the dependent variable. Being Native *and* adopted was forced to enter the regression equation last, and this variable retains its significance in predicting low self-esteem even when the effects of age at adoption are accounted for.

Parental descriptions of adolescent problems are tabulated in Table 3.4. Although issues surrounding ethnicity were often perceived as problematic, these figures suggest that the adoptive parents were unwilling or unable to come to grips with issues of ethnic identity and respect for the child's original ethnic group. The parents of both Native and intercountry adopted children put little stress on identity and ethnic issues, preferring instead to treat the child "just like one of us." A measure of identity integration (Weinreich 1979) indicated, however, that failure to integrate or respect ethnic identity was present in half of the Native adolescent adoptees. In the ICA group, only 10 percent (two individuals)

Table 3.3

Multiple Regression of Variables Predicting Poor Self-Esteem in 159 Canadian Adolescents

Variable	Simple	_r_ After Multiple Regression	Multiple Correlation
Subject's age	-.16	-.16	.16
Sex: female	.13	.09	.17
Maternal education	-.15	-.14	.20
Age in months when child was adopted (0 = nonadopted)	.26	.20	.28
Ethnicity: nonwhite	.24	.12	.33
Maternal age	-.09	.03	.33
Child is Native <u>and</u> adopted	.39	.25	.44

Note: Variables entered into the regression analysis in steps, ordered as above, with "Native" entered last. Partial correlations of 0.18 and above after regression are significant at the 5% level or beyond.

had similar identity conflicts. In the nonadopted Native group, three adolescents (13 percent) showed marked identity confusion.[1]

We conclude from this analysis that Native children do have significantly poorer adjustment than white adoptees. The exact cause of this poorer adjustment is unknown, but conflicts over ethnicity might be a factor. These results and other clinical data suggest that Native adoptees are usually brought up with a consciousness of themselves as white, but increasingly find themselves subject to the stereotyping and rejection experienced by the average Native adolescent in urban Canada. Intercountry-adopted children, despite their differing ethnicity, do not seem to experience similar kinds of rejection or conflict. This is a tentative conclusion that needs testing and exploration in future work.

It is not entirely clear from the data why outcomes for Native adoptees should be so much worse than the outcome for white children adopted by white parents and for intercountry adoptees. What is clear, however, is that Native children adopted by white parents in this sample did have much lower levels of adjustment, more problems with depression, low self-esteem, and suicidal ideas, and much higher levels of acting-out behavior. Table 3.5 shows that failure to integrate concepts of ethnic, social, personal, and sexual identity (as indicated by Weinreich's measure) was the most powerful predictor of adolescent problems. Identity integration problems account for most of the variance in correlation of being adopted with marked behavior problems, as well as the correlation of being Native in predicting serious behavior problems in adolescence.

Table 3.4
Problems of Childrearing Identified by Parents of Adopted and Nonadopted Children in Canada

Variable	Natives Adoptees ($\underline{n}$=37)	White Adoptees ($\underline{n}$=42)	Intercountry Adoptees ($\underline{n}$=20)	Nonadopted White Adolescents ($\underline{n}$=40)	Nonadopted Native Adolescents ($\underline{n}$=23)
Child suffered racial harassment or insults in elementary school	51.3%	0.0%	15.0%	0.0%	34.8%
Lack of identity integration[a]	48.6%	14.3%	10.0%	7.5%	13.0%
Child had neurological or learning problem needing specialist treatment	10.8%	2.4%	0.0%	5.0%	4.3%
Up to age 12, marked signs of anxiety/depression/ psychosomatic signs[b]	32.4%	11.9%	5.0%	13.0%	38.9%

(continued)

Table 3.4
Continued

Variable	Natives Adoptees ($n=37$)	White Adoptees ($n=42$)	Intercountry Adoptees ($n=20$)	Nonadopted White Adolescents ($n=40$)	Nonadopted Native Adolescents ($n=23$)
Up to age 12, marked signs of aggression/ overactivity/conduct disorder[b]	43.2%	9.5%	5.0%	10.0%	21.7%
Marked behavior problems present at interview: one or more of rebellion; running from school or home; drug or alcohol use; delinquency; sexual acting out	59.5%	11.9%	15.0%	15.0%	17.4%

[a]Cut-off point indicated by Weinreich (1979).
[b]Clinical cut-off on Rutter's behavior disorder scale (Bagley, 1988a) completed by mother.

Table 3.5
Multiple Regression of Variables Predicting Marked Behavior Problems by Age 13 in 159 Canadian Adolescents

Variable	Simple	r After Multiple Regression	Multiple Correlation
Child has marked identity problems	.43	.43	.43
Child is adopted	.24	.18	.50
Sex: Female	-.14	-.10	.52
Child is Native	.33	.12	.55

Note: Variables entered into the regression analysis in steps, ordered as above. Partial correlations of 0.18 and above after regression are significant at the 5% level or beyond.

These findings leave us with the inference that, in more than one-fifth of the Native adoptees, identity problems and identity confusion are of major importance in the development of behavior problems associated with adoption breakdown. This inference will be explored in future research with these subjects.

There was also an implication that Native children adopted by white parents needed special support (which few of them got) to buffer them against what appear to have been acute role dilemmas—the conflicting roles of being a Native child in a white family, of being a Native child in a city with relatively few Native people, and of having to bear the brunt of ethnic stigmatization without the support of parents of similar ethnicity.

By contrast, the nonadopted Native children grew up on reserves in rural areas with cultural and family factors supporting their ethnic identity. It is also notable that the intercountry-adopted group appeared to have few current problems. These findings are similar to other work on the adjustment of intercountry-adopted children in North America (Feigelman and Silverman 1983). In Calgary, numerous people of Oriental, Central American, and South American origin are visible—commercially and professionally successful—and it may be that the intercountry-adopted children experienced fewer role conflicts with school and peers with regard to status, ethnic identity, and attachment to culture of origin. Ongoing work with this sample indicates that all of the intercountry-adopted children were comfortable and accepted in interethnic dating, whereas dating a white boy or girl was rare for the adopted Native adolescents.

A POTENTIAL SOLUTION

Child welfare programs in Canada have often undermined rather than supported Native families. Children have been removed by child protection workers, often on trivial grounds, and their extended families have been ignored as potential sources of care. Native children have been placed in various types of alternative care situations—from boarding schools (which were themselves abusive) and foster homes (which were uninterested in Native children) to white adoptive families (which were often unable to meet the identity needs of Native children).[2] Overall administration of almost every aspect of the life of Native people covered by the Indian Act is retained by central government. These powers include those of education and social service, which are usually delegated to the provinces. Only rarely are Native bands allowed to administer their own social service systems, and then only under the paternalistic guardianship of the federal government. In the present political climate, Canada seems unlikely to pass a law such as the Indian Child Welfare Act, which would allow autonomy in social service delivery in tribes so choosing (Simon and Altstein 1981). Yet it appears to us that allowing Native people in Canada such autonomy is the only way to solve the problems of Native child welfare. Likewise, the land claims made by many Canadian bands for return of traditional territory must also be conceded. These lands were either illegally seized or taken with so-called treaties that were signed under duress or without legal guidance as to their implications.

Native peoples in North America have traditionally formed nations with individual languages, customs, and territories. Native and Metis people in Canada are seeking to reinforce their group identity through the negotiation of their rights as individual nations. Within this search for political recognition lies a potential solution—namely, applying the rules that control and monitor ICAs to adoptions of Native children by white adoptive families and Americans.

Any number of approaches could be used. First, independent Native nations could enact laws that govern the removal of children from the band for purposes of adoption.[3] In addition (or alternatively), both Canada and the Native nations could adopt the United Nations (U.N.) principles on ICA that emerged from a conference at Leysin, Switzerland, addressing the many problems surrounding such adoptions (Delupis 1976).

The Leysin principles (United Nations 1960) have been revised and updated in subsequent international meetings (Lueker-Babel 1986), and the revised principles presented to the U.N. (United Nations 1985) are broadly as follows:

a. The first priority is for a child to be cared for by his or her own parents.

b. Where adoption is considered to be a suitable solution to the problem of providing a permanent family environment for a child, the informed consent of the child's biological parents should be sought before any legal proceedings regarding adoption are undertaken.

c. ICA should only be considered when no permanent home within the child's own country can be found.

d. ICA should only be undertaken when governments of the respective countries have agreed on the professional and legal principles to be followed in monitoring and supervising such adoptions.

e. All assessments of children and potential parents should be made by properly qualified professionals according to standards set down by the two countries involved. In no case should the placement result in improper financial gain for those involved. Professionals involved should receive normal fees, but no financial inducement should be offered to any biological parent, or to any official.

f. Special legal precautions should be taken to control the activities of third parties who attempt to arrange international adoptions.

g. The order for adoption should be made in the country in which the child is born, and the prospective adopters should travel to that country for purposes of such legal hearings. The laws and rules concerning adoption should be agreed on by both countries involved.

h. Prospective adopters should be professionally assessed in their country of domicile: if they are unsuitable as in-country adopters, then they would certainly be unsuitable as intercountry adopters.

i. The receiving country shall appoint professionals to monitor the child's progress in the receiving country for at least six months.

j. All actions taken with regard to ICA shall be taken in the best interests of the child and for no other reason. The child's potential for healthy psychological growth in the country of the adopters—in terms of adaptation and acceptance by the wider community—should be carefully considered before making an adoption order.

Adoptions of Native children from Canada, many of whom have been taken to the United States and elsewhere, have not followed these principles. Children have been handed to prospective adopters by child welfare authorities who were clearly pleased to be relieved of a financial burden.[4] Adoption orders have been made by the country, province, or state in which the adopter resided, with no social work or legal monitoring undertaken once a child has been placed.

The case of Carla W., who returned to Canada in November 1989 at the age of 25, illustrates the problems that can arise in an unsupervised ICA when the Leysin principles are entirely ignored (York 1989). Carla, a

Native child, was removed from her parents by social workers in Winnipeg when she was five. As usual, the option of placing Carla with members of her extended family was not considered. The social workers involved in this case—like adoptive parents and many other Canadians— seemed to view aboriginal culture and social organization with distaste, not as something to be taken seriously or respected.

When Carla was eight years old, she was placed with a Dutch couple in Manitoba. The couple immediately left for the Netherlands, and there were no further checks or follow-ups on Carla's status. Although application of the U.N. principles on ICA might have prevented the disasters that followed, Canada has never followed these principles.[5] Carla was one of thousands of Manitoba Indian children adopted by white parents in the 1960s and 1970s. Hundreds of these children were sent to the United States, and some went even farther, to Europe.

After six months in the Netherlands, Carla's adoption broke down for unexplained reasons. She was initially placed in a children's home where she recalled that nuns beat her when she wouldn't obey instructions—apparently because she didn't understand Dutch. She was then placed in a series of foster homes where, by her own account, she was both acutely depressed and rebellious. In the final home, she was sexually abused and had two children by her foster father. Both children were placed in care, and the foster father denied responsibility. When Carla returned to the Anishinaaboin nation, she was met by the traditional chief in full regalia and 50 members of her extended family. The Anishinaaboin and other nations in Canada are trying to locate the thousands of children taken from them and placed for adoption.

CONCLUSIONS

Native people in North America are struggling to survive, both culturally and physically, following the devastations imposed on their traditional ways of life and family systems by white settlers and their administrative apparatus. The approach of white settlers can be described as institutional racism, just as the approach used by whites in North America to control blacks and exclude them from many arenas of public and social life is institutionalized oppression. And just as the adoption of black children by white parents has been problematic compared with within-race adoptions and ICAs (Feigelman and Silverman 1983), so the adoptions of Native children by whites appears to be fraught with difficulty.

Although there is some evidence of positive trends in identity development in black children adopted by white parents, Bagley and Young (1979) and Simon and Altstein (1981) have argued that the case of Native Americans is a special one. Native Americans have been subjected to a singularly tragic fate, and their children have been particularly vulnerable. Our own research supports such a conclusion.

The majority of adoptions of Native children by white parents in our survey (based on random sampling) had experienced difficulties, often profound. And it should be added that attempts by some of these white parents to give their children a sense of identity as a Native person were not particularly successful: Native adolescents with profound identity problems were equally divided between parents who ignored identity issues and those who tried to emphasize Native identity. From these results, we conclude that the extreme marginalization of Native people in Canada allows little possibility for a Native child to adapt successfully in a white family. The few truly "successful" Native-white adoptions in our series involved children with mixed ancestry who were able to pass themselves as white.

Our study is unique in including a control group of native children who grew up with their parents on rural reserves. These controls—who had relatively good psychological outcomes in adolescence—were not randomly selected, but came from families identified by the band as needing help and support following the removal of an older child by provincial social services. The findings from these nonadopted, Native adolescents are important, and this work deserves replication.

Answers to the problems of Native communities lie, we have argued, in a combination of political, social, and economic development. The Native communities in Alberta with the fewest problems (of crime, suicide, family breakdown, alcoholism, and removal of children by external authorities) are the larger reserves in the south, communities with diversified economies that provide income through ranching and leasing oil, coal, and natural gas reserves (Bagley, Wood, and Khumar 1990). It is also these nations—particularly the Blackfoot, with whom we have worked extensively (Bagley 1985)—who are closest to organizing indigenous systems of child welfare and adoption. Not only must the white power structure concede land claims by Native peoples, it must also foster development of Native nations the same way they foster the development of Third-World peoples. If Native nations and communities choose to allow some of their children to be adopted by white families, then internationally accepted rules for ICA must be observed.

NOTES

1. Weinreich's method of identifying acute identity problems in adolescence is based on the theoretical merging of Kelly's personal construct theory, Eriksonian notions of identity formation, and Hauser's work on identity problems in black adolescents (Kelly 1955; Hauser 1971). Each adolescent tested produces a unique

collection of elements (individuals or groups) that are construed in ways given by the subject. Each personal construct is then interpreted in the light of Hauser's work on identity formation. Because there is a subjective element in this interpretation, each set of personal constructs was interpreted by the writer and/or the two research assistants (Michael Wood and Helda Khumar) who did the interviewing; each profile was rated "blindly" by two individuals who had not interviewed the subject. When there was complete agreement between the two raters on profound failure of identity integration, a subject was assumed to have acute identity problems.

For example, John (age 14) identified 11 elements relating to himself, his ethnic group, his school peers, his past self, his ideal self, his white parents, his Native parents, and Native people in general. As "a person with white parents" he evaluated himself positively in the past, but negatively now. Native people in the past were evaluated positively in the past, but negatively now. His white brother had very positive ratings, while he had very negative current ratings on the strong-weak dimension. White peers were seen as unfriendly, successful, and strong. We used Weinreich's formulation for assessing the ratio of current identification with contra-identifications (past, present, and future) to obtain measures of identity integration failure or identity fixation. For further details on the methods of analyzing the personal constructs that we use, see Fransella and Bannister (1977).

The identity problems of the Native adoptees in this study appear to be much more profound than those of adolescent black subjects adopted by white parents analyzed by McRoy and Zurcher (1983).

2. It is ironic that only in 1988 in Canada did details begin to emerge of the sexual abuse (among many other types of abuse) in the boarding schools for Native children run by Catholic and Anglican missionaries. In September 1989, the Canadian Broadcasting Company ran an hour-long documentary in which many adult Native people spoke about these abuses. The last of these schools, in Manitoba, was closed in October 1989 after parents complained about the severe and regular beatings their children received. The missionaries defended such beatings on biblical grounds.

3. What are needed for both sending and receiving countries involved in ICA are model acts of the kind outlined by Simon and Altstein (1981) in their chapter on ICA.

4. The readiness of child welfare authorities to unburden themselves of seemingly unadoptable children is illustrated by the State of California, which in the late 1970s gave into the care of a religious organization 150 permanent wards, all of them black. The cult, called the People's Temple, took 39 of these children to Guyana with the tacit approval of the State of California, but in contravention to California law, which forbids the removal of permanent wards. Once in Guyana, the children were beaten, terrorized, raped, and sexually tortured. They had to regularly rehearse taking poison. Wooden (1981) devotes a good part of his book on the Jonestown massacre to describing how easily children can be given away or disposed of once the state has assumed the role of legal parent. As Wooden points out, some 300 of those who died by poisoning in Guyana did not commit suicide: they were children and minors who had no option but to obey the adults who had terrorized them. In other words, these children were murdered.

5. There is an "Adoption Desk" at the federal government headquarters in

Ottawa, with the role of advising parties in ICAs. The writer asked the director of this agency in 1984 whether the Leysin principles were followed in Canada. The director replied by letter, saying that he had never heard of these principles! For a statement of federal policy on adoptions of Native children, see *Adoption and the Indian Child*, available from the Adoption Desk, National Health and Welfare, Brooke Claxton Building, Tunney's Pasture, Ottawa, K1A 1B5, Canada.

REFERENCES

Bagley, C. (1984). Child protection and the Native child. *Perception*, 28, 17–20.

Bagley, C. (1985). Field dependence and verbal reasoning in Blackfoot, Japanese and Anglo-Celtic children in Southern Alberta. In R. Diaz-Gurrero (Ed.), *Cross-cultural and national studies in social psychology* (pp. 191–208). New York: North Holland Publishing.

Bagley, C. (1986). Child abuse by the child welfare system. *Journal of Child Care, 2*, 64–69.

Bagley, C. (1988a). Lies, damned lies, and Indian ethnicity in the Canadian census. *Ethnic and Racial Studies*, 11, 230–233.

Bagley, C. (1988b). Child abuse and the legal system: The question of bias. In S. Martin (Ed.), *Judges and equality issues* (pp. 140–149). Toronto: Carswell Legal Publications.

Bagley, C. (1988c). Day care and child development. *Early Childhood Care, Health and Development*, 39, 134–161.

Bagley, C. (1989a). Profiles of youthful suicide: Disrupted development and current stressors. *Psychological Reports*, 65, 234.

Bagley, C. (1989b). *The prevalence and long-term sequels of child sexual abuse in a community sample of young, adult women.* Manuscript submitted for publication.

Bagley, C. (1989c). Development of a short self-esteem measure for use with adults in community mental health surveys. *Psychological Reports*, 65, 13–14.

Bagley, C., Wood, M., & Khumar, H. (1990). Suicide and careless death in Native populations: A Canadian case study. *Canadian Journal of Community Mental Health*.

Bagley, C., & Young, L. (1979). The identity, adjustment and achievement of transracially adopted children. In G. Verma & C. Bagley (Eds.), *Race, education and identity* (pp. 192–219). London: Macmillan.

Bagley, C., & Young, L. (1981). The long-term adjustment and identity of a sample of inter-country adopted children. *International Journal of Social Work*, 4, 1–7.

Buchignani, N., & Engel, J. (1983). *Cultures in Canada: Strength in diversity.* Edmonton: Weigl Publishers.

Byler, W. (1977, Summer). Removing children: The destruction of American Indian families. *Civil Rights Digest*, 19–27.

Campagna, D., & Poffenberger, D. (1988). *The sexual trafficking in children.* Dover, MA: Auburn House Publishing.

CJPH. (1982). Editorial: Health of Native Canadians—its relevance to world health. *Canadian Journal of Public Health*, 73, 297–298.

Coopersmith, S. (1967). *The antecedents of self-esteem*. San Francisco: Freeman.

Delupis, I. (1976). *International adoptions and the conflict of laws*. Stockholm: Almquist and Wiksell.

Ellestad-Sayed, J., Haworth, J., Coodin, F., & Dilling, L. (1981). Growth and nutrition of preschool Indian children in Manitoba. *Canadian Journal of Public Health, 72*, 127–133.

Evers, S., & Rana, C. (1983). Morbidity in Canadian Indian and non-Indian children in the second year. *Canadian Journal of Public Health, 74*, 191–194.

Fanshel, D. (1972). *Far from the reservation: The transracial adoption of American Indian children*. Metuchen, NJ: Scarecrow Press.

Feigelman, W., & Silverman, A. (1983). *Chosen children: New patterns of adoptive relationships*. New York: Praeger.

Fransella, F., & Bannister, D. (1977). *A manual for repertory grid technique*. New York: Academic Press.

French, L. (1980). An analysis of government sterilization and adoption practices involving Native Americans. *International Child Welfare Review, 45*, 37–40.

Government of Alberta. (1984). *The Child Welfare Act of Alberta*. Edmonton: Government of Alberta.

Hauser, S. (1971). *Black and white identity formation*. New York: Wiley.

Hepworth, H. (1980). *Foster care and adoption in Canada*. Ottawa: Canadian Council on Social Development.

Hepworth, H. (1981). *Trends and comparisons in Canadian child welfare services*. Ottawa: Health and Welfare Policy Development Branch, Government of Canada.

Johnston, P. (1983). *Native children and the child welfare system*. Toronto: James Lorimer and Company.

Kelly, G. (1955). *The psychology of personal constructs*. New York: Norton.

Kimmelman, J. (1984). *Report on the adoption of Native children*. Winnipeg: Government of Manitoba.

Luecker-Babel, M. F. (1986). International adoption: Agreement at last? *International Children's Rights Monitor, 3*, 7–13.

MacDonald, R. (1978). *Canada Ill: The uncharted nations: A reference history of the Canadian tribes*. Vancouver: Evergreen Press.

McRoy, R., & Zurcher, L. (1983). *Transracial and inracial adoptees: The adolescent years*. Springfield, IL: Charles C Thomas.

Morrison, R., & Wilson, C. (1986). *Native peoples: The Canadian experience*. Toronto: McClelland and Stewart.

Morse, B. (1984). Native Indian and Metis children in Canada: Victims of the child welfare system. In G. Verma & C. Bagley (Eds.), *Race relations and cultural differences* (pp. 141–156). London: Croom-Helm.

Nuttall, R. (1982). The development of Indian Boards of Health in Alberta. *Canadian Journal of Public Health, 73*, 300–303.

Ramsay, R., & Bagley, C. (1986). The prevalence of suicidal behaviors, attitudes and associated social experiences in an urban population. *Suicide and Life-Threatening Behavior, 15*, 151–160.

Sachdev, P. (1984). *Adoption: Current issues and trends*. Toronto: Butterworths.

Siggner, A., & Locatelli, C. (1980). *An overview of demographic, social and economic conditions among Manitoba's registered Indian population.* Winnipeg: Government of Manitoba, Corporate Policy Research Office.

Simon, R., & Altstein, H. (1981). *Transracial adoption: A follow-up.* Lexington, MA: D.C. Heath.

Spady, D. (1982). *Between two worlds.* Edmonton: The Boreal Institute, Occasional Publication No. 16.

Talbot, P. (1983). *Tuberculosis on Indian reserves in Manitoba.* Winnipeg: Federal Health and Welfare, Regional Office, Manitoba.

Tervo, R. (1983). The Native child with cerebral palsy at a children's rehabilitation center. *Canadian Journal of Public Health, 74,* 242–245.

Thomlison, R. (1985). *Report on the death of a Metis foster child.* Edmonton: Alberta Social Services, Government of Alberta.

Unger, S. (Ed.). (1977). *The destruction of American Indian families.* New York: Association on American Indian Affairs.

United Nations. (1960). *Report of Leysin seminar on inter-country adoption* (Document UN/TAO/SEM/Rep. 2). Geneva: United Nations.

United Nations. (1985). *Draft declaration on social and legal principles relating to the protection and welfare of children, with special reference to foster placement and adoption nationally and internationally* (General Assembly Document A/40/998-6 Dec. 1985). New York: United Nations.

Weinreich, P. (1979). Cross-ethnic identification and self-rejection in a black adolescent. In G. Verma & C. Bagley (Eds.), *Race, education and identity* (pp. 157–175). London: Macmillan.

Wooden, K. (1981). *The children of Jonestown.* New York: McGraw-Hill.

York, G. (1989, November 11). Carla comes home. *Toronto Globe and Mail,* p. 14.

Young, L., & Bagley, C. (1982). Self-esteem, self-concept and the development of black identity: A theoretical overview. In G. Verma & C. Bagley (Eds.), *Self-concept, achievement and multicultural education* (pp. 41–59). London: Macmillan.

Young, T. (1983). The Canadian North and the Third World: Is the analogy appropriate? *Canadian Journal of Public Health, 74,* 239–241.

II

WESTERN EUROPE

4

Norway: Intercountry Adoptions in a Homogeneous Country

BARBRO SAETERSDAL
MONICA DALEN

What does it mean for intercountry-adopted children to grow up in a small, homogeneous country unaccustomed to living and interacting with colored minorities, a country where, until recently, racism never appeared on the political agenda? How does such a context affect the adoptive family? Is it easier to grow up in a country where color prejudice has no historical roots, or will a colored intercountry-adopted child be even more stigmatized in such a setting? The Norwegian situation provides an interesting context for a discussion of these questions.

FROM A HOMOGENEOUS TO A MULTI-ETHNIC SOCIETY

Norway is a sparsely populated country—as big as California, but with only 4.5 million inhabitants. Norway's gross national product (GNP) equals that of the United States, and the difference in standard of living between rich and poor is not very great. There is one government-run school system with a uniform core curriculum, private schools are extremely rare, and universities are free for all who meet admission requirements. The majority of Norway's population is Lutheran. The health and social security systems include everyone.

Except for a small minority of Laps who live in the northern part of the country, Norway has traditionally been ethnically homogeneous. The immigration of laborers from southern Europe to northern Europe in the 1950s and 1960s never reached Norway.

Until recently in Norway, racism was something that concerned others—blacks in the United States, Jews in Hitler's Germany, and apartheid in South Africa. It did not concern Norwegians, who had no colonial past and did not participate in the slave trades. Norwegians fought Hitler and Nazism during World War II. Their hands and consciences were clean—a wonderful state of innocence.

But things have changed. In the early 1970s, at about the same time that adoption agencies started ICAs, immigration from the Third World to Norway started steadily growing. Most immigrants live in the big cities: about 15 percent of newborn babies in Oslo are from Asia or Africa, and 20 percent of all pupils in the lower grades of Oslo's elementary schools are of foreign origin. In one inner-city school, 78 percent of the children were immigrant children in 1989. Over the past 20 years, Norway has become a multi-cultural, multi-ethnic society, and some of the social and economic patterns well-known in other multiethnic societies have appeared in Norway. The state of innocence is gone, and the glossy and self-contented Norwegian image has acquired some nasty rifts. The racism that self-contented Norwegians had once attributed only to other societies has become a part of Norwegian reality. These changes have had an important impact on the lives of the 7,000 intercountry-adopted children and their families.

TRANSRACIAL VERSUS INTERCOUNTRY ADOPTIONS

In a homogeneous country such as Norway, it is difficult to see the point of making a sharp division between "transracial" and "intercountry" adoptions. Whether adopted children go from black minority families to white majority families within the same country or from one part of the world to another, the basic facts remain the same—a child relinquished for adoption will always go from poor to rich, from underprivileged to privileged—regardless of whether the adoption occurs within the same country or outside the country. But political pressure against a family who adopts a child from abroad might be less severe if the same family were to adopt a black minority child from its own country. This might in turn lessen the psychological burden of these families.

The political aspect of ICAs might also be absent in the public discussion on adoption matters as has been the case in Norway. Neither public opinion nor adoption agencies have openly discussed the desirability of "same race–same culture" adoption practices in Norway. Nor has there been any reaction against transracial ICAs such as there has been in the United States and England (Chestang 1972; Chimezie 1975; Fanshel 1972; McRoy and Zurcher 1983; Simon and Altstein 1977, 1981, and 1987; Triseliotis 1988; Gill and Jackson 1983; Tizard and Phoenix 1989). This is due in part to the decreasing supply of Norwegian children relinquished for adoption. Free abortion is available through the 12th week of pregnancy, and social and economic conditions for unmarried mothers and their children have improved greatly in the last few decades. New infertility techniques such as in-vitro fertilization are not widely practiced, and surrogacy is not allowed. Thus, the only option for most infertile couples in Norway is either to accept their infertility or apply for adoption of a child born abroad. ICA in Norway has been viewed as a private, acceptable, and respected way of creating a family if a couple cannot have its "own" children.

FROM PRIVATE ADOPTIONS TO ADOPTION AGENCIES

Until the early 1970s, ICA in Norway was practiced only on an individual basis. Missionaries, diplomats, business people, relief workers, and Peace Corps participants often became attached to special children they had come to know while working abroad. The first adoption agencies working exclusively with ICAs appeared in the early 1970s. Transracial adoption (in the original sense of the term—from minority women living in Norway) has not been practiced so far, and that might be one reason why adoption across race and culture has never been a political issue in Norway.

FACTS ABOUT ICA IN NORWAY

As mentioned earlier, adoption of Norwegian-born children was the dominant way of creating a family for infertile couples until 1970. After that, the situation changed. Figure 4.1 shows that most infertile couples today adopt children from foreign countries.

Regulations

The law regulating all adoption practices in Norway was most recently revised in 1986. This law is based on the following principles:

Adoption is allowed only when there is a very good reason to believe that it would be "the very best" for the child.

The adopted child has the same legal rights in the family as the biological child.

An adoption cannot be canceled.

Unmarried couples are not allowed to adopt and single parents are very seldom given permission to adopt.

Private adoptions are not permitted.

Adoption Agencies

A couple wanting to adopt a child from a foreign country must go through an adoption agency, and there are only two licensed adoption agencies in Norway. These agencies have arranged adoptions from various countries, but mainly from countries in Asia, as Table 4.1 shows.

Figure 4.1
Adoption in Norway

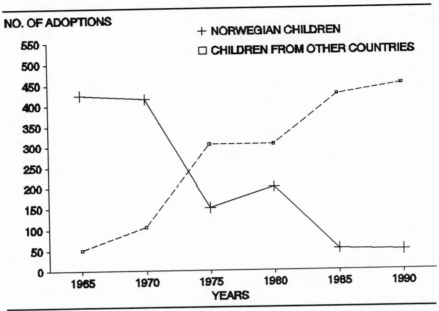

Notes: The law that regulates all adoption practices in Norway was last revised in 1986. This law is based on the following principles: adoption is allowed only when there is a very good reason to believe that it would be "the very best" for the child; the adopted child has the same legal rights in the family as the biological child; an adoption cannot be canceled; unmarried couples are not allowed to adopt and single parents are very seldom given permission to adopt; private adoptions are not permitted.

Procedure

A long application procedure is required before a couple is accepted as adoptive parents. Applicants must first be accepted by Norwegian authorities and then by the government in the child's birth country. Restrictions connected with permission to adopt which concern the following areas:

Age of the applicants
Length of their marriage
Fertility status
Religious status
Economic status

Table 4.1
Adopted Children in Norway and Their Countries of Origin

Year	Norwegian-born children	Europe	Asia	Latin America	Africa	Unknown
1967	381	26	46	4	–	–
1968	386	16	58	1	–	–
1969	392	32	31	2	–	–
1970	411	28	80	5	–	2
1971	342	20	135	2	–	–
1972	205	15	189	5	–	4
1973	198	23	255	10	6	–
1974	221	20	361	13	1	2
1975	157	17	260	15	1	3
1976	184	26	300	56	3	5
1977	139	11	338	61	1	1
1978	135	5	312	39	–	1
1979	134	17	197	58	–	3
1980	190	15	216	52	1	3
1981	174	10	265	77	2	5
1982	106	13	435	97	–	2
1983	93	13	398	85	2	–
1984	106	12	395	109	4	–
1985	90	7	344	88	–	–
1986	106	9	304	172	3	–
1987	91	3	306	160	7	–

Educational and professional status
Motivation for adoption
Unblemished record

Research

Norwegian social scientists have not shown much interest in ICA as a social phenomena, and only a few ICA studies have been carried out over the past 20 years (Lehland 1971; Schjelderup-Mathiesen and Nytrohaug 1977; Berntsen and Eigeland 1987). Recently, Dalen and Saetersdal (1987; Dalen 1988; Saetersdal 1988) investigated Indian- and Vietnamese-born adoptees, and Kvifte-Andresen investigated inter-country 12-year-old adoptees from several different countries (1989). Because Dalen and Saetersdal's findings are so far the only ones published, the following discussion is based on them.

Using a variety of research methods, the Dalen and Saetersdal project investigated Indian and Vietnamese adopted children and their Norwegian families. These particular groups of adoptees were chosen because they had the same ethnic origins as two of the largest immigrant and refugee groups in Norway. Dalen and Saetersdal's findings are based on a survey of 182 parents (81 percent of the population) with adopted Indian and Vietnamese children under age 17 and on in-depth interviews with Vietnamese-born adopted boys and girls aged 17 to 22 years and their parents, for a total of 98 persons. Children's drawings and questionnaires to teachers were also used.

The families represent various socioeconomic and demographic backgrounds from different parts of Norway. Most parents had been married for many years before adopting, half more than ten years. Stability also characterized the adoptive families after the adoption. Among the 182 families with children under 17, there were only two deaths, three divorces, and two separations. Only one-quarter of the families moved to another place after the adoption, and most of them had only moved once. The adopted children seemed to grow up under more stable circumstances than most other Norwegian-born children.

Only one-third of the adoptees grew up as only children. Half of the children were adopted by families who already had biological children, and almost one-quarter later acquired siblings. Most of these siblings, however, were also adopted. The belief that infertile women who adopt later become pregnant seems to be a myth. Out of the 182 families with adopted children younger than 17, only 19 mothers later became pregnant.

We now consider three important aspects in the lives of these inter-country adopting families: the initial period of adjustment to the new family constellation, the school situation, and the identity problems these children and adolescents struggle with in Norwegian society. Finally, we propose a new theoretical psychosocial model for understanding the ICA dilemma.

INITIAL PERIOD OF ADJUSTMENT

Physical Health

A common belief in Scandinavia is that foreign-adopted children arrive in very poor physical condition, but according to several recent studies, this seems to be a myth. That does not mean that many children have not experienced difficult living conditions in their birth countries, but reflects instead the fact that institutions and foster homes are able to provide improved living conditions for the children, especially in the transitional phase before adoption.

Adoption agencies often informed parents-to-be that children might arrive in poor physical condition and might exhibit symptoms of tropical and other diseases due to malnutrition. But even when parents were intellectually well-prepared, some of them reported that they were shocked by their children's poor medical condition. This was especially true for Vietnamese children who arrived during the war.

Parents were asked to estimate their children's health upon arrival. (Most of the 182 adoptees under age 17 came from India.) The most remarkable finding was that 73% of the children had arrived in very satisfactory or satisfactory physical condition. The remaining 27% were judged to be in not very satisfactory or poor physical condition, but most of these were children who had arrived in Norway during the Vietnam War. These findings correspond with another Norwegian investigation (Berntsen and Eigeland 1987) on Colombian- and Korean-born adopted children.

According to official sources, 4 percent of all intercountry-adopted children in Norway arrive with some form of physical or mental handicap. The proportion of handicapped children in the Dalen-Saetersdal investigation was, however, 8 percent. Most of these children came from Vietnam.

Mental Health

Even when the parents were prepared for a difficult initial period, the psychological adjustment problems of many children seemed to have come as a surprise. Once medical problems were overcome, psychological problems surged to the surface. These problems varied from child to child and family to family, and some children seemed to manage the first adjustment period in the family without any difficulties.

More than half the children in the Saetersdal-Dalen investigation showed adjustment problems. Sleeping and eating problems were common in all age groups: children had difficulty falling asleep and woke up several times during the night. Some children did not want food, while others swallowed anything they could lay their hands on so that parents had to hide or ration food. Children displayed various forms of regressive behavior in the initial six months, including wetting their pants, excessive clinging and attention seeking, whining, and tantrums. Many parents also told of difficulties they had communicating with their children in the beginning.

One-third of the children studied had serious adjustment problems. These varied, of course, according to the children's age upon arrival. The group that clearly stood out were children between one and three years old at adoption, findings that are in accordance with a Swedish investigation (Gardell 1980). It is obvious that the period of psychological and social adjustment between parents and child also is a period of strain for both parties. But how could one expect anything else? Perhaps a more remarkable finding is the fact that a relatively high percentage of adopted children do not show any great initial adjustment problems.

If it is true that a fairly large proportion of the children had initial adjustment problems, it is also true that these problems diminished over time. Changes in adjustment from the initial period to the time of investigation is shown in Table 4.2.

The changes in the psychological condition of the oldest children were remarkable. The most vulnerable group again seemed to be children adopted between one and three years old. Even though this group showed substantial improvement, they still exhibited many symptoms at the time of the investigation. Language problems were accentuated for children who had been more than four years old at the time of adoption. It is also remarkable that some of the original problems seemed to "wander" into other areas.

The Vietnamese "Babylift" Children

Vietnamese-born adoptees who arrived in Norway during the Vietnam War were in extremely poor physical and mental condition and in many ways represent an extreme group. Few groups of adoptees have had more traumatic early childhood experiences. Although this group may not be representative of intercountry-adopted children, and certainly not of adopted children in general, their fate is of special interest in a discussion about the reversibility of early childhood trauma. Their story provides an interesting illustration of how children raised in extremely difficult conditions develop and adjust socially and psychologically. Because

Table 4.2
Adoptees' Difficulties at Time of Arrival and Time of Study by Age at Adoption

Areas of Difficulty	0-3 Months Old (n=38)		4-11 Months Old (n=57)		1-3 Years Old (n=43)		4+ Years Old (n=42)	
	Arrival %	Today %	Arrival %	Today %	Arrival %	Today %	Arrival %	Today %
Sleep	40	15	28	10	40	8	26	5
Eating	27	24	25	8	14	8	17	0
Bowel & bladder control/day	–	–	–	–	29	6	14	0
Bowel & bladder control/night	–	–	–	–	34	6	24	8
Play	–	–	–	–	28	8	33	8
Contact with children	–	–	–	–	9	3	27	5
Anxiety	–	–	–	–	29	6	20	6
Language development	–	–	–	–	17	6	21	25
Temper	–	–	2	11	26	22	41	14
Clinging	–	–	12	9	44	14	22	6
Attention seeking	–	–	8	17	35	19	38	14

these were also the children we interviewed as adolescents, their adjustment and experiences form the basis for our reasoning on identity formation of intercountry-adopted children in Norway.

Physical and Emotional State at Adoption

Most of these Vietnamese-born children were between two and five years old when they arrived in Norway. They were in very bad health and extremely developmentally retarded. Some had severe physical handicaps, and a few were mentally retarded. Many of the three-year-old children could not walk or talk. They were passive, apathetic, frightened, retarded, underweight, and sick. The parents were told by medical authorities that these children had very little chance of growing up without mental and physical defects.

The following description is typical:

When she came to us she was at least two years old, but we believe she was older. She was in a pitiful condition and weighed only seven kilos. The hospital told us she was enervated, dehydrated, and on the verge of shock. She had boils, infections and diarrhea. She had no expression on her face of either joy or sorrow. I carried her close to me day and night for at least three months. She always carried a rusk and a tangerine in each hand, and whenever she dropped either of them, she became hysterical. She sometimes had convulsions and fits of temper at night, so we understood that she suffered. When she first started to stand, she began to make rapid progress.

Many parents were surprised that their children did not talk—even children who were three years and older—and they found this lack of language and communication skills most difficult to handle.

And when she smiled, she just imitated the others. Nothing was obvious or simple for her. She would sit with her glass of milk in front of her and pour it out, or she would take a bowl with flowers and throw the flowers away. And I let her do this because it was just bewilderment with this strange new world that she discovered when she was almost four years old. It took quite a while until she actually could begin to understand the world around her. But she did not manage to get the words. Not a single one until late.

Descriptions of disorientation and bewilderment were typical in the parents' accounts of the initial adjustment period. Many parents expressed worry and anxiety about the heavy responsibilities they had undertaken. One parent of an older child who refused in the beginning to have anything to do with her new family said, "At first I thought, I can't manage this, I can't. And we were desperate and depressed at least the first couple of months."

Reviving a Lost Childhood Together

Along with this anxiety and feelings of inadequacy, many parents also emphasized how much they were moved by the helplessness and pathetic condition of their children. They were moved the same way parents of newborns are—by the total dependence and vulnerability of their children.

We believe that the adoptees' total helplessness *intensified the attachment and promoted the bonding* between parents and children in a way that is difficult to achieve with older adopted children who arrive in better physical and age-relevant mental states. The initial period was not only difficult and exhausting, but it also gave parent and child a chance to revive parts of the child's lost infancy.

Most of the couples who adopted the Vietnam children already had biological children, and we believe that this fact partially explains their ability to cope with the strains and challenges of the adjustment period. They were not becoming parents for the first time with the insecurity that that implies. They already were parents and, according to their own accounts, quite sure of themselves in that role. Their previous experiences as parents enabled them to rely on their own judgments and feelings about what was right or wrong in situations and they could resist contradictory advice from both professionals and friends.

As one mother put it:

And everybody said that she would become impossible if we continued to carry her with us everywhere. We had an uncle who was a child psychiatrist, and he also emphasized that. But we had to trust our own feelings. She *needed* us all the time then, and that was most important. Once secure, she remained so from the time she was five years old.

Another factor that helped these families cope was the presence of older siblings, who often acted as intermediaries in families with adoptees who were too afraid of adults in the beginning to be able to relate to their adoptive parents.

For most of these Vietnamese-born adoptees, the adjustment period lasted between three months and a year. Then their development came "as an explosion." Once they had overcome their initial medical problems, they developed "iron health." Psychologically and socially, the majority of these Vietnamese-born adoptees have since developed well. They have close relationships with their parents and have experienced little bullying and discrimination at school or in their neighborhoods. In fact, as children, they may well have been subjected to positive discrimination.

In other words, they present in many ways a positive picture. Our findings suggest that early childhood traumas do not necessarily deem a child to a bleak future. The effect of privation and deprivation can be reversed or modified by a caring and devoted family setting. Our findings support those of Harvey (1982), Kadushin (1970), Feigelman and Silverman (1983), and Clarke and Clarke (1977). And it should be noted that some of the children in those investigations had even more traumatic early childhood experiences than did the Vietnamese baby-lift children.

Meeting these children as adolescents also made us realize how much we have, in our psychological training, been influenced by the classic studies of Bowlby (1969), Ainsworth (1973), and others that emphasize the importance of early emotional relationships. In recent years, such pessimistic views have been reinforced by psycholinguistic research on the importance of early communication between mothers and neonates (Condon and Sander 1974; Trevarthen 1979)—not to mention the pessimism of psychoanalysts such as Alice Miller (1981, 1984). Perhaps it is time to reevaluate some of these findings and put more effort into investigating mechanisms that counteract, heal, and soothe the effects of early childhood trauma.

SCHOOL SITUATION AND ACADEMIC PERFORMANCE

Intercountry-adopted children seem to be in danger of being underachievers in school. In other words, there appears to be a mismatch between their abilities and potentials and what they actually achieve academically. On the other hand, results also indicate that these children are happy at school, and their social development is considered very good. They are seldom teased or tormented by others, and they appear to have good relationships with their teachers and fellow pupils.

As we stated earlier, many of the intercountry-adopted children we studied had serious adjustment problems when they arrived in their new families. Such children need a long time to settle into their new surroundings, and psychological adjustment problems are particularly serious and long-lasting for older children. This means that those who were oldest at arrival started school before the upsetting transition phase was over, and this transfer from home to school represented still another change of circumstance for the adopted child.

A large number of these children had their start in school postponed, and most of these were children who were more than four years old when they arrived in Norway. Language difficulties were often given as the reason for the delay, and sometimes there were problems with determining a child's precise age. However, no special arrangements were made to help these children educationally during this waiting period, and many parents reported considerable adjustment problems when their children finally did start school. The change from home to school often reawakened earlier, perhaps suppressed, feelings of separation. The children became insecure and anxious. Moreover, the school system required a much greater degree of independence, and it represented the child's first confrontation with formal, academic learning.

Intercountry-adopted children often lack the emotional security necessary for a good school start. This often manifests itself in the form of concentration difficulties in the classroom, a characteristic that both teachers and parents agree seems to be one of their main problems.

Language Problems

Gradually, the adoptive parents and teachers became aware that, even though the children had a good command of the spoken language, they still lacked a deeper understanding of many everyday words and expressions. This, in turn, created problems both in Norwegian and in other subjects and consequently affected the children's general intellectual development. Many of these language problems were misinterpreted as being the same ones that Norwegian-born dyslexic children have. However, the language problems of intercountry-adopted children seem to be qualitatively different, and they are generally not discovered until the teenage years, when a greater degree of abstract thinking is demanded. Our findings clearly show that as adopted children move up in the school system, their learning difficulties become more and more apparent.

Many of these children have not been able to keep up academically in secondary school. The teaching at this level is far more theoretical and abstract than at the primary level, where more concrete examples are used and teaching is more visual. Many of the parents expressed early optimism that their children had progressed well in the first few years in school. Then, gradually, some of the children started to do poorly. "We thought she knew more than she actually did," was a typical parental statement.

Why is it that these parents and teachers were not aware of the adopted children's language problems at an earlier stage? To begin with, it may be that everyone was taken in by the rapid language learning of these children. Both parents and teachers were blinded by the facade of language, by the children's accent-free intonation and by their command of the language in everyday situations. Second, perhaps they failed to notice the extent to which inadequate language connects up with later learning difficulties and the problems this group had with various subjects in school.

Given these findings, it is very important that the parents of intercountry-adopted children be made aware of these children's particular form of language development. From the start, adoptive families should aim to provide stimulating and positive language environments for their children.

Special Education: Useful or Harmful?

One sign that learning difficulties have become apparent is if a child is given special education. According to Norwegian law, children can only be given special education after they have been officially assessed as having special needs. A relatively large number of the adopted children we studied had been given special education, particularly in the higher grades. This confirms the fact that schools only gradually have become aware of the special academic problems of intercountry-adopted children. However, it is also true that special education was provided only for students with the most pronounced language problems. Most often, these were children who came to Norway when they were a bit older.

The parents also had problems getting people to understand their adopted children's particular difficulties, precisely because they function so well in their everyday language usage. The special education these adopted children received was not adapted to their special problems, and the help they did receive was provided at a stage when it was already too late.

As mentioned earlier, starting school is a difficult period for intercountry-adopted children, a period during which they seldom are given the extra help and consideration they need. Perhaps this is because both parents and teachers want to protect these children from standing out even more in the school environment.

Our research project has shown that few of the adoptive parents asked for special help during the preschool years. This may be because many of them were afraid of unnecessarily stigmatizing their children. Or did these parents feel that they ought to be able to cope with their difficulties themselves? They all had to endure long, drawn-out procedures before finally being allowed to adopt. Now they had to show that they really could master the task.

It does not appear that the Norwegian schools have been paying enough attention to intercountry-adopted children's special difficulties at the start of school. This may be because neither the parents nor the schools are aware of the difficulties. On the other hand, it may be that both parties want to make starting school as ordinary as possible for these children so as not to exaggerate their differences from the other pupils. Perhaps the solution is to wait and see what happens, then to provide help when there is a visible need for it.

In Norway today, these children start school after their problems have already become manifest, and we have shown that the help they do get in school is not tailored to their special learning needs. This is almost certainly because the experts have not had sufficient insight into the difficulties with which intercountry-adopted children are struggling. The special education that has been provided was designed to meet the needs of Norwegian-born children and based on knowledge of and experience with the learning difficulties experienced by these children, primarily dyslexia.

Mother Tongue Teaching: Yes or No?

Some intercountry-adopted children have been taught their mother tongues at their Norwegian schools, mainly children who were somewhat older when they came to Norway, but experience from this type of teaching has been mixed. Many adoptive parents want their children to maintain their original languages and to learn about the culture and traditions of their countries of origin. The adopted children themselves have a more ambivalent attitude. Many do not want this type of teaching, and their teachers report a determined unwillingness to speak or listen to their mother tongues. Is it possible that the language brings back memories of the time spent in a child's native country, memories that may be threatening to the child? Perhaps it is necessary to suppress both language and memories in order to fit into a new environment, especially when a child is still not secure in his or her new surroundings. We know too little, however, about what it means for a child's cognitive development to have his or her first language drastically cut off.

Underachievers in Education and Work

Most of the adolescents we talked to were still attending secondary or high school, and they were more or less evenly distributed between vocational and general academic studies. Many had already decided on the kind of work they wanted to do. If one can point to a common feature, it is that they were very down-to-earth: they limited themselves to the range of what they thought they could cope with. With the exception of one girl who wanted to go into film and media, none of the youngsters gave the impression that they considered any of the "dream jobs" that teenagers usually think about. It also appears as if inter-country-adopted children go in for non-academic careers.

Lack of educational attainment appeared to have an effect on these youngsters' future working lives. Many who struggled with the academic side of school did not want to continue their education beyond secondary school. However, other possible reasons for this lack of ambition should be considered. The parents of some of the brighter pupils commented on their children's caution in their choice of careers. Were these youngsters afraid of failing if they set their sights too high? Did adopted children think that failure for them would be far more noticeable than for others? Or were they afraid they would come up against what black Americans call "the glass ceiling"—the unseen but all-too-real barrier that prevents them from reaching the top?

We feel it is important to encourage adoptive parents to ask for professional help for the serious adjustment and language problems that their children sometimes have. Perhaps these families should be offered professional advice and follow-up from the moment a child arrives from abroad. It is equally important that schools be made more aware of the fact that starting school is an extremely difficult time for intercountry-adopted children. Systematizing experiences thus far and developing suitable methods designed to satisfy the particular academic needs of intercountry-adopted children must be seen as a professional challenge to those working in this area. Perhaps a greater and more goal-oriented effort in this field would result in fewer of these children becoming underachievers at school.

CONCERNS FOR THE CHILDREN'S FUTURE

Why, then, are we so concerned about the future of these intercountry-adopted children, and why do we feel it necessary to emphasize the shadows in an otherwise rather rose-colored picture? Our concern, which grew gradually as we conducted our interviews, can be summarized in the following manner. Many of the young Vietnamese-born adoptees we interviewed seemed, in spite of their good adjustment, unable to realize their full potential. We found high levels of anxiety and insecurity in many of them. These traits seemed to be independent both of the adoptees' intelligence and abilities and of the economic and social standing of their adoptive families. The same personality traits were described independently by the parents and the adoptees themselves. On the basis of these findings, we believe it is appropriate to talk about an "intercountry-adopted personality," even though we fear that such a term might stigmatize or label the children in an unfortunate way.

Typical teenage or young-adult Vietnamese-born adoptees might be described as follows: Young, well-adjusted, and strongly attached to their families; somewhat insecure, uncertain about whether they will be able to manage life on their own, and afraid and unwilling to take risks. They show fewer than usual signs of typical teenage protest and exhibit less of a desire to move out of the protective family circle than their Norwegian-born counterparts. They do not like to "stick out"—to be noticed or remarked upon—even when such remarks are positive and encouraging. They do not deny their adoptive status or their racial and cultural background, but they underplay these characteristics and refuse to admit them as important parts of their identities. Sexually they are uncertain of their value as partners in lasting relationships and marriage. Socially, they have many friends but few deep and long-lasting friendships. They are hard-working without really obtaining the results or the marks they are due. Some of their personality traits can be attributed to traumatic experiences in early childhood: basic insecurity and deprivation experienced in early years seems to linger on even when they seem to function well in their everyday lives. The adoptive family thus comes to represent the basic security in their lives—especially psychologically, because the surrounding society seems somewhat reluctant to integrate and accept them as full Norwegian citizens.

The Psychological Paradox

Psychologically, these teenagers live in a paradoxical situation. They are Norwegian citizens. They have grown up in Norwegian families that, psychologically, are theirs, families whose values and beliefs they share. They want to be treated as "everybody else." They have, as one father put it, "a Norwegian soul in a Vietnamese body." As children, they have been sheltered and protected against discrimination by their families. Their parents have been active, sensitive, and outgoing in order to prevent incidents involving discrimination at school and in their neighborhoods. Their close surroundings have usually identified them as members of Norwegian families and treated them as such. But then the shield that their adoptive families have provided during childhood is torn apart when they come into their teens and must face many situations on their own. Strangers might not identify them as Norwegian and might treat them as migrants or refugees. Their identity is constantly questioned. One adoptee put it this way:

If I go in the shop, they will perhaps think I am a refugee, will try to help me, or old ladies will pity me and tell me how well I speak Norwegian. At secondary school when we had new teachers, they all asked if I knew Norwegian, or if I should have extra Norwegian lessons. I said that I had grown up here and considered myself Norwegian. When I go out at a restaurant, people come up and ask all kinds of questions.

It is fair to say that, in many respects, these young people live in a psychological no-man's-land: they both belong and do not belong. Their position is marginal. Their behavior indicates that they must fight to be accepted as Norwegian citizens, although fight might not be the right word. They would rather withdraw from awkward or difficult situations. They avoid contact with unknown people and social situations where they might be rejected, discriminated against, or subjected to embarrassing positive behavior. They try to surround themselves with "secure" friends who can protect them. In doing so, they also restrict their circles:

I did not dare to go in there and pay for the petrol. I do not know why I was afraid. It was perhaps that deep inside I felt that they knew that I was different. I am better now, but I still think it is horrible. I try to avoid doing a lot of things. I try to pluck up courage and now it is better. Perhaps I am subconsciously afraid of being spoken to if I am alone. It is usually when I am on my own that people begin making nasty comments.

The adopted teenagers want by all means to keep a low profile, and they do so in different arenas, privately and politically. They express, for example, very little social and political interests, even those who have grown up in politically and socially active families. One might have thought that their own marginal position would have made them particularly sensitive to social injustice and prejudice, but most of them apparently feel that they cannot afford to show any solidarity with low-status migrants and refugees. We interpret this as one of many coping techniques in their low-profile strategy.

A Model Toward Understanding the Intercountry Adoptee's Dilemma

What happens to individuals in such a complex and double-bind situation? In 1964, David Kirk developed a theory of adoption that has had a profound impact on adoption research and practice ever since (Kirk 1964, 1985). According to Kirk, adoptive parents live with particular dilemmas and with what he calls a "role handicap," because there are no well-defined social roles for adoptive parenthood. Adopters have to fight society's devaluation of their special kind of parenthood and, in doing so, must choose between different strategies—either a "rejection of difference" or an "acknowledgement of difference" of their special kind of parenthood. They also have to pay the price for the choice they do not make. For example, because of the undeniable visible difference between themselves and their children, intercountry adopters must engage in differentiation acts practically from the start (Costin and Wattenberg 1979). They must recognize that their child is different at the very time that they feel an especially strong desire to attach the child to themselves and themselves to the child. Unlike the in-ethnic adopters, intercountry adopters do not have any choice but to acknowledge the difference. However, acknowledgement of the child's origin, which Kirk says is crucial for the good outcome of the adoption, does not automatically mean that there will be a total acknowledgment of all differences. Rejection can be transferred to other arenas.

Differences Between In-ethnic and Transracial Adoptions

Kirk's theory does not truly explain the transracial, intercountry adoptees' situation. Only if we add a third dimension "stressing of difference" to his model (thus making the model more complex) can we obtain a deeper understanding of what goes on with ICAs. By "stressing the difference" we mean those psychological mechanisms that enhance, underline, and stress the ethnic and psychological differences in such a way that they overshadow other (perhaps equally strong) traits in an adoptees' psychological make-up. Racist groups in the society, for example, will always stress ethnic differences and treat intercountry adoptees as a marginal or outcast group.

In Figure 4.2, A, B, and C are different dimensions in a psychosocial system. The degree of difference will vary according to an adoptee's personality and attitudes in his cultural subgroups. Relations within the family system, social and economic factors, and existing networks will determine with which force and in which direction of A, B, and C the intercountry adoptee will turn.

A (acknowledgment of differences) might easily be the dominating factor in family situations, B (rejection of differences) in school situations, and C (stressing of differences) in social situations outside family and school. Such a psychological situation means that the intercountry-adopted child simultaneously might be subjected to three-fold cross-pressure. He or she has to cope with three different sets of value systems for behavior, according to the given social context. It is obvious that such an ambiguous and controversial situation would be a mental strain on any young person, but especially on someone who, for obvious reasons, has difficulties coming to terms with the question, *Who am I?*

Our research indicates that attitudes in all three directions vary from time to time and from arena to arena. We can illustrate this with an example from the school situation. In Scandinavian schools, the dominating philosophy stresses equality among all human beings regardless of their backgrounds or abilities. In such a context, teachers often reject any hint of difference and thereby neglect an adopted child's special educational needs. We have also seen that, if an adoptee displays asocial behavior, school authorities rapidly turn from a "rejecting the difference" to a "stressing the difference" attitude. By stressing the dif-

Figure 4.2
Theories of Adoption

Kirk:
Rejecting-the- difference ←——→ Acknowledge-the-difference

Dalen/Sætersdal:

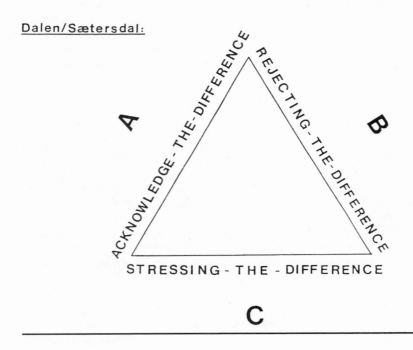

---

ference—whether it is the child's background, early traumatic experiences, ethnic characteristics, or adoptive status—authorities free themselves from responsibility. The same mechanism—moving from acknowledging or rejecting the difference to stressing the difference—also occurs within the adoptive family if a child displays psychological or social problems. For obvious reasons, adoptive parents can more easily than biological parents absolve themselves from responsibility by referring to early traumas or heredity as the cause of problems.

We used our model to analyze our interview data from four different aspects of the situation, namely:

1. Attitudes toward adoption
2. Attitudes toward one's own ethnic characteristics
3. Attitudes toward one's own cultural background
4. Attitudes toward ethnic minorities in Norway

A brief summary of our findings follows.

Attitudes Toward Adoption

Their adopted status did not seem to be a major problem for the Vietnamese adolescents we interviewed. A majority of the statements represent an "acknowledgment of differences" attitude. Their adoptions had been openly discussed since they came into their families. Some of the adoptees had had periods, especially between 12 and 14 years old, when they thought a lot about their families in Vietnam. Most of the adoptees, however, did not want to seem disloyal or hurt their parents' feelings by discussing their thoughts about their origins.

Attitudes Toward Ethnic Characteristics

The Vietnamese adolescents were ambivalent about their ethnic characteristics. Their attitudes can be characterized by a mixture of rejection and acknowledgment. None of them showed a "stressing the difference" attitude by dressing or making themselves up in a way that emphasized their ethnic origins. As children, most of them had received a good deal of positive reinforcement about the way they looked. As adolescents, however, they resented being a visible minority. They were annoyed at always being remarked upon in public places, even when such remarks were approving and positive.

We were surprised that none of the adolescents mentioned their ethnic background when we asked them to describe themselves. Nor did their parents do so when we asked them to describe their children. It is difficult to interpret this lack of racial references as colorblindness in the positive sense of the word. The adoptees seemed to want to deny or minimize their feelings of differentness and dismiss the importance of ethnic identity.

In this connection, we want to mention our survey of 182 intercountry-adopted children less than 17 years old. In that group, more than 50 percent of the parents claimed that their children had not been preoccupied with their looks. (Only three percent felt it had been a problem.) The accompanying comments, however, gave a somewhat different impression and clearly showed uneasiness and mixed feelings. Some of the children's remarks reminded us of the classical studies in the United States where black children turned out to prefer white dolls. We assume that the intercountry-adopted child, recognizing that he or she looks different from family members, also learns about the negative connotation that society places on membership in his or her ethnic group.

Attitudes Toward Cultural Background

Most of the adoptees (and their parents) had positive feelings about their country of origin and showed an open-minded, "acknowledging" attitude. In some cases, the children's background was also regarded as an asset, a desirable exotic spice in the family setting. Most of the parents had been eager to tell their children what they knew, at times perhaps too much. As one father put it: "When she was in primary school, she held a speech about Vietnam. When she was in grammar school, she talked about her canary birds." As adolescents, many of the adoptees were uneasy when reminded of the war in Vietnam and the circumstances that brought them to Norway. However, unlike in transracial adoptions (from minority to majority status within the same country), in ICAs cultural background represents few threats to the family unit. Parents know that if their children want to go back and trace their origins, they will do so more or less as tourists. Language and cultural barriers will be difficult to overcome, a hindrance to a feared reunion with the biological family or a permanent return to the birth country. For adoptive parents in general, a geographically present minority group is much more threatening, especially when such a group has marginal or low status in the society.

Attitudes Toward Ethnic Minorities in Norway

The adoptees' attitudes toward ethnic minority groups, migrants, and refugees were mixed and ambivalent. Most of the Vietnamese-born adoptees wanted to distance themselves from Vietnamese refugees, and they "stressed the difference" between themselves and other minorities. This distance might actually be physical, marked by staying deliberately apart from refugee children or adolescents on the playground, at school, on buses, at social gatherings, and in public places. Psychologically, most of these adoptees denied any common interests with refugees. By doing so, they avoid situations where they might gain firsthand knowledge of their own ethnic and historical background. Obviously, this is an awkward situation that might be difficult to handle in the long run because by denying the refugees, they are also denying a part of themselves. The risk for self-hate and double communication is obvious. Some of the older adoptees in our sample were aware of this; others denied any such feelings. Many stressed their belonging and loyalty to Norway and their Norwegian families. They voluntarily underlined their perception of likeness in manners, attitudes, and behavior with their adopted parents. At the same time, many adoptees also admitted to having periods when they had thought a lot about their Vietnamese background and fantasies about visiting Vietnam as adults. Some also described their relief when they were able to "disappear" in the streets— when, for example, they were visiting England and other multiethnic societies. They felt less psychological strain if they knew that black or non-European people probably also had low status in those settings.

What Is a Successful Adoption?

When discussing the outcome of ICAs, it is important to remember that the whole concept of a successful adoption is a social as well as psychological construct that varies from society to society and family to family. The behavioral content of adjustment will vary depending on the ruling ideologies and social values of the society and the subculture to which the family belongs. Raynor (1980) found that 85 percent of British adoptive parents were either very or reasonably satisfied with their in-racial adoptions, and 80 percent of the adult adoptees in the study claimed the same. Feigelman and Silverman (1983) were struck "by the lack of problems encountered in most homes with adolescent Korean transracial adoptees" in the United States. Harvey (1982) found that a couple years after adoption, the Australian parents of young Vietnamese adoptees rated their adoptions as very successful for themselves; 91 percent rated their adoptions as successful for their families, and 90 percent for the adopted children.

But "success" is an ambiguous concept, and we must acknowledge the difficulties in interpreting it. It is sobering to consider how biological parents would answer the same question: How many of them would declare their parenthood a failure? Perhaps we should also ask ourselves what kind of standard we dare to set as an ideal for adoptive families: a life without problems, a life without shadows?

Bridge Builders Between Races and Cultures

The intercountry-adopted child's position is by definition a difficult and vulnerable one. So far, Vietnamese-born adoptees in Norway have developed surprisingly well, especially considering the poor state in which they arrived. How will they and other groups of adoptees fare in the future? We believe that much of the answer lies in how racism will be fought in Norway.

If racism increases in the future, these children will be driven further into a marginal position, with all the psychological and social difficulties such a position implies. Their situation will be less problematic if Norway develops into a more open, multicultural and multiethnic society. If that happens, intercountry-adopted children will dare to stand forward as the people they truly are, people with roots and solidarity in two cultures. They will be, as one father put it, "bridge builders between races and cultures in our society."

REFERENCES

Ainsworth, M. D. 1973. The development of infant-mother attachment. In Caldwell and Riccuti (eds): *Review of Child Development Research*, Vol. 3, pp. 1–94. Chicago: University of Chicago Press.

Berntsen, M., and Eigeland, I. 1987. *Intercountry Adopted Children and the New Language*. Oslo: Norwegian Institute of Special Education. (Thesis.)

Bowlby, J. 1969. *Attachment and Loss*, Vol. I. London: Hogarth Press.

Chestang, L. 1972. The dilemma of biracial adoption. *Social Work*, 17: 103.

Chimezie, A. 1975. Transracial adoption of black children. *Social Work*, 20: 296–301.

Clarke, A., and Clarke, A. D. 1977. *Early Experience: Myth and Evidence*. London: Open Books.

Condon, W., and Sander, L. 1974. Synchrony demonstrated between movements of the neonate and adult speech. *Child Development*, 45: 456–462.

Costin, L., and Wattenberg, S. 1979. Identity in transracial adoption. In Verma and Bagley (eds): *Race, Education and Identity*, pp. 220–35. London: Macmillan.

Dalen, M. 1988. *Intercountry Adopted Children: Underachievers at School?* Paper presented at the International Conference on Adoption, Melbourne, Australia.

Dalen, M., and Saetersdal, B. 1987. Transracial adoption in Norway. *Adoption and Fostering*, 4: 41–49.

Fanshel, D. 1972. *Far from the Reservation*. Metuchen, NJ: Scarecrow Press.

Feigelman, W., and Silverman, A. 1983. *Chosen Children: New Patterns of Adoptive Relationships*. New York: Praeger.

Gardell, I. 1980. *A Swedish Study on Intercountry Adoption*. Stockholm: Liber Tryck.

Gill, O., and Jackson, B. 1983. *Adoption and Race*. London, England: St. Martin's Press.

Harvey, I. 1982. Transracial adoption in Australia. *Adoption and Fostering*, 2: 843–50.

Kadushin, A. 1970. *Adopting Older Children*. New York: Columbia University Press.

Kirk, H. D. 1964. *Shared Fate: A Theory of Adoption and Mental Health*. New York: Free Press.

Kirk, H. D. 1985. *Adoptive Kinship: A Modern Institution in Need of Reform*. Toronto: Butterworths.

Kvifte-Andresen, I. L. 1989. *Internationally Adopted Children in Norway: Adjustment at 12 Years of Age*. Unpublished manuscript, Department of Psychology, University of Oslo.

Lehland, K. 1971. Children of different race in Norwegian schools. *Norwegian Journal of Education*, 55: 297–305.

McRoy, R., and Zurcher, L. A. 1983. *Transracial Adoptees*. Springfield, IL: Charles C Thomas.

Miller, A. 1981. *Prisoners of Childhood*. New York: Farrar, Straus & Giroux.

Miller, A. 1984. *For Your Own Good: Hidden Cruelty in Childrearing and the Roots of Violence*. New York: Farrar, Straus & Giroux.

Raynor, L. 1980. *The Adopted Child Comes of Age*. London: Allen & Unwin.

Saetersdal, B. 1988. *What Became of the Vietnamese ''Baby-Lift'' Children? Early Childhood Trauma Revisited*. Paper presented at the International Conference on Adoption, Melbourne, Australia.

Schjelderup-Mathiesen, K., and Nytrohaug, L. 1977. *Vietnamese Children in Norway*. Oslo: Groendahl.

Simon, R., and Altstein, H. 1977. *Transracial Adoption*. New York: Wiley.

Simon, R., and Altstein, H. 1981. *Transracial Adoption: A Follow-up*. Lexington, MA: Heath.

Simon, R., and Altstein, H. 1987. *Transracial Adoptees and Their Families*. New York: Praeger.

Tizard, B., and Phoenix, A. 1989. Black identity and transracial adoption. *New Community*, 15: 427–437.

Trevarthen, C. 1979. Communication and Cooperation Understanding. In Bullowa (ed): *Before Speech*. London: Cambridge University Press.

Trevarthen, C. 1982. "The Primary Motives for Cooperative Understanding." In I. G. Butterworth and P. Light (eds): *Social Cognition Studies of the Development of Understanding*, pp. 77–109. Brighton: Harvester Press.

Triseliotis, J. 1988. *Some Moral and Practical Issues in Adoption Work*. Paper presented at the International Conference on Adoption, Melbourne, Australia.

5

International Adoption in West Germany: A Private Affair

MARTIN R. TEXTOR

HISTORY

International adoptions in Germany began during the Third Reich, when a great number of children born to Aryan women in occupied countries and fathered by German soldiers were brought to the "fatherland" and placed in adoptive families. For example, about 300 children of Norwegian mothers were relinquished for adoption for adoption by German couples; many of these children had been born in one of nine institutions in Norway operated by "Lebensborn e.V.," an SS organization furthering eugenics (Kunst 1988).[1]

After World War II, the situation changed and West Germany became an exporter of children relinquished for adoption. According to Table 5.1, the number of children adopted by foreigners increased from 489 in 1950 to a peak of 2,628 in 1957. Most of these children were sent to the United States, Scandinavian countries, the Netherlands, Belgium, and other Western countries. Some of these children (including many of mixed race) had been fathered by soldiers of the occupation forces. The parents of others had died during the War or were unable to feed and house them due to widespread destruction, poverty, and famine. In recent years, some of the children adopted by foreign couples during the late 1940s and early 1950s have been searching for their birth parents. Many have been aided by search groups and consultants, and lately by a newsletter (*Geborener Deutscher*) and computer bulletin board (WOMB BBS) for German-born adoptees living in the United States. Many of these searches have been successful because birth and adoption records are not sealed in West Germany (Textor 1988b).

Table 5.1
Adoptions in the Federal Republic of Germany

Year	Total	Number of Children and Adolescents Adopted By Relatives and Stepparents	By Foreigners	Applicants
1950[a]	4,279		489[a]	2,434[a]
1951[a]	5,430		709[a]	3,019[a]
1952[a]	5,820		872[a]	3,165[a]
1953[a]	6,189		1,376[a]	2,917[a]
1954	6,423		1,840	2,771
1955	8,433		2,618	2,643
1956	8,285		2,383	2,882
1957	8,396		2,628	2,909
1958	7,873		2,279	2,950
1959	8,003		2,307	3,074
1960[b]	6,416		1,649	3,024
1961	7,673		1,776	2,921
1962	7,472		1,555	3,345
1963	7,608	2,169	1,557	3,828
1964	7,684	1,928	1,380	4,257
1965	7,748	2,058	1,226	4,455
1966	7,481	1,984	1,219	4,512
1967	7,249	1,887	908	4,861
1968	7,092	1,761	772	5,224
1969	7,366	1,952	743	5,345
1970	7,165	1,918	645	6,009
1971	7,337	2,037	628	6,537
1972	7,269	1,848	590	7,632
1973	7,745	2,017	533	9,211
1974	8,530	2,218	440	12,210
1975	9,308	2,540	414	15,674
1976	9,551	2,564	373	17,909
1977	10,074	2,959	336	18,817
1978	11,224	3,555	333	18,884
1979	9,905	3,867	339	20,014
1980	9,298	3,102	295	20,282
1981	9,091	3,602	322	19,180
1982	9,145	3,968	256	20,746
1983	8,801	3,814	300	21,249
1984	8,543	4,008	266	20,003
1985	7,974	3,871	247	19,726
1986	7,875	3,867	238	21,071
1987	7,694	3,873	215	20,806

[a]Without West Berlin.
[b]Including Saarland.

After 1960, there were enough German couples interested in adopting children that the number of international adoptions dropped quickly—from 2,307 in 1959, to 743 in 1969, and 247 in 1985 (see Table 5.1). Until the end of the 1960s, however, advertisements were still placed in German newspapers by American or Scandinavian couples searching for children to adopt—offering mothers money, material goods, or trips to their countries. But they were less and less successful because a growing number of German couples were competing with them for a dwindling pool of available children. On the one hand, the number of children relinquished for adoption in Germany was decreasing (as it was in most other Western countries). There were only 4,008 nonrelated adoptions in 1986, down from a high of 7,669 children in 1978 (Linder 1987). On the other hand, the number of registered couples willing to adopt rose from 3,024 in 1960 to 6,009 in 1970 and to more than 20,000 since 1979 (see Table 5.1). Due to the small supply of German children, more and more German couples have turned to Third-World countries for children to adopt.

PRESENT SITUATION

Slightly more than 1,000 ICAs take place in the Federal Republic of Germany each year, adding up to one-fourth of all nonrelated adoptions. More detailed statistics about these adoptions were presented by Bach (1988), who evaluated data about 1,046 ICAs registered between 1984 and 1987 in the West German states of Bremen, Hamburg, Lower Saxonia, and Schleswig-Holstein. Altogether, 69 nationalities were involved. Sixteen percent of these ICAs involved German children adopted by foreigners, foreign stepparents, or couples of mixed nationalities. Thirteen percent of the adoptees came from Eastern and southeastern Europe, especially Turkey, Yugoslavia, and Poland. Another 10 percent came from other European countries or North America, often the children of German mothers and American, Canadian, British, or French soldiers stationed in the Federal Republic of Germany. The majority (61 percent) of ICAs involved children from Third-World countries. Out of 638 children, 506 came from the following 10 countries: South Korea (141), India (74), Philippines (64), Colombia (47), Chile (46), Brazil (36), Sri Lanka (33), Thailand (33), Peru (19), and Ghana (13). Children from South and Southeast Asia and Latin American children make up most of those adopted from Third-World countries.

Bach (1988) presents more detailed information about 300 ICAs, all of which involved children from Third-World countries. Seventy-three percent of these children were less than one year old at the time of placement, and 19 percent less than two months old—which means that, according to West German law, they had not been relinquished legally. A child must be at least eight weeks old before he or she may be relinquished in West Germany. Eighteen percent were between one and three years old, 5 percent between three and six, and 4 percent over six years old. In 50 percent of these cases, the birth parents (at least the mothers) were known. In 43 percent, mothers were listed as unknown in the foreign adoption papers. In 7 percent, no information at all was given about birth parents. Half of the children had been in children's homes before placement, and 41 percent had lived with parents, relatives, or foster families. No information was given for 9 percent. The percentage of children from children's homes seems to have declined during the past 10 years, however. A study from the early 1970s (Weinwurm 1976) found that about 80 percent of 71 Korean and Vietnamese children had been in children's homes, which might be related to the fact that they tended to be adopted at an earlier age.

A state agency or an organization approved by a government was involved in only 45 percent of the 300 cases studied by Bach (1988). In 55 percent of cases, parents obtained children through personal contacts or with the help of private or commercial organizations. Seventy of the 300 cases involved commercial, illegal, or criminal practices. According to Bach, "That means that 23 percent of all adoptions of children from the Third World, or 42 percent of all private adoptions contradict the adoption regulations of the Federal Republic and, in general, also those of the countries of origin" (Bach 1988). Moreover, in a great number of the private adoptions, the papers were incomplete (e.g., no statement of relinquishment) or open to doubt. In general, however, Bach concluded that commercial and illegal practices are employed less often today than they were a few years ago.

Private adoptions by German citizens are rare in Argentina, Uruguay, Venezuela, Mexico, Thailand, and the Philippines. (They are forbidden in Sri Lanka, Indonesia, Taiwan, and South Korea.) Most adoptees from these countries come to Germany via state-approved agencies. Some children from Thailand and the Philippines, however, are adopted by German men who marry the child's mother or other relative. Most of the private (and illegal) adoptions take place in Chile, Peru, Colombia, Brazil, India, and Sri Lanka. In these countries, large amounts of money are sometimes paid to children's homes, birth parents, or middlemen in exchange for the children. In a few cases, children are even stolen or registered immediately after birth as the biological children of a German couple (Bach 1986; 1988). After some of these cases were discovered and received a lot of publicity, many people criticized ICAs.

Negative experiences involving ICAs have led the two largest organizations involved with foreign adoptions in Germany to turn against them. Since 1987, the German branches of *Terre des Hommes* (Osnabrück) and *Internationaler Sozialdienst* (Frankfurt)—both of which had always considered international adoptions only a small part of their work—decided to place foreign children into West German adoptive families only if no solutions could be found for the children in their birth countries. A third organization, *Pro Infante* (Kempen), had planned to stop placing foreign children by the mid-1980s, but it still continues to place about 120 children a year. A fourth state-approved organization, *Eltern für Kinder E.V.* (Essen), was formed in 1987 by a group of parents who split from *Terre des Hommes* because they did not agree with the decision to curtail placements. This organization, however, has only placed a couple of children so far.

When couples interested in adopting foreign children realize that they will not find much help at the aforementioned agencies, they often turn to private contacts in Third-World countries (e.g., German clergymen, nuns, businessmen, and individuals working for development institutions) or to foreign private or commercial organizations. Thus, according to Bach (1989), state-approved agencies were involved in only 10 percent of the ICAs registered in the aforementioned four northern states of West Germany during the first half of 1989. Criticism of this development has led many experts, journalists, and representatives of adoption agencies to call for state intervention, a description of which follows.

At present, if a foreign child is brought to Germany to be adopted by a German couple, the case is treated according to the same laws as a case involving a German child. The birth parents (or the natural mother if the father is unknown) must unconditionally relinquish the child for a type of adoption similar to a German one and must do so in writing (using a form accepted by the government of their country), no sooner than eight weeks after the child's birth, and on a form referring to the respective German couple. If these and other requirements (e.g., minimum age limits for adoptive parents) are not fulfilled, the responsible agency in the child's country of origin is contacted and asked to obtain a statement from the birth parents (or biological mother if the father is unknown) on the form required by German law. If there is no reply, or if the natural parents cannot be found or are deemed to have disappeared, then the adoption is finalized.

When a German couple adopts a foreign-born child in its country of origin according to regulations passed by that country's government, then the adoption is in principle recognized by the German state as required by the International Private Law. The adoption then has the same legal effect in the Federal Republic of Germany as it has in the country where it took place. However, because these effects are often different from those stipulated by German law, it is usually recommended that the couple adopt the child a second time in West Germany (*Bundesarbeitsgemeinschaft der Landesjugendämter und überörtlichen Erziehungsbehörden* 1988; *Internationaler Sozialdienst, Deutscher Zweig* 1988).

The Adoptive Parents

In the previously mentioned study involving 300 adoptions of children from Third-World countries (Bach 1988), 1.5 percent of the adoptive parents were less than 30 years old, 67 percent were between 30 and 40, and 31.5 percent were over 40 at the time of placement. Similar results were also reported by Kühl (1985). This means that about half of these couples were over the upper age limit of 35 recommended by the *Bundesarbeits-gemeinschaft der Landesjugendämter und überörtlichen Erziehungsbehörden* (1988). Because these recommendations are also considered by the four German organizations placing children from Third-World countries, the percentage of private adoptions is especially high among couples over age 35 (Bach 1988). It can be assumed that these marriages are very stable because the divorce rate in this group seems to be below average (Kühl 1985; Weyer 1985).

Economically, 3 percent of the 300 couples belonged to the lower-middle, 22 percent to the middle, 65 percent to the upper-middle, and 10 percent to the upper class. Forty-five percent of the adoptive parents had graduated from universities [with even higher percentages reported in the less representative studies of Kühl (1985) and Weyer (1985)]. Most of the mothers did not work outside the home, at least not while their adopted children were small. Many of the adoptive families lived in one- or two-family houses (Schreiner 1984). Thus, the standard of living in these families was very high. Forty percent took vacations twice a year, and 24 percent three times a year. Favorite hobbies included reading books and newspapers, which might indicate an intellectual atmosphere in these homes. Many parents were active in politics and showed great interest in Third-World issues. According to Kühl (1985), these parents were often members of organizations that provide aid to developing countries.

According to a study of 71 parents who had adopted Korean or Vietnamese children via *Terre des Hommes* (Weinwurm 1976), the most common motive for adoption was a wish to help a child in need, followed by the wish for a child, the feeling of responsibility for Third-World children, and the wish to give a child a chance in life. Schreiner (1984) found that couples who adopted children from Third-World countries were less inclined to instrumentalize their children (i.e., use them to find meaning in life, to fulfill a partner's wish, or to improve the marriage). Those who already had biological children were especially prompted by altruistic motives.

But both Kühl (1985) and Eisenblätter (1989) convey the impression that humanistic motives have become less important in adoption since the late 1970s. Most couples who try to adopt children from Third-World countries are looking for substitutes for biological children they cannot conceive or German children they cannot adopt. Consequently, they want to adopt infants and are less willing to adopt older children.

Integrating the Child

Many adoptive parents, especially those adopting privately or via foreign organizations, fetch the children themselves from the respective Third-World country, which allows them a view of their child's motherland and living conditions. By doing so, couples become acquainted with older children on their "home turf" and can accompany them through the sometimes horrifying experiences of traveling to their new country (which may intensify the first bonds). Other couples meet their adoptees at the airport. Parents' first impressions are frequently ones of shock because many children are undernourished and sick. For example, in a study of 71 Vietnamese- and Korean-born children (Weinwurm 1976), less than 10 percent were healthy at the time of placement. Thus, some children have to be hospitalized directly after their arrival, although ambulatory treatment is sufficient in most cases. Usually the children recover in a short time from illness, undernourishment, and developmental delays (Weinwurm 1976). With some children, however, medical exams reveal retardation or handicaps that lead to great sorrow and grief on the part of the parents.

Integrating a newborn from a Third-World country into a family's life does not usually cause any more problems than integrating a biological newborn. Older infants, however, may not react to objects and people, may be apathetic or auto-aggressive, and may exhibit behavior stereotypes or other symptoms of deprivation. Older children exhibit a wide range of behaviors in the months after arrival. Some are conforming, subservient, pliant, and passive; others are anxious, clinging, and fearful of separation. Some are shy, reserved, timid, and distrustful; others are outgoing, positive, and happy. Some reject any approach by their new parents. Others are aggressive, destructive, incalculable, and without self-control. Many are insecure, lack self-confidence, are unable to play, cannot get along with siblings or other children, are voracious eaters, regress, do not want to go to bed, or exhibit symptoms such as sleep disorders, enuresis, encopresis, trance-like states, fits of rage, and auto-aggression. They may steal out of habits acquired in their birth countries or lie out of fear of punishment or loss of love.

They often behave in these ways or otherwise provoke their parents in order to test the parents' love or to gain the parents' continuous attention. These behaviors are also frequently caused by culture shock and the problems associated with integrating two lives and two worlds in a short period of time. For older children, it may be extremely distressing to suddenly not be able to communicate and have to learn a new language. They usually stop speaking their mother tongues completely. They may also deny their origins and try to adapt totally to the role of a German son or daughter (Weinwurm 1976; Weyer 1979, 1985; Schreiner 1984).

According to adoptive parents, older children usually require complete attention in the months after arrival, which continuously taxes the parents' love, patience, and understanding. These couples often feel overburdened and experience great stress, doubt, and many sleepless nights. Frequently they have to reduce contacts with relatives and friends. Comparing the reports of 163 parents who had adopted children from Third-World countries with those of 42 parents who had adopted German-born children, Kühl (1985) concluded that the integration peri-od is much harder on the first group of parents. Weinwurm (1976) re-ported that problems occurred in three-fourths of 71 cases. Adoptive parents must help their children develop self-confidence and trust. They have to give lots of love, support, encouragement, praise, and stimula-tion. They also have to set appropriate limits, to find the right combina-tion of pampering and discipline. Often they need to help their children verbalize experiences of desertion, abuse, or maltreatment (or enact them in play) so that these children can recover. If there are biological children in a family, they are frequently disappointed because the adopted child does not or cannot play with them, is aggressive, or gets too much parental attention. Sometimes biological children feel neglect-ed, become jealous, and even develop behavioral problems.

In an intensive study of 12 Vietnamese and 8 Korean children, Weinwurm (1976) found that the effects of early deprivation can be total-ly alleviated if adoptive parents pass through the following three phases: (1) They stimulate needs in the child, especially if the child is apathetic. (2) They satisfy the child's needs totally for quite a long time. This means that they must postpone satisfaction of their own needs and wishes, which is made easier by the child's poor physical state and frequent regression. Thus, the parents confront the extreme experience of depri-vation with an equally extreme experience of total needs satisfaction. The contradiction between these experiences allows the child to negate both and thereby overcome the deprivation. (3) The absolute satisfaction of needs is gradually faded out. The child learns to postpone some needs and develops normally.

Parents are less successful at alleviating the effects of deprivation if, for example, they treat the adopted child from the beginning like his or her siblings, if they allow too short a period of total needs satisfaction, if they confront the child from the start with norms, rules, high expectations, and punishment, or if they continue to satisfy all the child's needs for too long.

According to interviews with adoptive parents, several months are usually needed to integrate a child into a family and to find a new family equilibrium (Weyer 1979, 1985; Schreiner 1984). Parents sometimes need the help of other adoptive parents, child specialists, or other third par-ties. Relationships between adoptees and their parents develop in totally different ways; even two adoptions by the same family can produce diverse experiences. From the beginning, there may be a close relation-ship (even with older children), or such a relationship may take a long time to develop. There may be a positive and unproblematic relationship during the first weeks that suddenly turns into a negative one as the child starts to test the parents' love. Or there may be a negative relationship at the beginning that slowly develops into a positive one. Sometimes one parent is more successful than the other at stimulating a child's trust.

In a few cases, no positive relationship develops between the adoptive parents and the child. *Terre des Hommes* reported that it had to remove children from homes in 1.8 percent of its cases (Kühl 1985). Winter-Stettin (1984) studied 37 removals that took place between 1971 and 1983, most of which occurred either shortly after a child's arrival or after a child had been in a home for more than four years. Removals were more frequent if: (1) the child's age at arrival was higher than average; (2) the child's age was between those of older and younger children already living in the family; (3) the child had a very problematic biography [i.e., had spent a long time in (several) children's homes]; (4) it was discovered some time after placement that the child was handicapped; or (5) there were great discrepancies between the wishes of the applicants with respect to the child they wanted to adopt and the characteristics of the child who was placed with them. About two-thirds of these parents reported behavior disorders similar to those reported by other adoptive parents during the first months after their children arrived. In contrast to other adoptive families, however, the families from which children were removed were unable to alleviate the problems. Winter-Stettin (1984) believes that these parents did not behave adequately toward their adopted children. For example, they may not have known how to deal with behavior disorders or how to reduce sibling rivalry. They may also have used the children to fulfill unconscious needs such as saving their marriages.

Family and Social Relationships

In only one German research project has empirical data been collected about the integration of adoptees from Third-World countries into their adopted families. Kühl (1985) interviewed 145 adolescents and young adults with an average age of 16.7 years who had been adopted via *Terre des Hommes*. Nearly 80 percent of them were born in either South Korea or Vietnam. Eighty-nine percent described their relationships with their mothers as "very good" or "pretty good," and 88 percent rated their relationships with their fathers the same way. Eighty-three percent definitely rejected the statement "Adopted children are children of second choice." Kühl (1985) compared a subgroup of these adolescents with matched groups of 43 German-born adoptees and 50 adolescents living with their biological parents and found that the first group rated the emotional climate in their families more positively. The mutual understanding between themselves and their parents was similar to the controls.

Three-quarters of the adoptive parents interviewed by Kühl (1985) described their relationships with their adopted children as being comparable to the ones they had with their biological children. According to Kühl, these results show that the relationships between adoptive parents and adopted adolescents are strong and survive the challenges of adoption, puberty, and leaving home. In only one-fifth of all cases did parents and children not feel close to one another or only slightly close. In four of those cases, the adolescents were living in children's homes or foster families at the time of the interview.

Not much can be said about the relationship between foreign-born adopted children and their siblings because three-quarters of all ICAs in West Germany today involve childless couples (Bach 1988). In the 1960s and 1970s, however, it was common for families with above-average numbers of children to adopt (Kühl 1985; Weyer 1985). Weinwurm (1976) reported that the reactions of siblings to newly adopted children were positive in about two-thirds of the cases studied. Jealously and rivalry were reported in about one-third of the families. Weyer (1985), who studied 50 adoptive families with 100 adopted and 86 biological children, found more sibling rivalry between adopted children than between adopted and biological siblings. She reported that natural children were more likely to feel secure about their places in the family and were therefore less likely to be jealous. Adopted children were more willing to accept the presence of biological siblings than of other adopted ones; thus, they often reacted negatively to further adoptions. In most cases, however, the relationships between siblings were similar in adoptive and natural families. Siblings often showed great solidarity if the adopted child was handicapped, retarded, or symptomatic.

Schreiner (1984) reported that adopted children from Third-World countries often experience extremes in the ways they are treated. They are either treated with special attention or are rejected by others, and sometimes there is a change during the course of their lives. They may be awarded much attention during early childhood, then later rejected when they are perceived as competitors. Weyer (1985) stipulated that Asian-born adoptees experienced less hostility than South American ones. The latter are often counted among the 1.5 million Turks living in West Germany who are the least integrated of all guest workers.

Adopted children from Third-World countries are less discriminated against by people of their own age and young adults than by older adults. Half of the 145 adolescents interviewed by Kühl (1985) mentioned that they had been teased "somewhat" or "much" because of their appearance, with girls being overrepresented. Thirty percent considered their looks to be an advantage in dating, in school, or at work, whereas 15 percent considered their looks a disadvantage. According to Weyer (1985), reactions of other people also depend on how the adoptees behave and whether they emphasize their foreign looks in their style of dress. Most of the adolescents she interviewed tended to be optimistic that their strangeness would not be a problem with respect to dating and work. In general, foreign-born adopted children seem to develop strategies for dealing with curiosity, teasing, prejudices, and discrimination. However, many still feel hurt by these reactions or become fed up with questions concerning their origins and their adoption.

Adoptive parents seem to fear that their children will be discriminated against (Weyer 1985). More than half of the 27 fathers and 28 mothers interviewed by Schreiner (1984) were concerned about increasing hostility toward guest workers and foreigners. But the parents themselves often experienced positive reactions to the adoption: 92 percent had been praised by others "because of their good deed," and 26 percent believed that they were more respected by their neighbors since the adoption. Sometimes, however, they found prejudices in themselves, especially if their children behaved in unexpected or unwanted ways.

School and Work

In the West German school system, children attend the same type of school (*Grundschule*) for only the first four years (except for handicapped and retarded children, who go to special schools, the so-called *Sonderschulen*). After that, children are split and go to three different branches of the school system according to their achievements, aptitudes, and interests: (1) the *Hauptschule*, for those who are expected to hold blue-collar jobs later on; (2) the *Realschule*, for those who are interested in white-collar jobs; and (3) the *Gymnasium*, for those who want to study at a university. Of less importance are other types of schools such as the *Gesamtschule*, which is similar to U.S. high schools.

Many adoptive parents seem to have high expectations with respect to the education of their children (Weyer 1979, 1985). More than half of the 27 fathers and 28 mothers interviewed by Schreiner (1984) planned to send their children to a *Gymnasium* or *Realschule*. About one-third were undecided, and only a few considered the *Hauptschule* (mostly foster parents of German-born children who were used as controls).

Of the more than 150 adopted adolescents and young adults studied by Kühl (1985), 89 percent were still in school: 4 percent in *Sonderschulen*, 18 percent in *Hauptschulen*, 31 percent in *Realschulen*, 29 percent in *Gymnasium* (especially those who were adopted at a young age), and 18 percent in other types of schools. Similar results were reported by Weyer (1985). These data show that intercountry adoptees receive a more intensive education than the average German student. However, 28 percent had to repeat a grade at least once, and adoptees who were older at the time of placement were overrepresented in this category. Most adolescents reported problems at school such as being frustrated, having difficulties in specific subjects, suffering from learning disorders, or not getting along with teachers or peers.

According to Weyer (1985), most adoptees from Third-World countries were optimistic about their futures. Many of them planned to work in the social services or as artisans. Apprenticeships are the most common form of professional training for technical, blue-collar, and white-collar jobs in West Germany, and they are readily available.

Self-Concept and Identity

Using the Frankfurt Self-Concept Scales, Kühl (1985) compared the self-concepts of 43 adopted adolescents from Third-World countries with matched groups of 43 German-born adoptees and 50 nonadopted adolescents who lived with both biological parents. He found only one significant difference among the three groups: nonadopted adolescents felt less valued by others. There were no significant differences in the adolescents' ratings with respect to sociability, social integration, efficiency, capacity to solve problems, self-acceptance, ability to fulfill one's needs, sensibility, irritability, and acceptance of one's looks.

Adoptees from Third-World countries are faced with some extra difficulties in the development of a secure identity: they have to cope with the fact that part of their origin is unknown, that they have two sets of parents, and that they were relinquished for adoption. They must also deal with different looks, their ethnic heritage, and the task of having to integrate two different cultures.

According to Weyer's (1985) study of 50 adoptive families, many adopted children rejected their origins and repressed their memories at the beginning. They tried to become typical Germans. During adolescence, however, they tended to reflect upon their origins with great intensity. They asked themselves why they had been relinquished for adoption and revived negative memories of their birth families or of time spent in children's homes. Some looked back with hate and condemnation, others with distance and calmness. A few were attracted by their countries of origin, were interested in traveling there, or wanted to visit their biological parents and relatives. But only two of the 94 adoptees wanted to return permanently to their birth countries—one of them a boy who came to West Germany at the age of 10 and still had contact with his biological siblings. The few adoptees who traveled with their adoptive parents to their birth countries lost any romanticized memories and illusions, recognized how they would live if they had not been adopted, and found that they reacted like Germans and not like people from their former motherlands. Most adoptees were well-informed about the Third World and the countries they came from, partly as a result of their parents' efforts. According to Schreiner's (1984) study, nearly 80 percent of 27 adoptive fathers and 28 mothers deemed it right to acquaint their adopted children with their countries of origin via storytelling, books, movies, and photos. Kühl (1985) reported that slightly less than 80 percent of 163 adoptive parents talked with their children about their origins.

Kühl (1985) also interviewed 145 adopted adolescents and young adults and found that 15 percent "often," 40 percent "sometimes," and 45 percent "rarely" or "never" thought about the time before their placement. They tried to fill the genealogical void with memories and fantasies. One-third of the adoptees were "much" or "pretty much" interested in their countries of origin, another third "somewhat," and the last third (mostly adoptees who had been adopted at a very early age) "hardly" or "not at all." Those who were interested learned about the present situation in their birth country, read books and watched movies about it, fitted their rooms with items from it, or even learned their native language. Two-thirds of the adoptees said they would like to visit their country of origin, and one out of two wished to meet his or her birth parents. Psychologically healthy and socially integrated adoptees were more interested in their countries of origin, whereas those who were unstable and dissatisfied with their relationships with their adoptive parents more often wanted to meet their biological parents. Most adoptees reported that they belonged partly to West Germany and partly to their birth countries. For example, 66 percent said they felt "much" and 28 percent "somewhat" as Germans, whereas 16 percent felt "much" and 32 percent "somewhat" as Vietnamese, Koreans, or South Americans.

ADOPTION SUCCESS

Like their biological counterparts, adopted children develop in many different ways (Weyer 1985). Weinwurm (1976) reported that 69 percent of 39 Vietnamese and 47 percent of 32 South Korean adoptees had reached developmental stages appropriate to their ages. Kühl (1985) found that a high percentage of 163 adopted adolescents and young adults had behavior problems. According to their parents, these foreign-born adoptees had difficulties at school (35 percent), a lack of concentration (34 percent), a lack of ambition (33 percent), a lack of perseverance (25 percent), a lack of self-confidence (21 percent), great egoism (20 percent), a habit of lying (20 percent), a wish to be at the center of attention (20 percent), passivity (18 percent), and rebelliousness (17 percent). But when Kühl compared a subgroup of these foreign-born adoptees with a matched group of 48 German-born adoptees, he found no significant differences.

Weyer (1985) also reports that some of the 50 adoptive couples she interviewed were still worried by their adolescent children's behavior (e.g., fits of rage, distancing, provocative behaviors, rejection, lies, lack of self-confidence, etc.). The parents often reacted with guilt feelings if problems started some time after the adoption, and many felt a great deal of pressure from third parties to get help for their children. Sometimes they blamed the child's genetic heritage and early experiences for present problems.

Despite all the difficulties, 44 percent of the 163 parents interviewed by Kühl (1985) were "very satisfied," and 37 percent were "satisfied" with their adoptions; only 14 percent were "partly satisfied." Their 145 adolescent and young-adult adopted children were even more content: 65 percent were "very satisfied," 19 percent "satisfied," 13 percent "partly satisfied, partly unsatisfied," and 3 percent very "unsatisfied." No significant differences were found when these results were compared with a matched group of 43 German-born adoptees. In general, there were positive correlations between satisfaction with adoption, good understanding between parents and adopted children, closeness, adoptees' positive self-concept, and a lack of behavior disorders. Weyer (1985) reported that most of the adoptees interviewed said that they would adopt children themselves. Their parents also noticed positive changes in themselves brought about by their adopted children: they had learned a lot from these children and viewed them as enriching their lives.

Kühl (1985) found that adoption success was more likely and an adoptees' self-concept more positive (1) the shorter the time the child had spent in a children's home; (2) the less often the child had changed from one children's home to another; (3) the younger the child had been at the time of placement; (4) the less the discrepancy between the child's age and the wishes of the parents in this respect; (5) the less delayed the child's cognitive development had been at the time of placement; (6) the older the adoptive parents had been at the time of the child's arrival; (7) the longer the time between two adoptions by the same couple; and (8) the more the family had been characterized by: open expression of emotions and opinions, solving problems in undestructive ways, lack of conflicts, independence of family members, a positive attitude with respect to achievement and competition, a focus on intellectual and cultural topics, and flexible rules (according to ratings on Family Climate Scales). Moreover, adoption success was greater and self-concept more positive if the family belonged to the lower-middle class, if the parents had no biological children, and if there were no younger children at the time of placement. No correlations were found between adoption success and the child's sex, age at time of relinquishment, physical state (illness, undernourishment, etc.) at time of placement, parents' motives for the adoption, and number of children in the family.

CRITICISM AND ALTERNATIVES

It is evident that research about ICAs is still in its infancy in West Germany. We have discussed here mainly the families of children placed by *Terre des Hommes*, but research results about private adoptions and children placed by other agencies are lacking. Moreover, the studies discussed here were unrepresentative. They were based on voluntary participation and often do not meet the standards widely accepted by social scientists. They are exploratory at best. On the other hand, these problems are common to nearly all studies in the field of adoption (Textor 1988a). The results reported here are similar to those found in other countries.

Research about the ICA placement process and about the work of agencies is lacking. Only in Kühl's (1985) study were adoptive parents asked how they felt about the work of *Terre des Hommes*, and nearly one-third of them were critical of the preparations made for the adoption, the lack of consideration given to their wishes with respect to a child, and the lack of support after the adoption.

In West Germany during the last couple of years, the opponents of ICA seem to have triumphed over the proponents, even though the opponents' arguments are based neither on German research results nor on results from American, British, or Scandinavian studies. Opponents' opinions, however, greatly influence the policies and practices of the major German agencies placing children from Third-World countries. The opponents of ICA regard such adoptions as a new form of exploiting the Third World and as a kind of trade in human beings. Moreover, they criticize the egoistic motives of many adoptive parents and point to the use of bribery, forgery, and money in private adoptions (Bach 1988; *Bundesministerium für Jugend, Familie, Frauen und Gesundheit* 1988; *Terre des Hommes* 1989).

The opponents of ICA also refer to the negative attitudes that are spreading in Third-World countries, where increasing numbers of citizens supposedly feel impotent about the problem of deserted children and ashamed about the attention given to it in the First World. They demand, and often win, restrictions on ICAs—which are seen as a symptom of neocolonialism (*Bundesarbeitsgemeinschaft der Landesjugendämter und überörtlichen Erziehungsbehörden* 1988; Baer 1989). Eisenblätter (1989) stipulates that the demand by the First World for children from the Third World is greater than the number of children available; therefore, single mothers or poor birth parents are sometimes pressured into relinquishing their children for adoption. Alternatives such as in-country adoptions are not considered.

Criticism has also been directed at German courts and youth services (at both the local *Jugendamt* and state *Landesjugendamt* levels) for the practice of providing applicants with copies of their homestudies. Many couples have their homestudies translated and sent to foreign organizations and agencies that place children. Or couples sometimes travel to Third-World countries themselves and adopt privately using these homestudies to obtain the necessary permission. The German courts and youth services are often unable to check whether these children were relinquished according to the respective laws and whether all regulations had been followed. Adoptions are sometimes finalized even when there are doubts about the legality of the placement procedures and the qualification of the adoptive parents. There have also been cases in which children were brought to West Germany for adoption by couples who had not been approved by the respective German agencies (Bach 1986; *Terre des Hommes* 1989).

Many critics maintain that ICA should be reserved only for extraordinary cases, for children for whom no help is available in their birth countries (Kühl 1985; Bach 1988; *Terre des Hommes* 1989). Eisenblätter (1989) stipulates that German agencies placing children from Third-World countries act responsibly only if they further and finance projects that offer those countries alternatives to ICA. Therefore, he and his colleagues at *Terre des Hommes* (1989) demand more programs to prevent the desertion of children, to support families in need, to find jobs for single mothers, to finance the construction of day care centers, to provide information about sex and family planning, to improve the situation in children's homes, to support street children, and to reintegrate children into their birth families. Like the *Internationaler Sozialdienst, Deutscher Zweig* (1988), *Terre des Hommes* is trying to further in-country adoptions in the Third World.

The *Bundesarbeitsgemeinschaft der Landesjugendämter und überörtlichen Erziehungsbehörden* (1988) recommends that ICAs should take place only in cooperation between German and foreign institutions (e.g., adoption agencies, children's homes, courts and youth authorities). All necessary information about the child and the couple applying for adoption should be exchanged. This means that homestudies would not be handed over to applicants, but only to collaborating institutions. Moreover, foreign agencies should be informed about how placements have progressed in Germany during the waiting period, usually a year, before the adoption can be finalized. *Terre des Hommes* (1989) demands even more: it wants the same regulations to apply for ICAs that apply for in-country adoptions. This means that about 90 percent of all ICAs presently taking place via private adoptions and those using agencies not approved by the state would be forbidden. Individuals who take part in the "trade of children," fake documents, or claim that a foreign-born baby was born to them should be severely punished. And children adopted by those individuals should be removed and returned to their birth parents. Some of these demands were considered by the German parliament, which revised the law about the arrangement of adoptions (*Adoptionsvermittlungsgesetz*) on 27 November 1989. Individuals trading in children now face high fines and prison sentences of up to five years.

The aforementioned demands by *Terre des Hommes* were not well-received by the German organization of foster and adoptive parents. In a public statement dated 29 May 1989, the organization's chairwoman commented that *Terre des Hommes* and the German media present ICAs as if children were being bought from "good" parents and given to adoptive parents who fulfill their wish for children by resorting to criminal practices. In fact, the statement goes on, many state and private agencies in Third-World countries that place children often demand less, rather than more, bureaucracy (Baer 1989).

In general, if one considers the alternatives facing a deserted child in some Third-World countries, ICA may often be the best solution (Weyer 1985; Baer 1989).

NOTE

1. Some of the children born to Norwegian mothers and adopted by German couples during the Third Reich were returned to Norway. Following a resolution passed by the Norwegian parliament in November 1947, about 150 of these children were tracked by United Nations organizations or the Red Cross and returned. Most had to spend months or years in children's homes because their mothers did not want them (sometimes for fear of discrimination) and because few Norwegian couples were interested in adopting relatively old, German-speaking children. Some of these individuals later joined a self-help group of children born to Norwegian mothers and German fathers.

REFERENCES

Bach, R. P. 1986. *Gekaufte Kinder: Babyhandel mit der Dritten Welt*. Reinbek: Rowohlt.
Bach, R. P. 1988. Daten und soziale Hintergründe der Adoption von Kindern aus der Dritten Welt. Eine Untersuchung der Gemeinsamen Zentralen Adoptionsstelle der vier norddeutschen Bundesländer in Hamburg. *Zentralblatt für Jugendrecht*, 75, 328–333.
Bach, R. P. 1989. Personal communication with author, July 24.
Baer, I. 1989. Zur Problematik der Adoptionsvermittlung von Kindern aus der "Dritten Welt." *Nachrichtendienst des Deutschen Vereins für öffentliche und private Fürsorge*, 69, 2–5.
Bundesarbeitsgemeinschaft der Landesjugendämter und überörtlichen Erziehungsbehörden. 1988. *Empfehlungen zur Adoptionsvermittlung*, Vol. 2, rev. ed. Köln: Bundesarbeitsgemeinschaft der Landesjugendämter und überörtlichen Erziehungsbehörden.

Bundesministerium für Jugend, Familie, Frauen und Gesundheit. 1988. *Bericht über die Entwicklung der Adoptionsvermittlung in der Bundesrepublik Deutschland seit 1984*. Bonn: Bundesministerium für Jugend, Familie, Frauen und Gesundheit. (Unpublished paper.)

Eisenblätter, P. 1989. *Die Situation verlassener Kinder in Entwicklungsländern: Lösung durch Auslandsadoption—oder bessere Alternativen? Überlegungen zur Interessenlage der Betroffenen*. Osnabrück: Terre des Hommes. (Unpublished paper.)

Internationaler Sozialdienst, Deutscher Zweig. 1988. *Tätigkeitsbericht 1987*. Frankfurt: Internationaler Sozialdienst, Deutscher Zweig.

Kühl, W. 1985. *Wenn fremdländische Adoptivkinder erwachsen werden . . . Adoptionserfolg und psychosoziale Intergration im Jugendalter. Erste Ergebnisse einer Befragung*. Osnabrück: Terre des Hommes.

Kunst, L. 1988. Der Makel eines Deutschen Vaters: Die Geschichte der Kinder von Wehrmachtssoldaten in Norwegen wirkt bis heute nach. *Abendzeitung*, 6 April.

Linder, P. 1987. Adoptionen: Trend, Strukturen und Bestimmungsfaktoren. *Baden-Württemberg in Wort und Zahl*, 35, 458–467.

Schreiner, H. 1984. *Zur pädagogischen Situation von fremdrassigen Adoptivkindern*. Frankfurt: R. G. Fischer.

Terre des Hommes. 1989. *Massnahmen gegen Privatadoptionen/Kinderhandel*. Osnabrück: Terre des Hommes.

Textor, M. R. 1988a. *Offene Adoptionsformen. Abschlussbericht zu Projekt 05/87/1a/MT*. München: Staatsinstitut für Frühpädagogik und Familienforschung. (Unpublished manuscript.)

Textor, M. R. 1988b. Adoptierte auf der Suche nach ihrer Herkunft. *Soziale Arbeit*, 37, 456–462.

Weinwurm, E. M. 1976. *Mutter-Kind-Interaktion bei asiatischen Kindern in Deutschen Adoptivfamilien. Begleitende Verhaltensbeobachtung von Terre des Hommes Kindern hinsichtlich des Deprivationssyndroms*. Münster: Westfälische Wilhelms-Universität Münster. (Unpublished dissertation.)

Weyer, M. 1979. *Die Adoption fremdländischer Kinder: Erfahrungen und Orientierungshilfen*. Stuttgart: Quell.

Weyer, M. 1985. *Adoption gelungen? Erfahrungsberichte über die Integration fremdländischer Kinder*. Stuttgart: Quell.

Winter-Stettin, A. 1984. *Die bei Terre des Hommes Deutschland e.V. im Rahmen der Auslandsadoptionsarbeit vorkommenden Replacements: Eine Aktenanalyse*. Osnabrück: Terre des Hommes. (Unpublished manuscript.)

6

The Conditions of 18- to 25-Year-Old Foreign-Born Adoptees in Denmark

METTE RORBECH

In earlier days, there was a surplus of children in Denmark who wanted parents; today there is a deficit. The need to relinquish children for adoption has declined because only a few childbirths are unwanted and because it is now more acceptable to be a single mother.

According to the Danish Adoption Act, the legal implication of an adoption is a complete change of family for the child. The legal relationship between the child and biological family lapse and, for all purposes, an adopted child has the status of the adopter's legitimate child.

CHILDREN ADOPTED FROM ABROAD

Since 1970, Danes have adopted almost 10,000 foreign-born children. Well over one-half are from Korea, and most of the rest are from other Asian countries. In 1987, 537 foreign-born children came to Denmark for adoption, 64 percent of them from Korea. South Korea has been and continues to be of great importance for the adoption pattern in Denmark (see Table 6.1).

During this period, twice as many girls as boys were adopted. The number of girls from Korea is twice that of boys. For other Asian countries, girls outnumber boys four to one. But from Africa, the numbers of boys and girls are almost equal. From Latin America, there are twice as many boys as girls, although the total numbers of children adopted from Latin America and Africa are very modest.

After the Korean War, private Western organizations established a number of well-organized children's institutions with a view to providing Korean children for adoption in Western countries. These institu-

Table 6.1
International Adoptions from 1970 to 1988 by Adoptees' Native Countries

	Europe	Korea	Asia Other	America	Africa	Other	Total
1970	183	25	7	5	3	3	226
1971	195	196	20	3	5	2	421
1972	190	332	32	17	2	1	574
1973	121	432	117	15	2	0	687
1974	91	560	91	13	2	2	759
1975	75	525	147	18	4	1	770
1976	74	226	172	19	9	2	502
1977	59	457	165	23	10	1	715
1978	42	446	211	22	15	2	738
1979	18	312	123	29	5	4	491
1980	24	450	226	59	5	2	766
1981	23	381	197	51	6	0	658
1982	15	387	187	44	8	0	641
1983	13	373	134	43	3	0	441
.							
.							
1987	5	345	123	61	1	2	537
1988	2	282	94	71	6	4	459
Total	1,144	5,974	2,192	528	87	26	9,951

Note: The figures for 1970 to 1972 have been counted by the Ministry of Justice and for 1972 increased by one-fourth for the sake of comparison, since only the three first quarters of that year had been counted. The source of all figures up to 1984 is Report No. IV of the Ministry of Justice 1053/1985. The source for 1987 is "Population Movements," *Danmarks Statistik 1987,* Copenhagen 1989. For 1988, Population and Elections, Statistical Intelligence No. 6, 1989.

tions include Korean Social Services and Holt Children's Services. From 1973 to 1984, the yearly number of adoptions from Korea averaged 400, or approximately 62 percent of all ICAs in Denmark.

In addition to being an act to which a number of legal rights and obligations are attached, adoption is also a social and mental process that develops throughout life between the adoptee, the adopters, and perhaps the biological parents. According to Danish law, adoptees are assured of rights on an equal footing with biological children in terms of support and inheritance.

ABOUT THE STUDY

ICA assures children a secure, emotionally rich development and upbringing. They grow up in families, and relationships between parents and adopted children are mostly good and deep ones. This is one of the principal findings of a study based on children aged 8–12 years by the Institute of Social Research in 1977, "Born Abroad—Adopted in Denmark."

The present study is principally concerned with adolescent and young-adult, foreign-born adoptees as they are about to enter "lives of their own." They may begin to seek training and education, housing, jobs, possibly a permanent partner, and perhaps beginning their own families. How do they fare in terms of education, jobs, money, and social life compared to others of the same age? Do they stay at home longer for fear of fending for themselves? Do they defer the meeting with society at large by seeking parental protection longer than other young people?

The study included 18- to 25-year-olds from Asia, Africa, and Latin America who were adopted by Danish parents. None of the parents and adoptees were related before adoption (i.e., no stepchild or family adoptions were included). Adoptees studied were born between 1 January 1963 and 30 August 1970.

The study was prepared by desk research and loosely structured, indepth qualitative interviews with 10 adoptees. Adoptees were asked a number of questions about their identity formation, feelings of a double cultural attachment, and strategies for working within their own roots and cultural origins. All 10 interviewees were from Asia: 8 from Korea, and 2 from India. The interviews lasted from one to two hours and were conducted by the researcher herself.

In the autumn of 1988, information from the nationwide questionnaire was collected. A total of 455 adoptees from three continents were randomly selected from adoption files. Those selected received a letter briefly describing the study. Next, they were visited in their homes by an interviewer from the Institute of Social Research. The interviewers asked questions on the basis of a questionnaire with fixed response categories; individual interviews lasted approximately 40 minutes. There were 384 total respondents, which is 84 percent of the planned interviews. This high response rate enhances the credibility of the research results. The study is thus representative of adoptees 18–25 years old from Asia, Africa, and Latin America.

ARRIVAL IN DENMARK

Most of the respondents were born in Asia, especially Korea. Two-thirds were more than three years old when they arrived, a status applying to very few children being adopted today (see Table 6.2). Many of them had already acquired a language; more than half could remember speaking another language, but hardly any speak it today. Because of the high average age at adoption, one-third of them could remember people and violent incidents from their lives before coming to Denmark.

Children who were slightly older at adoption commonly retained one or more of their original names. Children who were younger most frequently retained one name, and then as a middle name. One-third of the children had all their names replaced by Danish names.

Almost all respondents had both an adoptive father and an adoptive

Table 6.2
Ages of Adoptees on Arrival in Denmark (%)

	Study Participants	Children Arriving in 1987
0-2 years	34	81
3-5 years	50	11
6 years or older	16	8
Total	100	100

Source: "Population Movements." *Danmarks Statistik 1987*, Copenhagen 1989.
Note: Total number of study participants was 384. Total number of children arriving in 1987 was 537.

mother, but a few were adopted by single mothers, and a few lost one parent during childhood to divorce or death. Most had siblings, about half of whom were their parents' biological children, which means that they were the only children with adoptive status in their families. This is also different from the situation today where most children are adopted by parents who are unable to have children themselves.

ADOLESCENCE

From the earlier study, we know that the discrimination to which these adoptees were exposed as 8- to 12-year-old children was not serious— neither negative nor positive. The region in which they grew up determined to some degree how often they felt discrimination. Large towns (with more than 40,000 inhabitants) were the most frequent scenes of teasing. This may be because towns of that size do not have as many foreign-appearing residents as the capital region, but neither are they small communities where everyone knows each other. According to the respondents, the teasing they were exposed to was not extensive.

The attitudes of schools and teachers were important to the respondents during their school years. Fourteen percent reported teachers treating them better than other pupils, and nine percent said they were treated worse because of their appearance. A slightly higher number of males reported occasions of feeling uncomfortable in school. Most of the respondents started in the ordinary school system, where they completed their first nine or ten school years. A very small number shifted schools due to teasing.

The respondents were always aware of their status as adoptees—some added, "deep inside." The intensive interviews often produced reports on to whom they talked about these feelings, and whether they still talked to anybody about them. It was to their adoptive parents that they talked about their feelings regarding being adopted, coming from another culture, and having a different appearance. At the time of the interviews, many of them also talked to their boyfriends or girlfriends. Most felt comfortable discussing their adoption-related problems with their parents, but there was a small group who felt they could not, and for them it was a problem.

It is one thing to talk to parents about being adopted from a distant country, but quite another to discuss the motives of their birth parents with their adoptive parents. More than half of the adoptees had no information on why their birth parents acted as they did. Those who had been informed were most frequently given positive accounts of birth parents' motives. They said things such as, "My parents wanted to assure a good and better life for me."

Most respondents had spoken to their adoptive parents about their different appearance, but one-third had not. All in all, there was openness between these adoptive parents and their children about their being adopted and not looking the same as others, but a small group (15 percent) had neither read their adoption files nor discussed their appearance with their parents. Boys especially had not discussed their foreign appearance or read their adoption files. One reason to discuss these things is that a person's identity is formed and affected by the feelings and the self-understanding brought about by these problems. Talks may thus be postponed for too long.

TOWARD ADULT LIFE

Between the ages of 18 and 25, 42 percent of the respondents were still living at home. This percentage is lower than that among nonadoptees of the same age (65 percent). Those who have not yet moved out are the youngest. Thus, adoptees do not stay at home longer; in fact, the opposite is true. Like all other adolescents, adoptees move out when they are finished with their schooling, when their education and finances permit. Those who finish school early, after nine or ten years, and then start basic vocational training, complete their training correspondingly early and, consequently, they leave home earlier than those who attend upper secondary school and then start further education. It should be noted that twice as many adoptees as nonadoptees had left home early (i.e., before their eighteenth year).

More than one-half of the adoptees left school after they passed the ninth or tenth form examination; one-fifth attended upper secondary school. Sixteen percent had continuously been upper secondary school students, which is the same rate as for nonadoptees. Most of the adoptees between 18 and 25 years old (like others of this age) were concluding their training or education and entering the labor market (and thus the financial and social conditions for an independent life).

A relatively large group (27 percent), however, left secondary or upper secondary school without really starting training or education (see Table 6.3). One-fourth of these had passed an upper secondary examination, so there were approximately 20 percent who finished school with only ninth or tenth form examinations. This 20 percent is the residual group in terms of education. One-half of these were unemployed and the other half had unskilled jobs. Many adoptees in this group had left home very early (i.e., before their eighteenth year). They are in many ways vulnerable in terms of what we usually consider a good starting point for a materially secure life. They are an "at-risk group" who never really get on, and some in this group might be expected to have social problems later in life. But these would be the same problems experienced by non-adopted Danes who do not go on for further training or education after secondary school.

Of the few adoptees who had experienced unemployment, most had only had one such period, and only for a short time (up to six months). Almost all planned to continue their training or education. Because many of them were 18 to 20 years old, it is possible that they will carry through with their plans. The parents of adoptees were more often in socioeconomic positions above parents of nonadoptees the same age. Whether the adoptees will realize their educational plans is impossible

Table 6.3
Training and Education of Adoptees and Nonadopted Agemates (%)

| | Adopted | | | Comparison Group* | | |
	Male	Female	Combined	Male	Female	Combined
Have completed vocational training	16	17	17	25	25	25
Are in the course of vocational training	37	27	30	32	15	25
Are in the course of education	9	9	10	13	24	18
Are still in school (upper secondary)	15	17	16	13	20	16
Not in education or training	23	29	27	17	15	16
Total	100	100	100	100	100	100
Numbers	125	259	384	300	237	537

*This group does not represent all Danes aged 18–25 years. It is weighted with an age bias for the purpose of comparing respondents in this study with nonadoptees aged 18–25 years.

to know, but the basic conditions and support from their families seem to exist.

The purpose of integration is to avoid segregation (i.e., separation or isolation) of those who are different. Integration of adoptees is aimed at assuring them an active life in interaction with others and in close contact with the society in which they live. In terms of training, education, jobs, housing, and the number who had not yet started training or education after secondary school (the "educationally weak residual group"), the respondents appeared not to be fully up to their non-adopted peers.

FAMILY, NETWORK, AND LEISURE TIME

The respondents' social lives in Denmark had begun in their adoptive families. In adolescence, they were taking the first steps toward forming their own core families. After they left home, which more than half had done, they lived alone for short or long periods. One-fifth were living with a Danish-born partner in permanent cohabitation or marriage. Young women, especially, got established early.

Most respondents expected to have families of their own some day. Although only a few had children at the time of our interviews, most of them wanted to have two or more. About one-fourth of the adoptees wanted both biological and adopted children.

Whether the respondents were 18 or 25 years old, male or female, they had contact about once a month with family members with whom they were not living. Parents and siblings were the most common contacts; visits with other relatives (grandparents, uncles, aunts, and cousins) were less common. It should be noted, however, that 20 to 25 percent of the respondents rarely met with their parents and siblings.

In addition to family contacts, almost all of the respondents have contacts with friends. More than half felt that they had many friends, which was equally true of both sexes. A full 75 percent of the respondents had no other foreign-born adoptees as friends, and two-thirds had no foreigners as friends. The adoptees appeared to live as other Danes do, forming friendships with people they meet and like. Thus, these adoptees did not isolate themselves from other foreign-appearing people, nor did they isolate themselves within minority groups.

In their leisure time, respondents read about the same amount as other youngsters. Almost none of the respondents, male or female, were regular readers of books and periodicals about ICA or the history and development of their birth countries. The same difference between males and females existed among adoptees as exists among other young people: more men tend to read newspapers and cartoons, whereas slightly more women tend to read magazines and fiction.

Entertainment such as movies and TV is enjoyed by all young people, adoptees and nonadoptees, to the same extent. Art exhibitions, museums, and lectures were attended by several respondents, mostly women. A few more adoptees than nonadoptees attended arts activities and events.

DISCRIMINATION

Had the respondents experienced discrimination by way of differential treatment in everyday life, and what was their attitude toward foreigners living in Denmark? Had recent social tensions between immigrants and other groups in Denmark been important to the foreign-born adoptees or affected their own attitudes toward immigrants and refugees?

In the earlier study by the Institute of foreign-born adopted children, a small group of parents (14 percent) expressed concern that their children might be subjected to some form of racial discrimination in the future. This concern was voiced more frequently for sons than for daughters. Irrespective of sex, age, and birth country, the discrimination to which the children were exposed between 8 and 12 years old was usually not serious, and it did not inhibit the adopted children's social integration among others of the same age.

The situation changed, however, as these children got older. Ten years later, intolerance to foreigners had gained ground and become visible. During childhood and through adolescence, the respondents believed other people viewed them as Danes. These experiences, combined with their own views of other people, were part of the background on which their assessment of life in Denmark was based.

Had ethnicity been important to them during childhood and adolescence? To elucidate this issue, respondents were asked whether, while growing up, their appearance had caused them to be treated better or worse than others, to be teased, or to feel uncomfortable or different. They were asked about family members other than parents, about siblings, teachers, and schoolmates—and finally about other children and adults (see Table 6.4).

Most had practically never been treated worse than others, and about 20 percent felt that they had been treated better than other children. A few more female than male respondents felt that teachers treated them better than other pupils because of their background.

Teasing was more widespread: about one-half of the adoptees had been teased in school and elsewhere. (There are no differences between the sexes.) For most respondents, however, teasing had been a rare incident.

About one-third had felt different when they were among other people, and one-fourth had felt uncomfortable.

Table 6.4
Adoptees' Exposure to Positive and Negative Discrimination (%)

	Often/At Times	Rarely	Never	Total
In their families (not parents and siblings)				
Were treated better	15	4	81	100
Were treated worse	3	2	94	99
Were teased	6	7	87	100
In school				
Were treated better	11	3	86	100
Were treated worse	5	4	90	99
Were teased	27	33	40	100
Among other people				
Were treated better by adults	7	9	83	99
Were treated worse by adults	8	12	80	100
Were teased	18	29	52	99

The adoptees' replies indicate that the closer the knowledge and personal contact they had with others, the less exposed they had been to teasing and differential treatment. On the other hand, the more remote their relations and personal contacts with others had been, the more frequently they were teased and felt uncomfortable or different.

This finding was true for both the open replies to the questionnaire and the intensive interviews. In the open replies to the questionnaire, some adoptees explained that they had been mistaken for immigrants and addressed in derogatory language in the street or at parties. If they then told insulters that they were adopted, they were offered apologies.

On the basis of Table 6.4, we have created one measure for positive discrimination and two slightly different measures for teasing. Positive discrimination occurs when a child is given better treatment either by a teacher or by an extrafamily adult. One of the teasing measures concerns teasing in the near environment (i.e., being teased by both extended family members and in school). The other measure concerns teasing by strangers and includes those teased only in school and those teased by other people in general (see Table 6.5).

Table 6.5 illustrates that one-fourth of the adoptees had experienced positive discrimination outside their family frameworks. It also shows that most of the adoptees had been teased, and most frequently in school. These experiences may conceivably influence the respondents' further personality development and their later ability to cope.

We now discuss the correlation between these measures for discrimination and feelings of national and familial identity. First we considered whether teasing had influenced the way respondents coped in the edu-

Table 6.5
Adoptees' Exposure to Various Types of Positive (A) and Negative (B and C) Discrimination

	Percentage	Number
A. Positive discrimination in school/ among other people		
A teacher and another adult treated me better than other children	5	
Have only been treated better than other children by one of those	20	
Neither teachers nor other adults have treated me better than other children	76	
Total	101	376
B. Teasing in school/the family		
Have been teased both by relatives and in school	10	
Have only been teased in one of those cases	52	
Have never been teased by relatives or in school	37	
Total	99	379
C. Teasing in school/among other people[1]		
Have been teased both in school and by other people	35	
Have only been teased in one of those cases	31	
Have never been teased in school or by other people	33	
Total	99	333

[1]This measure does not include the respondents who have been teased by relatives.

cational system. Our findings prove that there is no correlation between being teased as a child and starting or completing education or training. The question is: Do children who feel teased at school and by relatives find consolation in knowing that they can talk to their parents about these feelings? Those who felt they couldn't talk to their parents—and at the same time felt they had been teased within their families, felt they had been treated worse than other children in their families, or felt uncomfortable at family events—have major problems. But only 4 percent of our respondents fit this description.

ATTITUDES TOWARD IMMIGRANTS AND REFUGEES

Some within adoption circles argue that, in everyday life, adoptees with a foreign appearance dissociate from refugees and immigrants because they do not want to be assumed to belong to those groups and thus risk discrimination and harassment.

In Sweden and Norway, foreign-born adopted children are registered as immigrants, but in Denmark they are granted Danish nationality in connection with their adoptions. And in debates among adoptive parents, the view may be heard that their children are "a kind of" immigrant. But what do the adoptees themselves think? We asked them about their own attitudes toward refugees in Denmark and also whether they felt immigrants were welcome. They were also asked to assess whether they considered themselves immigrants. Finally, they were asked if they thought that, as Danes with a foreign appearance, they might contribute to bridging the gap between nations.

Two-thirds supported the view that greater control of the refugee flow into Denmark is needed, which correlates with the response by an equally large percentage who did not want Denmark to totally open its frontiers to refugees. Three-quarters agree or partly agree that immigrants were welcome but subject to adjustment to the Danish way of life, Danish culture, and Danish standards. They often indicated that the latter statement also applied to themselves. They were Danish and felt Danish because their way of life was Danish, and Danish culture and standards were ingrained in them.

Seventy percent of the respondents did not feel that they were a kind of immigrant in Denmark—which they are not in terms of Danish legislation and practice.

About one-half agreed that, with the status they have, they may be bridge builders between nations. Whether there will be a need for them as bridge builders depends on the development of Danish society.

We asked the adoptees whether they had met people in Denmark who considered them foreigners, and 30 percent replied that they had. A closer analysis of respondents' views on the number of refugees in Denmark and their opinions regarding control of the refugee flow reveals a correlation between their own feelings of being considered foreigners and their own attitudes to the views presented.

Respondents who felt they were foreign were more frequently in favor of allowing more refugees and immigrants into Denmark, perhaps because they would like their own appearance to be more common in our society. Accordingly, those who felt they were considered Danes by others indicated that immigrants were welcome but subject to adjustment to the Danish way of life.

The degree to which ethnicity was important was related to how adjusted and accepted the foreign-born adoptees felt in Denmark. The more adjusted and accepted they felt, the less important their own ethnic background was. We may conclude that the vast majority were integrated and accepted in Denmark, both by their families and by their friends and acquaintances. Only a few had experienced discriminatory behavior of any importance. But significant numbers had felt uncomfortable among other people (13 percent), different (21 percent), and as immigrants (24 percent).

DANISHNESS

More than 90 percent reported that they felt mostly Danish. This was true of both males and females, regardless of their age when they came to Denmark. It was also true when there were other adopted children in their families, and when their only siblings were their parents' biological children.

Only a small group (about 10 percent) had visited their birth countries. Among those who had, 50 percent thought of themselves as something other than Danish while they were visiting. Two-thirds of the respondents felt no major emotional attachment to their birth countries, and an equal number were content with having come to Denmark. Only 7 percent said they would have preferred to stay if they had to choose anew.

The one-third who felt an attachment to their birth countries were not different from the other two-thirds with respect to age, sex, schooling, and so on. A common feature among those who felt an attachment to their birth countries was that they wanted to visit there. One-half of the respondents thought at times of their birth mothers or families. One-third wanted to seek information about their birth families, but two-thirds knew for certain that they did not (see Table 6.6). A large percentage were curious about seeing their native countries again, but this did not necessarily imply that they wanted to seek information about their roots. A desire to learn their native language was more common among those who either sought or wanted to seek information. However, there were also some who only wanted to learn the language in order to visit their native countries as tourists.

A desire to seek information about their biological families was more common among the small group (17 percent) who felt they could not discuss their adopted status with their parents. This implies that fewer wanted to seek information about their birth families when dialogue with adoptive parents about adoption was open. It may, therefore, be concluded that words give relief and are an important part of developing a sense of community in an adopted country.

The one-third who felt an attachment to their native countries were asked to whom they talked about their feelings. About 25 percent said

Table 6.6
Characteristics of Adoptees Who Sought or Did Not Seek Their Roots

	Sought roots (%)	Did not seek roots (%)
Three years or older at placement	81	60
Spoke the native language at time of placement	79	59
Belong to the educational residual group	27	15
Have felt different	35	12
Have felt uncomfortable among other people	16	11
Have experienced teasing among other people	28	13
Feel like a kind of immigrant	28	19
Feel mostly Danish	31	61
NUMBER OF RESPONDENTS	85	150

Note: The roots are the biological family.

they talked to siblings, especially siblings who were also adopted from abroad.

The group who sought their roots was principally characterized by having been older on arrival and having retained their national language. Among those who sought their roots, a relatively high number had felt different, teased, and like a kind of immigrant. Although seeking one's roots is not in itself negative and implies no negative consequences, for some of the respondents it reflected a kind of maladjustment to Danish society.

Finally, a desire to seek one's roots (see Table 6.6) may be something that an adoptee feels at certain times of life. For example, the desire to seek one's roots may arise in connection with the adoptee's giving birth to a child or with the death of the adoptive parents.

CONCLUSION

All in all, we concluded that the Danish adoption policy has been successful. Most of the young people we studied were integrated into Danish society: they lived like their nonadopted peers and they felt Danish. Only a minority had experienced negative or positive differential treatment during childhood and education. And only occasionally do these adoptees think back to their native countries and their birth families.

7

Intercountry Adoption Coming of Age in The Netherlands: Basic Issues, Trends, and Developments

RENE A. C. HOKSBERGEN

INTRODUCTION

Even though Holland is a small country, with a population of almost 15 million, on certain issues it seems to have a lot of influence in the world—especially in Indonesia, Australia, South Africa, the United States, and Central and South America. This might have to do with the way in which the Dutch have always been connected to people in other parts of the world.

One of the consequences of these contacts is that Holland is quite multiracial in structure. About 7 percent of the total Dutch population is of some other national and racial origin. Do all these groups live together in harmony? Are there no problems of discrimination or conflict? Several studies done by Dutch and foreign researchers have been carried out to find reliable and valid answers to these questions (Bovenkerk 1978; Bagley 1973). They have found that, although there is some discrimination, it is not more than one would expect when people of different groups live closely together. The Dutch law and culture—which are rather open, tolerant, and progressive—plus a sound economic situation seem to prevent discrimination from worsening.

The phenomenon of intercountry and interracial adoption then, more of less fits into Dutch history and culture. For the population at large, there is nothing new in seeing children from Asia, South America, or Africa. Does this also mean that ICA is easily accepted and properly dealt with by responsible authorities and organizations and by the population at large? Responding to these questions will be the main topic of this chapter.

ADOPTION IN HOLLAND 1956-1990

On 1 November 1956, after a long and difficult process of negotiation, the first law on adoption in Holland came into effect. Attempts had been made to enact legislation on adoption since the 1930s, but blood ties were generally believed to be more important than the interests of children or foster parents. Until 1956, for example, foster parents were never completely sure of being able to keep their foster children. For such reasons, the Dutch Association for Foster Families and the Federation of Institutions for Unmarried Mothers (both of which still exist) decided to pressure the government, and their efforts were successful (Hoksbergen and Bunjes 1986).

The first Adoption Act restricted and reduced the existing adoption possibilities, which were viewed as being too liberal. Foster parents, for example, had to care for a child for three years before they could apply for juridical adoption. In 1974, the waiting period was reduced to one year. Only married couples were accepted as adoptive parents. There were no provisions for ICAs because they did not exist yet. Between 1957 and 1969, 600 to 700 children were relinquished annually through ICAs.

ICA really began in the early 1960s with the adoption of children from Greece (almost 400, completely stopped in 1979), Austria (about 300, stopped in 1984), Germany (about 150, stopped in 1982), and other European countries. Table 7.1 provides data on the number of inter-country-adopted children and their countries of origin between 1970 and 1988. In 1969, the first 10 children from South Korea arrived in Holland. Between 1970 and 1988, more than 17,000 children were adopted by Dutch families, most of them less than two years old and from Asia or South America (see Table 7.2). Five years of age is generally the upper limit for ICAs, although exceptions may be made to keep siblings together.

How did the phenomenon of ICA begin? Television broadcasts about the wars in Biafra, Korea, and Vietnam exerted a great influence by showing what those wars meant for millions of displaced and orphaned children in those countries. Committees were established that set up assistance for "children in need"—a concept that gained ground among large groups of Dutch society. One outcome of this was that, in the 1970s, 2,000 to 3,000 couples (about 70 percent involuntarily childless) applied for ICA annually. Another result is that there are now about 50,000 children who have been adopted financially—a procedure whereby children remain in their home countries, but receive financial support from families and organizations abroad. Organizations such as Foster Parents Plan and World Children (the largest adoption organization, established in 1971) are working toward the sponsorship of Third-World children.

Table 7.1
Intercountry-Adopted Children and Their Countries of Origin, 1970–1988

	1970	1972	1974	1976	1978	1980	1982	1984	1986	1988
Korea	101	122	269	342	321	180	247	129	157	107
Indonesia	–	–	22	110	249	669	279	31	–	–
Colombia	–	–	32	124	151	214	146	172	151	165
Sri Lanka	–	–	1	23	18	81	140	458	565	24
India	–	–	21	154	145	196	149	155	161	113
Bangladesh	–	–	–	88	141	34	1	–	–	–
Brazil	–	–	9	22	22	10	–	28	56	68
Lebanon	–	–	49	32	42	26	5	3	–	–
Austria	?	?	64	44	14	5	2	–	–	–
Chile	–	–	–	15	17	34	17	13	12	6
Other Countries[a] (including Lebanon and Austria until 1972)	41	81	130	125	79	83	50	59	61	49
Peru	–	–	1	17	7	61	9	2	1	3
Haiti	–	–	–	–	–	–	–	48	25	29
Thailand	–	–	21	29	5	1	–	1	9	13

Source: Ministry of Justice.

Note: Included 1971, 1973, etc. Before 1970, there were about 1,200 ICAs. These are not
included here.

[a]Between 1986 and 1988, the most important countries were Ethiopia, the Philippines,
Poland, Bolivia, and Costa Rica.

POLICY AND LAW

From the beginning, the policy of adoption organizations was to find
families for children in need, not the other way around—to find children
for childless parents in need. Partly because of this policy, many couples
with one or more children of their own offered themselves for ICA. Until

Table 7.2
Age of Intercountry-Adopted Children Placed in Dutch Families, 1984–1988

	1984		1985		1986		1987		1988	
Age	n	%	n	%	n	%	n	%	n	%
0	682	59	629	68	787	70	838	69	378	66
1	200	17	91	10	98	9	142	12	60	10
2	87	8	57	6	71	6	70	6	45	8
3–4	90	8	67	7	84	8	79	7	48	8
5 and older	95	8	87	9	83	7	77	6	46	8
Total	1154	100	931	100	1123	100	1206	100	577	100

1982, about 25 to 30 percent of all couples trying to adopt had children of their own (see Table 7.3). And all parents were prepared to do "project help" as well—that is, to sponsor children financially or to financially support special projects involving children in the Third World. All large ICA organizations arranged some sort of project help, but project help can easily be misused by organizations in the countries of origin. This danger may increase when project help is sent directly to institutions that give up children for ICA. The work of adoption organizations demands a lot of discipline and care. Can we conclude that the high quality of their work is guaranteed? The answer must be yes and no. Yes because there is so much social control—via the media, official reports of the organizations, and reports of parents—that intercountry adoptees in Holland can be assured that they were never bought or sold.

The quality of their work in other areas, however, could stand improvement. To better understand the reason for this, we will look briefly into history. In Holland and other European countries (i.e., Sweden, Belgium, Switzerland, Germany), the phenomenon of ICA from Asia and South America started partly on the basis of ideology. It would be

Table 7.3
Foreign-Adopted Children in Residential Care (by Country of Origin) as Percentages of Total Foreign-Adopted Children in Holland

Country of Origin	Children Placed		Foreign Adopted Children in Residential Care	
	Year	Number	Number	Percentage
Korea	1978	1787	101	5.6
Indonesia	1979	1119	17	1.5
Colombia	1980	872	64	7.3
India	1980	718	14	2.0
Sri Lanka	1983	410	5	1.2
Bangladesh	1978	317	15	4.7
Lebanon	1978	216	13	6.0
Chile	1980	80	2	2.5
Europe	1978	2139	53	2.5
Other Countries	1978	633	62	9.8
Unknown	-	-	3	-
Total		8291	349	5.7

imprudent to attribute either too much or too little weight to the impact of ideology on individual behavior. In many cases, children in need had to be helped and there were enough parents and possibilities in Europe to do so. Of course, the prevailing attitude was that only children who had been abandoned, orphaned, or officially relinquished should be adopted; the others should stay within their families and, if necessary, become sponsored. It was also believed that child welfare institutions in the Third World should be helped as much as possible, and that if the choice was between ICA or sponsoring a family, financial support for the family should win out. This was part of the ideology that very much influenced aspirant parents.

In the early 1970s, little consideration was given to political problems on the part of the children, who were considered the most wished for children of the world. That they sooner or later might suffer from psychological and educational problems was rarely considered before 1975 or 1976.

There was another difficulty. There were no official qualifications required to organize ICAs so anyone could act as an intermediary between aspirant adoptive parents and a country of origin. Some couples became so deeply involved with the needs of those children—often adopting a child themselves—that they began to organize ICAs. World Children, established in 1971 and the largest and oldest agency of its kind, started in this way.

By the end of the 1970s, several books and articles (Wolters 1978; Hoksbergen, et al. 1979, 1982) had revealed that the operations of adoption organizations needed more stringent controls and, the quality of their work needed to be upgraded.

In 1979, the late Minister Ed Nijpels, then still a member of the House of Commons, asked the Minister of Justice to improve the official regulations concerning ICA. In 1980, the Minister's official report recommended the legalization of regulations for intermediary organizations. These regulations held until 1988, when a new law on ICA was enacted.

There will be two important changes in the practice of ICA when this new law takes effect in 1990. First, all Dutch organizations involved in ICA will need an official permit when they place foreign children with Dutch couples. In addition, there will be other special requirements for such organizations, including the following:

They must be nonprofit corporations.
Their board members must guarantee the interests of both adoptees and adoptive parents.
Adoption work must be done by qualified psychologists and social workers.
Organizations must cooperate with organizations in the countries in which they work.

As a result of these changes, it is expected that aspirant adoptive parents will be much better prepared for the adventure of ICA. The Adoption Center at the University of Utrecht was asked to organize a course that would better prepare prospective adoptive parents. The course will consist of six to eight study evenings during which couples will acquire a variety of useful information, learn to recognize educational problems that occur frequently, and acquire feelings of empathy for the adoptee and his adoptive status.

The future adoptive parents will also learn something about the special characteristics of adoptive kinship. They should be prepared to recognize and acknowledge the differences between adoptive and natural kinship (Kirk 1981) and the attitude of other-orientedness—that is, a kind of cosmopolitan directedness in their behavior vis-à-vis the child (Hoksbergen 1985). They should accept the child as an independent human being for which they, most of all, are responsible. Any rights parents have over their children are less in the case of adopted children, and these limited rights might disappear as soon as the child acquires sufficient understanding and maturity to decide matters for him or herself. On the other hand, adoptive parents also have more obligations. For instance, they should respect the background of an adopted child and supply him or her with as much information about it as possible. Later, the adoptive parents should be prepared to help the child obtain more information about his or her country of origin (by traveling there, for example), help the child to find his or her place in society, and help in finding answers to basic questions such as "Who am I?" and "Why do I exist?" and "What are my relatives like?" In short, the adoptive parents need to support their adoptee in finding a satisfying identity.

It is hoped that adoptive parents will be able to love their adopted children and vice versa. Later, when the adoptee slowly moves away (or suddenly, as we so often see during adolescence), the adoptive parents will have to be able to let go with love. We emphasize again that it is very important for parents to recognize from the beginning that their child has a different background, and that background will influence their kinship and relationship with the child. It will also influence the child's feelings toward them as parents. Depending on the child's temperament and history, feelings of loyalty toward natural and adoptive parents (and toward Holland and the birth country) may be complicated—but they will nearly always exist. Adoptive parents will always have to deal with such feelings in intercountry-adopted children, and the children will have to cope with feelings of loyalty. Parents may have all sorts of expectations about the behavior and temperament of the adoptee with which they will have to deal.

Returning to the purposes of the new law, I conclude that there is hope in Holland that with better preparation for parents and the special requirements imposed on the adoption organizations, there will be fewer problems in intercountry-adoptive families.

RESEARCH ON ICA IN THE NETHERLANDS

Considering how deeply intercountry (and in-country) adoptions affect the lives of so many people, it is not surprising that they have become subjects of research in several disciplines. To give a realistic overview of research in this field, I have differentiated between juridical, medical, and psychological/psychiatric approaches.

The Juridical Approach

The work of Cloeck (1946) was the earliest important juridical study leading to the first adoption law 10 years later. In addition to his interest in ICAs, Cloeck also examined important differences between fostering and adoption.

The next influential juridical work was done by Nota (1969), who evaluated the results of the adoption law passed in 1956 and compared it to legal developments in other European countries. He considered it very useful to compare the laws in different countries in the interest of the growing unity of law in Europe. One of his recommendations was followed in 1979 when the first act on stepparent adoption was introduced. Nota also proposed to limit the probationary period from two years to one. Goudsmit's *Adoption in the Netherlands* (1971) provided an inventory of the statutes related to adoption in 40 countries.

Between 1971 and 1988, little was done concerning juridical matters vis-à-vis adoption. By 1988, however, it became clear that new developments would require important changes in the law. One rule that needed to be changed was the requirement that only married couples (with a minimum of five years of marriage) are able to adopt in Holland. Since about 1978, it has become obvious that this regulation is not in the best interest of children. Though single-parent adoption will always be unusual, there are several situations in which it might be important for the well-being of a child—for example, when an unmarried person working in a Third-World country accepts responsibility for a child because the mother died right after the child's birth. Or when a child is left with a single person by parents who then disappear. Or when an institution in the birth country has placed a hard-to-place orphan with a single person.

The Dutch government was confronted by articles in the media and remarks in the House of Commons with the fact that Holland is one of the few countries that does not permit single-parent adoption. Consequently, a study was conducted to investigate how single-parent adoptions were regulated in France, Belgium, Germany, Denmark, Sweden, and Great Britain. Released in 1988, the official report exuded an atmosphere of much more openness to the idea of single-parent adoption. In the next few years, some liberalization can be expected in Danish law concerning single-parent adoption. At present, however, such adoptions are only possible for posthumous adoption or if a couple is divorced.

A second important change concerns the formal rights of an adoptee to know about his genetic background. In May 1988, the Dutch Gezinsraad (family counsel) published its report "Rights of Information of Descent; Modern Techniques of Procreation and the Interest of the Child." Again, data from other countries (Germany and Sweden) were used for purposes of comparison. The report concluded its research with the following recommendations:

1. All adopted children should be able to receive information about their genetic backgrounds. This information should be adapted to the age of the adoptee.
2. Parents must be made aware of this need to provide information to the child;
3. All sperm and ovum donors must be registered for medical and psychological reasons.
4. The donor should be known by the physician. Mixing of sperm of several donors should be forbidden.
5. General data about the donor should also be given to the parents and the adoptee.
6. A law concerning modern procreation and surrogate-motherhood techniques should be passed as soon as possible.

The Medical Approach

In 1979, we published a work (Hoksbergen, et al. 1979, 1982) that for the first time provided information about the medical situation of a large group of adoptees. The research showed that extra medical attention for intercountry-adopted children cannot be considered a luxury. When a physician examines an intercountry adoptee for the first time after arrival in Holland, he or she may be confronted with a great variety of medical problems. The study was done at our Adoption Center between 1976 and 1979, and it involved 350 intercountry-adopted children (Hoksbergen, et al. 1979, 1982). We found that malnutrition was the most common complaint, mentioned by 20 percent of all parents. Fifteen percent of the parents mentioned intestinal disorders; in many cases, the child had a severe worm infection resulting in persistent diarrhea.

Another important complaint (among 15 percent) was skin disease (i.e., scabies, eczema, mycosis, and abscesses). Many children carried vermin such as lice, and some had exotic infections and diseases with which their physicians were probably not familiar. For this reason, there is a small group of pediatricians in Holland specializing in tropical disease who can be approached by adoptive parents. Some of these physicians do empirical research as well. Sorgedrager, for example, studied about 1,000 children (72 percent less than twelve months old) from Sri Lanka, Korea, Colombia, India, Haiti, and other countries. In general, the medical research demonstrates how important it is for adoptive parents to have their foreign-born children undergo proper medical checkups immediately after arrival. These children often will need special medical care for a long time.

The Psychological/Psychiatric Approach

In 1975, about 1,000 intercountry-adopted children arrived in the Netherlands, many in a pitiable state from medical and psychological points of view. Regular appeals were made to the adoption specialists at the Institute for Pedagogic and Andragogic Sciences of the University of Utrecht (now the Adoption Center). The confrontation of various problems with intercountry-adopted children resulted in extensive investigation in this field beginning in 1975. Several studies were carried out between 1975 and 1989.

The first study (Hoksbergen, et al. 1979, 1982) involved the mailing of questionnaires to 500 adoptive parents and resulted in a response rate of 70 percent. The responses showed that adoptive parents were, on the average, six years older than other first-time parents. The upper-middle class was, and still is, strongly represented. Few in this group of adoptive parents attached much importance to background information about their children, but this attitude has changed completely. For medical and psychological reasons, parents today try to get much more information, and some of them travel to the country of origin for this purpose. Later, most parents adopting today will help their children when they want to visit their birth countries.

The motive for adopting was an important issue in the first study. The couples were divided into four groups: involuntarily childless couples (70 percent), involuntarily childless couples after the birth of one child (10 percent), couples with two or more children of their own (10 percent), and completely and secondarily voluntarily childless couples (10 percent).

For the first two groups, the main reason for adopting had to do with the composition of the family. These couples very much wanted a child—preferably a child born in Holland, but that had become almost impossible. These couples did not focus their intentions much on the situation of the child. In later studies, I have called this type of motivation *inner orientedness*, which is related to Kirk's "rejection-of-difference" attitude (Kirk 1981).

The other two groups had more idealistic motivations, such as the desire to care for a child in distress or concern about overpopulation—motivations I call *outer orientedness*. The child is seen, to a large extent, as a world citizen, and the parents have a cosmopolitan directedness in their wish to have a child. This abstractedness, however, might harm the adjustment of the child, especially if he or she shows serious behavioral troubles from the moment he or she arrives in Holland.

Since about 1984, the motives for ICA have changed, as is evident from the family composition of later groups, which contain many more involuntarily childless couples. The preferences of couples in terms of the type of child they want has changed as well. Most now prefer a child as young as possible—definitely not older than two. Ten years earlier, the preference regarding the age of the child was more open. These preferences have changed partly due to data from recent studies showing that older children present many more problems than younger children. Even more important, however, is that some parents who have experienced problems with older intercountry-adopted children have concluded that these children are not able to live in normal Dutch families. In general, adoptive parents are better able to realize that educating an intercountry adoptee requires a certain outer-orientedness and the acknowledgment-of-difference attitude (Hoksbergen, Juffer, and Waardenburg 1987).

In our first study, we received many signals that, in addition to medical problems, there were also many examples of unusual behavior at home and at school. Therefore, the conclusion that these adoptive parents should be much better prepared for their task was largely accepted. The largest organization, World Children, which had already decided to provide more information to adoptive parents, now organized orientation meetings for all aspirant adoptive parents throughout the country. In 1980, the Minister of Justice established a new program with the special task of organizing an "adoption course for all aspirant adoptive parents" (about 1,600 couples).

Our second study (Bunjes 1980; De Vries 1988), involving 144 children from Korea, India, Colombia, and Bangladesh, was aimed at discovering how these children functioned in school. In 1979, a preliminary group was approached. The main group, consisting of kindergarten pupils and those in the first or second form of primary school, was approached in 1980 and again in 1983. The parents were also interviewed, making this the first time in Denmark that intercountry-adoptive parents and children had been approached in this way. The children were examined together with four classmates at school. The behavioral findings were not much different from those of the earlier study; in fact, they were rather positive. This result is related to the relatively young age of both groups of children in the 1975 and 1979 studies.

Language development was the important issue. Surprisingly, we found no alarming problem in the acquisition and use of the Dutch language in either the longitudinal study of 144 adopted children or a smaller cross-sectional study of 36 Korean children in secondary education (De Vries 1988). This finding was in accordance with reports from Hoksbergen and Bunjes (1986) and Schaerlaekens and Dondeyne (1985) for different samples of intercountry-adopted children in Holland and the Flemish part of Belgium. But these findings do not confirm the results of the investigations of Gardell (1980) in Sweden and Forrest (1981) in the United States. Both of these researchers describe prolonged language deficiencies in 43 to 54 percent of the intercountry-adopted children they met.

The Bunjes and De Vries studies were important because they showed that parents have become more alert to school adjustment problems. The general finding was that, depending on the age of arrival, intercountry-adopted children do not cause any more problems at school than do nonadopted children. The major conclusion (as of 1984) was that general outcomes were not negative.

THE STUDY OF CHILDREN FROM THAILAND

The third important study (Hoksbergen, Juffer, and Waardenburg 1987) was a follow-up of the former two, and all the knowledge obtained thus far was used. We decided to study a group that was relatively homogeneous concerning country of origin, age, and manner of placement. A group of children who arrived from Thailand between 1974 and 1980 made this possible. The study focused on a group of 121 children and 90 parents. Of these, 116 children and 87 parents entered the study (a response rate of 96 percent). The parents were interviewed and asked to fill out four instruments (a family dimension scale, Kirk's instrument for measuring adoptive kinship attitudes, a parents' list for measuring feelings of attachment, and a behavior list for the child). The children were also evaluated by their teachers at school through a behavioral assessment list, a teacher's questionnaire, and examination of their grades. At school, each adopted child was compared with two classmates. The interviews were carried out by the authors of the report, who all worked as lecturers for Utrecht University.

On the whole, this group of parents was not very different (in terms of high socioeconomic level and 76 percent childlessness) from other groups of intercountry-adoptive parents. Their children had been in Holland for an average of 8.6 years and had been less than 10 months old (11 percent were 25 months and older) when they arrived. Because these parents had traveled to Thailand for the adoption procedures, they had learned a great deal about their children's backgrounds. At the time of the study, almost all of the children were in good health compared to Dutch children of the same age. The general statement that intercountry-adopted children are often vital and strong (as is evident by their recuperative powers) held true for our group.

It should be emphasized that these parents did not find it difficult to accept their special form of parenthood; in fact, it seemed much easier for them than for parents involved in in-country adoptions. The acknowledgment-of-difference attitude was very strong. We found the same connections as Kirk: The greater the awareness of the special nature of adoptive parenthood, the easier the communication with the child about his or her adoption status and the greater the parental empathy concerning the child's perception of his or her environment. These children seemed to put more trust than most in their parents. Thus, the picture presented by these adoptive parents of their family systems showed adoptive families as rather closely knit compared to other Dutch families. They considered family life very important and had fixed structures that might make it easier for them to adjust to a child with special characteristics. This group of parents seemed to combine inner- and outer-orientedness attitudes.

The great effort and involvement of these parents had a positive effect on their children's functioning at school. In terms of their socioemotional behavior at school, adopted children from Thailand seem to be doing better than Dutch children. Children with problematic backgrounds have more trouble learning, but these Thai children tend to display more positive social behavior and are more likely to do their best with their schoolwork.

A large number of parents found it hard to react adequately to the problems of adaptation that nearly all children show. There are indications that temporary problems of adaptation may sometimes take on a more permanent character. Neglect, problematic background, and poor health give an unfavorable prognosis for a child's emotional and social growth. There is also an obvious relationship to later problems (most importantly lack of concentration, stealing, lying and denial, superficial relations, inaccessibility), although family situation and structure are important factors that may mediate these tendencies.

On the other hand, there may be protective factors in the adoption situation that reduce the risks of deprivation and separation experiences (Garmezy and Rutter 1983). Adoptive parents may have an educational "surplus," and these children are usually very much desired. There might also be protective factors on the part of the child, such as temperament or the will to survive.

In a few cases, the development of relationships was very problematic, and then the problems were immense. This brings us to our next large study, on the re-placements of intercountry-adopted children.

THE NEED FOR AFTER-CARE AND PROFESSIONAL ASSISTANCE BY ADOPTIVE PARENTS

Examining the appeals for assistance by adoptive parents provides an indication about the number of adoptions that have serious troubles. Between 1981 and 1982, an investigation was carried out among 60 arbitrarily chosen institutes for public health (now called RIAGG). It turned out that adoptive families ask these institutions for assistance four to five times more often than nonadoptive families. Socialization problems formed the main cause for seeking help. Adoptive children appear to make the process of forming relationships with their parents, contemporaries, and others difficult (Hoksbergen 1983).

During this same period, another study was conducted to find out how many ICAs could be deemed very problematic by examining the number of temporary placements in residential care. Using data from some of the organizations involved, we arrived at an estimate of about two percent of all intercountry-adopted children. Stimulated by the commotion from 1984 to 1986 about the problematic side of ICAs, we decided to conduct another national inquiry into the frequency and causes of placements in residential care (Hoksbergen, Spaan, and Waardenburg 1988). We concentrated on placement in residential care because this is a relatively objective approach to determining the extent to which ICA involves behavioral and educational problems.

We found that 5.7 percent of all intercountry-adopted children needed residential care at some time (see Table 7.3). Because we obtained our data from 670—or 93 percent—of the institutions involved and we could count the number of these problematic placements in two ways, we believe that this estimate of disrupted adoptions is almost exact.

For about one-quarter of the children studied, residential care was only a temporary disruption; after a time, they were returned to their adoptive parents. Age of arrival is very much connected to the chance of disruption (see Table 7.4). We also compared the numbers of Dutch-born and intercountry-adopted children in institutions (see Table 7.5), and the differences were striking, all the more so because these children had not yet reached their age of majority. The average age of the intercountry adoptees was still lower than that of the Dutch-born children. I expect that in a few years the need for residential care for intercountry adoptees will be about six times greater than for other children.

One of the main causes of problems was a child's history in his or her country of origin—more precisely, the amount of deprivation he or she experienced. One can also conclude this from the differences we saw

Table 7.4
Foreign-Born Adoptees in Residential Care by Age on Arrival

Age on Arrival (in Months)	Adoptees (total)	Adoptee Placements in Residential Care	Percentage of Adoptees in Residential Care	Period in Holland Before Placement in Residential Care of Less Than Six Months
0–6	6828	47	0.7	3
7–18	3255	43	1.3	3
19–30	1324	39	3.0	2
31–42	1267	43	3.4	–
43–54	1296	66	5.1	–
55–66	835	36	4.3	–
67–78	749	36	4.8	–
79–90	317	39	12.3	4
Totals	15871	349		

among the disrupted group and a control group of intercountry adoptees ($n = 30$) who were individually matched by age of arrival, sex, country of origin, and age at the time of investigation. We did this comparison via Achenbach's Child Behavior Checklist (CBCL), which was adapted by Verhulst, Althaus, and Versluis-den Bieman (1985). The differences between the two groups were significant. The main 10 (significant at the

Table 7.5
Dutch-Born Children and Foreign-Adopted Children in Residential Care

Year[a]	Percentage of Total Dutch-Born Children	Percentage of Total Foreign-Adopted Children
1980	0.33	0.75
1981	0.33	0.94
1982	0.33	1.10
1983	0.35	1.10
1984	0.35	1.50

[a]By December 31 of each year.

.01 level) were: "demands attention," "lacks feelings of guilt," "poor school work," "poor peer relations," "lying or cheating," "depressed," "secretive," "suspicious," "steals at home," and "steals outside home." Table 7.6 shows the results of the nine most important items for the disrupted and control groups.

In 1989, we obtained data from another study in which the CBCL was used (Verhulst, Althaus, and Versluis-den Bieman 1985), this time for a group of more than 2,100 intercountry adoptees (response rate: 65 percent) aged 10–15 years. Overall, the same results were found. For example, the older a child at placement, the greater the risk of delinquent and uncommunicative syndromes in boys, and cruel, depressed, and schizoid syndromes in girls. The significance of the high score on delinquent behavior is demonstrated by the fact that there are many more adoptees (in- and intercountry) than nonadoptees in criminal institutions for youth aged 12–18. Parents also reported more external behavior problems (conflicts with others and with their own expectations) among adoptees. Adopted children also had poorer scores than nonadoptees in social and academic functioning.

From earlier studies, we know that a major problem area in ICA is the attachment process between parents and child, so we decided to influence this process via experimentation. In 1985, we started a longitudinal study on responsiveness and attachment in adoptive parent-child relationships. Ninety couples with no biological children and 40 with at least

Table 7.6
Scores on Main Items of Achenbach's CBCL for Disrupted and Control Groups

Items	Disrupted Group	Control Group
Demands attention	48	14
Secretive	41	–
Poor school work	38	–
Lacks feelings of guilt	38	–
Can't concentrate	38	17
Stubborn		14
Argues a lot	–	16
Bragging		13
Likes to be alone	–	13

one biological child were followed for 30 months. The children were six months old, and their age at time of arrival had been four months or younger. The intervals for measuring the experimental and control groups were 6, 9, 12, 18, and 30 months. Various attitude and attachment tests were used, as well as observations of mother-child interaction. This study was conducted at the University of Leiden, and comparable studies were done at three other universities with three different groups of Dutch children: children born with psychoses, children born prematurely, and children of parents in low socioeconomic levels. The first articles and reports based on these studies are expected in 1990.

In another study (started in 1986) of 60 Indian children nine to eleven years old and a control group, we are trying to obtain a better understanding of the causes of problems in developing a healthy self-concept. We also plan to study children in India who will be sent for ICA at 12 to 36 months old and compare them to children who will remain in India.

THE DARK SIDE OF ICA

Until about 1980, public opinion about ICA in Holland was generally positive. There were, of course, reports of scandals and misbehavior on the part of some organizations and couples, but these were exceptions and often had nothing to do with the Dutch practice. This first stage of development of ICA is often called the "rose-colored period," and it was followed by a more realistic second stage.

During the past few years, Dutch ideas and policies concerning ICA have charged a great deal. It is of course positive that much more is being done to improve the preparation of aspirant adoptive parents. Parents have also become more realistic, and there are several books available that give them a lot of information.

But there is also a dark side. Fewer parents approach ICA with the idealistic, outer-oriented point of view. While ICA has become a more or less accepted phenomenon in Dutch society, the basic ideology that we should try to prevent ICA has decreased in importance. The transport of children from distant countries to give them a chance in Western families must be viewed ambivalently: it seems questionable to move children thousands of miles from their ancestors and origins. Let us hope that culture and economic circumstances in all Third-World countries change to the extent that it will be the exception when a child's only chance for a satisfactory upbringing exists with a family thousands of miles from its birthplace.

To conclude, the 20,000 intercountry-adopted children who have arrived in Holland in the last 20 years are very welcome and have a good chance of leading fulfilling lives. But we also have to see them as a symptom of ailing societies, societies that, in the interests of these children, have let them move far away from their homelands and birth parents.

REFERENCES

Bagley, C. (1973). *The Dutch Plural Society: A Comparative Study in Race Relations.* Oxford: Oxford University Press.

Bovenkerk, F. (ed.). (1978). *Omdat Zij Anders Zijn, Patronen van Rasdiscriminatie in Nederland* (Because They Are Different, Patterns of Racial Discrimination in the Netherlands). Meppel: Boom.

Bunjes, L. A. C. (1980). Ontwikkeling van Buitenlandse Adoptiekinderen (Development of Intercountry Adoptive Children). In: Hoksbergen, R. A. C. and H. Walenkamp, *Opgroeiende Adoptiekinderen* (Adoptive Children Growing Up). Deventer: van Loghum Slaterous.

Cloeck, H. P. (1946). *Adoptie als Vraagstuck van Kinderbescherming* (Adoption as Problem of Child Protection). Den Haag. (Dissertation.)

De Vries, A. K. (1988). Taalaanpassing van Koreaanse Adoptiekinderen (Language Adaptation of Korean Adoptees). In: de Vries, A. K. and Bunjes, L. A. C. (eds.), *A Fresh Start . . . A New Language*. Utrecht: Adoption Center.

Forrest, A. B. (1981). *Language Problems of Internationally Adopted Children*. Newark: University of Delaware. (Thesis.)

Gardell, I. (1980). *A Swedish Study on Intercountry Adoption.* Stockholm: Liber Tryck.

Garmezy, N., and Rutter, M. (eds.). (1983). *Stress, Coping and Development in Children*. New York: McGraw-Hill.

Goudsmit, H. R. (1971). *Adoptie in Nederland* (Adoption in the Netherlands). Den Haag: Vuga.

Hoksbergen, R. A. C., Bunjes, L., Baarda, B., and Nota, J. (eds.). (1979, 1982). *Adoptie van Kinderen Uit Verre Landen* (Adoption of Children from Far Countries). Deventer: van Loghum Slaterus.

Hoksbergen, R. A. C., et al. (1983). Adoptiefkinderen bij Medisch Opvoedkundige Bureaus (MOB) en Jeugd Psychiatrische Diensten (JPD) (Adoptive Children at Institutions for Child Care). In Hoksbergen, R. A. C. and Walenkamp, H. (eds.), *Adoptie uit de Kinderschoenen* (Adoption Coming of Age). Deventer: van Loghum Slaterus.

Hoksbergen, R. A. C. (1983). Adoptiefkinderen worden soms overgeplaatst (Adoptive Children are Sometimes Replaced). In Hoksbergen, R. A. C. and Walenkamp, H. (eds.), *Adoptie uit de Kinderschoenen* (Adoption Coming of Age). Deventer: van Loghum Slaterus.

Hoksbergen, R. A. C. (1985). *Een nieuwe kans, adoptie van Nederlandse en buitenlandse kinderen* (A New Chance, Adoption of Dutch and Foreign Children). Utrecht: Utrecht University Press.

Hoksbergen, R. A. C., and Bunjes, L. A. C. (1986). Thirty Years of Adoption Practice in the Netherlands. In Hoksbergen, R. A. C. and Gokhale, S. D. (eds.), *Adoption in World Wide Perspective, a Review of Programs, Policies and Legislation in 14 Countries.* Lisse: Swets & Zeitlinger.

Hoksbergen, R. A. C., Juffer, F., and Waardenburg, B. C. (1987). *Adopted Children at Home and at School*. Lisse: Swets & Zeitlinger.

Hoksbergen, R. A. C., Spaan, J., and Waardenburg, B. C. (1988). *Bittere Ervaringen* (Bitter Experiences). Lisse: Swets & Zeitlinger.

Kirk, H. D. (1981). *Adoptive Kinship*. Washington: Ben Simon.

Nota, J. A. (1969). *De Adoptie, Rechtsinstituut in Ontwikkeling* (Adoption, Institution of Jurisdiction Development). Leiden. (Dissertation.)

Schaerlaekens, A., and Dondeyne, N. (1985). Taalaanpassing bij buitenlandse adoptiekinderen (Language Adaptation of Intercountry Adopted Children). *Kind en Adolescent*, 6 (No. 4): 203–218.

Verhulst, F. C., Althaus, M., and Versluis-den Bieman, J. M. (1985). *I: Problem Behavior in International Adoptees, an Epidemiological Study; II: Age at Placement*. (Mimeo.)

Wolters, W. H. J. (1978). *Adoption of Foreign Children*. Nykesh: Callenbach.

III

THE MIDDLE EAST

8

Foreign Adoptions in Israel: Private Paths to Parenthood

ELIEZER D. JAFFE

INTRODUCTION

Intercountry adoptions was a nonsubject in Israeli child welfare until the late 1970s. During the British Mandate years (1917–1948), there were very few adoptions in general, and the emphasis was on placement of dependent children in orphan homes (built mostly in the 1880s), with some placements in foster care and financial support to help widows with children (Berger 1928; Weiner 1984). Institutional placement of infants was rampant from the 1930s to the late 1970s. The women's Zionist organizations, particularly WIZO (Women's International Zionist Organization), received funding from members abroad and built a large network of infant "homes" and "creches." These hospital-like facilities flourished until the late 1970s, when economic problems, negative research findings, and professionalization of social work forced most of them to close (Jaffe 1983). In 1960, 68.2 percent of all Israeli children living away from home were living in 142 institutions for dependent children (IMSW 1968).

The concept of adoption is not mentioned in or recognized by either the Torah (Jewish law) or the Koran (Moslem law). In both of these religions, "no legal act can supersede or annul the inalienable duties and privileges deriving from the natural bonds between parents and children" (Jacobovits 1969). With urbanization, acculturation, Westernization, war, mass migration, changes in sexual mores, infertility problems, socioreligious pressures toward family life and a desire for lineage continuity, Jews around the world turned to secular courts to establish legal rights (based on Roman law) regarding adopted children. In Palestine, too, Jews turned to the Mandate government's district courts for adoption decrees. The Orthodox Jewish view holds that "legal adoptions merely represent obligations which the parties have agreed to assume as a deed of supreme charity towards the ward" (Jacobovits 1969; Schachter 1982).

The scope of adoption in Palestine during the early years of the State of Israel was minimal, with only 44 cases in 1950. However, as the population doubled during the first decade of the State—from the original 600,000 inhabitants (primarily Ashkenazi Jews from Western countries) to 1.3 million—the number of nonrelative adoptions increased to 257 in 1967. In the first 20 years after the State of Israel was created in 1948, 81.7 percent of children adopted were illegitimate, and the biological mothers were mostly single (78 percent), under 25 years old (82 percent), relatively uneducated, and Sephardi (63 percent) who had come to Israel with the mass immigration of 700,000 Jews from Moslem Middle Eastern countries (Jaffe 1965; 1982). Only 8 percent of the biological mothers were married; 10 percent were divorced, and 2 percent were either separated or widowed. Only 3.3 percent were Moslem women.

In the 1960s, the majority of adopting couples (67.5 percent) were of Ashkenazi or European-American origin. The mass influx of Sephardi immigrants, and the family and personal disruption that many of them encountered, created a situation where the supply of children for adoption was greater than the demand. To this day, the Yemenite Immigrant Association claims that Yemenite babies from large families who were being treated in Israeli hospitals during the early 1950s were secretly adopted by Ashkenazi couples, and that false death certificates were issued to the biological parents living in the transient camps. No solid evidence of such a scheme has yet been discovered, but the Association insists on continuing the investigation of its claim.

Although the skin color of Sephardi babies is darker than that of Ashkenazi children, this was not a major barrier for Ashkenazi couples. This is in contrast to reports from other countries on the subject of skin color differences in adoption at that time (Fanshel 1957; Woods and Lancaster 1962). My assessment is that mostly necessity and convenience, combined with some Zionist ideology concerning Jewish peoplehood (i.e., a positive attitude toward the concept of the "Ingathering of the Exiles" into their ancestral homeland), made such adoptions natural, even nationalistic.

It is important to point out that the preceding data refer to nonrelative adoptions, which constituted 59 percent of all adoptions. During the 1960s, a study by Englard (1969) discovered that 12.1 percent of adoptions between relatives involved giving a child to a childless sibling of the biological parents. These family-related adoptions were primarily among Sephardi and Moslem families, whereas nonrelative adoptions were primarily by Ashkenazi couples. This practice (giving a child to relatives) is not uncommon in the Middle East.

The years before 1970 were marked by Jewish inter*ethnic* (not interracial or intercountry) adoptions. Only a very few researchers noted the possibility of ethnic exchange, cultural integration, and adjustment problems for children and adoptive parents coming from totally different social and cultural backgrounds (Jaffe 1965; England 1969). Unfortunately, there was no empirical research on this subject in Israel during this period, in contrast to the work done abroad by Simon and Altstein (1977), Fanshel (1972), Falk (1970), Grow and Shapiro (1974), and Fricke (1972). Some data and systematic review is available, however, regarding Sephardi children placed in private Ashkenazi foster homes from the overcrowded immigrant transient camps in the winter of 1950–1951, but nothing similar is available for adoption placements (Sapir 1953).

Indeed, the conceptual approach to Ashkenazi-Sephardi adoptions did not even recognize the possible questions involved. The whole matter was seen as a very small microcosm of the larger national goal: the rapid assimilation of the relatively "primitive" Sephardi culture into the modern, Western dominant Ashkenazi culture (Zipperstein and Jaffe 1980; Eisenstadt 1950). This was the essence of so-called nation-building until the mid-1970s, when cultural pluralism was substituted for the melting-pot approach, and then only after serious social disruptions by Sephardi youths (Cohen 1967; Cohen 1972; Cromer 1976). In the past decade, there has been a much greater sensitivity to ethnic issues, but never as an inter*racial* problem because of the common Jewish identity and common religious ancestral roots.

ORIGINS OF ICA IN ISRAEL

Like other Western countries, Israel does not have enough babies available for adoption to meet the requests of infertile couples seeking children. In fact, Israel is now poised at a crossroads that very likely will lead us to a situation similar to that of Holland: in 13 years, the bulk (80%) of Holland's adopted children now come from other countries (Hoksbergen 1984).

The reasons this situation has developed in Israel over the past 15 years are universal to the Western world. Unfortunately, very conservative attitudes and policies were adopted by the Israeli State Adoption Service and, coupled with the demographic change, this has created an adoption vacuum that has been filled by various devices, some with unfortunate consequences.

In 1988, only 154 nonrelative babies were adopted in Israel, up from 97 in 1985 and 85 in 1986. During the 1970s, only 44 percent of the couples approved for adoption actually received children. In 1982, the waiting period for a child was four years; by 1988, it was approximately six years. Each year, nearly 500 couples apply, and the backlog of those now waiting is approximately 3,000 couples (Tal 1985).

While infertility problems have continued at a regular pace, the number of children available for adoption has drastically declined due to changes in religious and cultural attitudes, better education, and social norms. As a result, approximately 80,000 abortions take place in Israel each year. Of these, 20,000 are legal (approved by appropriate hospital review committees) and another 60,000 are illegal (Glick 1989). Only a small minority of those undergoing abortions are non-Jewish women.

In 1985, 40% of all legal abortions were performed in three private Israeli hospitals. Pro-lifers claim that abortion is basically available on demand, depending on the interpretation of the phrase "danger to the mother." This category accounts for more than 6,000 of the legal abortions annually (Glick 1989).

In addition, better social welfare and income maintenance programs for single mothers have made the option of keeping their babies more feasible than previously. Also, there are increasing numbers of older single women choosing married biological fathers by whom to become pregnant, with the intent of raising the child alone.

Although the Israeli Adoption Service works hard to locate relatively older children and handicapped children (Bar-Am 1986; Orna Nenner 1989), most couples want to adopt infants, and there is simply no way of responding to this demand. As a result, criteria for adoptive couples are artificially stringent and the process lengthy: the chosen few may obtain babies, while the rest continue to wait and grow older. For example, a woman over age 38 and a man over age 42 cannot be candidates for the adoption of infants, but they can apply to adopt an older child or a handicapped child. The screening process includes individual and joint interviews with an adoption worker, a home visit, a group intake session, three to five group meetings, rating sheets, "Impression forms," and testing. Rejected candidates can reapply in a year or two (Jaffe 1982).

It was only natural and predictable for couples to begin looking outside Israel for infant children to adopt. Some turned to friends; others hired lawyers and intermediaries. Eventually, but quietly, the kibbutz movements began to assist kibbutz couples to locate and fund adoptions (Ben-Israel 1982; Jaffe 1986). Thus, a network of contacts, legal consultants, and Israeli and foreign go-betweens slowly developed that provided several thousand couples with the children they sought. Almost all of these adoptions took place abroad, and the children were brought to Israel with foreign passports.

Throughout this long "underground" period (which is still flourish-ing), the Adoption Service of the Ministry of Labor and Social Affairs chose a hands-off policy regarding foreign adoptions. The director of the Service, working with relative freedom and little public review (because of the secrecy of adoption work), had become entrenched in the ideology that only dependent Israeli children were clients of the Service: once these children found parents, the other waiting couples would have to fend for themselves. "The best interests of the child" became a slogan for neglecting eligible couples' abilities to help homeless children anywhere and to have a family. Even the name was deliberately changed, from the Adoption Service to the Service for the Child.

Basically, the Service abandoned these waiting couples and publicly stereotyped them (and those who championed ICAs and outreach pro-grams with social agencies in other countries) as egoistic, self-serving people thinking only of themselves and their needs. For most couples, the situation was devastating, and many turned to independent adop-tions abroad.

ISRAELI ADOPTIONS: A GOVERNMENT MONOPOLY

There are no private or independent adoption agencies in Israel. The only adoption services available are government-operated district offices of the national Adoption Service and the three largest municipalities. The high degree of cooperation between state and municipal adoption workers means that the government has a total monopoly over all adop-tion work. This arrangement is the cornerstone of the Israel adoption scene. In addition, Section 33 of the Adoption of Children Law totally bans private adoptions—both those by private, nonprofit social agencies with professional staffs and independent adoptions involving contracts between various individuals. A year of imprisonment is prescribed for anyone placing a child through channels other than the official Adoption Service.

Israeli adoption law requires that all adoption orders and related mat-ters must be determined and issued by the District Court. The law relies very heavily on testimony, liaison, and recommendations of "welfare officers empowered for the purposes of this Law. . . . The Minister of Labor and Social Affairs shall appoint for purposes of this Law, from among welfare officers defined by the Welfare Services Law of 1958, a chief (adoption) welfare officer and welfare officers who shall act in accordance with the directives of the chief welfare officer, either general-ly or in respect of any particular matter" (State of Israel 1981, Sections 6 and 36).

The adoption welfare officer of the Ministry of Labor and Social Affairs is charged with the following tasks, as mandated in the Adoption Law:

Handing over child for purposes of adoption

(a) Where a person has agreed to receive a child into his house with a view to adopt him, the child shall not be handed over to him except through a welfare officer. This provision shall not apply to the handing-over to an adopter who is the spouse of a parent of the adoptee.

(b) A welfare officer shall not hand over a child as stated in subsection (a) unless his parents have consented to the adoption or the court has declared the child adoptable.

(c) Where it appears to a welfare officer that the case suffers no delay and circumstances so require, he may even without the consent of the parents or the declaration of the child as adoptable, prescribe where the child shall stay or hand him over to a person who has agreed to receive him into his house with a view of adopting him. An act under this section shall require the approval of the court within fourteen days from the day on which it is done; the approval may be given *ex parte* (Section 12).

Probationary period

A court shall not make an adoption order unless the adoptee has lived in the adopter's household for at least six months prior to the making of the order; this period shall be reckoned from the day on which a welfare officer empowered for the purposes of this Law under section 36 (hereinafter referred to as a "welfare officer") is notified that the adopter has received the adoptee into his house with a view to adopting him (Section 6).

Consent of adoptee

Where the adoptee is nine years of age or over, or where he is under nine years of age but is able to understand the matter, a court shall not make an adoption order unless it is satisfied that the adoptee wishes to be adopted by the adopter: Provided that the court may, after hearing the adopter and a welfare officer, make an adoption order without disclosing the fact of the adoption to the adoptee if it is satisfied that—

(1) the adoptee does not know that the adopter is not his parent and

(2) there is every indication that the adoptee wishes his link with the adopter to continue and

(3) the welfare of the adoptee demands that the fact of the adoption not be disclosed to him (Section 7).

Declaration of child as adoptable

In the absence of a parent's consent, a court may, on the application of the Attorney-General or his representative, declare a child adoptable if it is satisfied that one of the following is the case:

(1) there is no reasonable chance of identifying, finding or ascertaining the opinion of the parents;

(2) the parent is the father of the child but is not married to his mother and does not recognize the child as his own; if he recognizes him, the child does not live with him, and he refuses, without reasonable cause to receive him into his home;

(3) the parent is deceased or has been declared legally incompetent or has been deprived of the guardianship of the child;

(4) the parent has abandoned the child or has, without reasonable cause, refrained from maintaining personal contact with him for six consecutive months;

(5) the parent has, without reasonable cause, refrained from fulfilling all or the main part of his obligations towards the child for six consecutive months;

(6) the child has been maintained outside the parent's house for six months beginning before the child was six years of age and he refuses, without justification, to receive him into his house;

(7) the parent is, due to his conduct or situation, not capable of taking proper care of the child, and, not withstanding reasonable attendance and economic aid towards his rehabilitation, *as usual with the welfare authorities*, there is no prospect of his conduct or situation changing in the foreseeable future;

(8) consent is refused from an immoral motive or for an unlawful purpose (Section 13).

Welfare officer as guardian

(1) Where a parent consents to his child being adopted or the court declares the child adoptable, and no guardian has been appointed of the child, the rights, duties and powers of the parent shall, until the court otherwise decides, vest in a welfare officer designated in that behalf by a chief welfare officer, as if the welfare officer had been appointed guardian of the child instead of the parent.

(2) The provisions of subsection (1) shall apply also to a child in respect to whom a welfare officer acts as provided in section 12 (c) (Section 15).

Report of welfare officer

A court shall not make an order under this Law until it has received a written report of a welfare officer. The provisions of sections 3 to 6 of the Welfare (Procedure in Matters of Minors, Mentally Sick Persons and Absent Persons), Law 5715-1955 shall apply *mutatis mutandis* (Section 22).

Inspection of register

(a) The Register of Adoptions shall not be open for inspection; it may, however, be inspected
   (1) by the Attorney-General or his representative;
   (2) by a marriage registrar, or a person empowered in that behalf by a marriage registrar, where the inspection is necessary for carrying out his official function;
   (3) by a chief welfare officer.

(b) On the application of the adoptee aged eighteen years or over, a welfare officer may permit him to inspect the register entry relating to him. If the welfare officer refuses the application, the court may permit the inspection after receiving a report from the welfare officer (Section 30).

Prohibition of handing-over

A person who hands over or receives a child for the purpose of adoption otherwise than through a welfare officer or otherwise than in accordance with a court order under this Law, is liable to imprisonment for a term of one year (Section 33).

From the above, it is clear that only a welfare officer appointed by the Minister of Labor and Social Affairs can appear before the Court, and these appointments have always been on the sole recommendation of the chief welfare officer who is the head of the Adoption Service of the Ministry. All of the adoption welfare officers are also employees of the Ministry, leaving private professionals no access to the court in adoption matters. The law created and perpetuates an adoption cartel by the government.

Section 22 of the Adoption Law restricts the court from making an order until it receives a written report from the welfare officer. This means that all intake, evaluation, and eligibility determination is entirely in the hands of the state welfare worker. Anyone rejected by the adoption worker would have no recourse, because the law does not include any appeal system. In 1982, Mrs. Lea Saporta received a baby for the six-month trial period, but she was subsequently discovered to be in a program for artificial insemination. The Adoption Service was displeased with the fact that she had withheld this information, revoked the placement, and demanded the return of the child (Hoffman 1982). Having no right of appeal, the Saportas went to the Supreme Court, and eventually were permitted to keep the baby after mediation by the judges. The former legal adviser to the Social Affairs Ministry, writing in the press under a pseudonym, made the following comments on the law and the Saporta case:

The revocation was made since it was claimed that the adoptive mother was absent from the adoptive home in order to undergo a test-tube pregnancy procedure during the critical period when the infant arrived at her home.

Yet, families who were initially rejected in the screening process have no access to the court or even to a quasi-judicial forum to appeal their rejection. . . .

The adoption service gives too much discretion to its professional social workers, who use their own values to choose among the competing applicants, possibly disadvantaging many potential adoptive parents. The review by the consultants of the adoption service bolsters this unfair use of discretionary power.

Our new Adoption of Children Law—1981 created a monopoly, which should give all families who deal with it a fair shake. When the Ministry of Labor and Social Affairs drafted this law in December 1980, it included a section providing for an officially appointed Appeal Board to hear appeals against rejection.

It is suggested that its chairman be either a supreme court justice or a district court judge, or one retired from these benches; and that the board include a psychiatrist or psychologist and a social worker. That section disappeared from the draft presented to the Knesset. This is most regrettable. It is unfair to many potential adoptive families and to the children who could benefit from their loving care. . . . (Assaf 1982)

There is no provision in Israeli adoption law for children brought from abroad for adoption in Israeli courts (Corinaldi 1986). Israel recognizes adoptions obtained abroad, and the Adoption Service will provide reports for legal professional agencies abroad if requested to do so by Israeli citizens. Israel provides equal rights and services for children who were adopted abroad, and the Ministry of Interior has promised to eliminate the code number "02" on identity cards of adopted children, which designated those adopted abroad. The Service does not serve as a broker between Israeli couples and social agencies abroad, but it does try to advise couples about some foreign services.

Israel has signed the General Assembly *Declaration on Social and Legal Principles Relating to the Protection and Welfare of Children, With Special Reference to Foster Placement and Adoption Nationally and Internationally* (U.N. 1986). These are very basic principles, recommending that governments establish policies regarding the protection of children involved in ICA, but relatively little work has been done in this area. However, a draft of detailed suggested guidelines and additions to the original Declaration was made by a U.N. committee and has been circulated to all member states, including Israel. These *Draft Guidelines for Intercountry Adoption* will require a thorough review of the topic in Israel. The same is true of another draft now being circulated in Israel regarding changes in the *Convention on the Rights of the Child* (U.N. 1989). This latter document has received broad review and attention due to special interest by the Israeli branch of Defense for Children International (DCI), which is trying to secure its ratification by the Israeli government. Article 21 endorses the importance of and the need for quality standards for ICA and the need to prevent improper financial gain for those involved in it. Adoption of this article and the guidelines may provide the needed stimulus to discuss an ICA program for Israel.

BRAZILIAN ADOPTIONS

In 1986, a female Brazilian tourist, Arlette Hilo, was arrested in Tel Aviv on suspicion of using a forged passport. The police were also very interested in clarifying allegations that Hilo had used forged documents to arrange the adoption of Brazilian babies for many childless Israeli couples. These couples had paid thousands of dollars each, and the police suspected that some of the babies may have been kidnapped. The trail apparently started in the United States when two Israeli couples who had adopted in Brazil were detained for questioning: one baby was discovered to have a forged passport and was returned to Brazil. Hilo eventually left Israel, but many observers were surprised at the large number of Israeli couples who appeared for her hearing and emotionally demonstrated on her behalf (Gazit 1986).

In the 1980s, the South American private adoption "market"—including Brazil, Argentina, Chile, Peru, Ecuador, Paraguay, El Salvador,

Venezuela, and Mexico—became very attractive worldwide (Pilotti 1985). Some Israelis were especially interested in certain provinces in Brazil where some of the early settlers had come from European countries. These settlers intermarried with natives, and their descendants are of lighter skin color than children in other provinces.

Figures vary regarding the number of babies adopted by Israelis in South America. Plea Albeck of the Ministry of Justice estimated that between 2,000 and 2,500 babies from Brazil lived in Israel in 1987 (Negev 1987). The first adoption from Brazil took place in 1977 by an Israeli tourist couple, and they encouraged others to do the same (Kadmon 1986). Adoptions from Cambodia in 1972 probably did not result in similar large-scale interest because of the skin color and facial differences of the children (Berkowitz 1987). Another estimate in 1988 placed the number of Brazilian-adopted babies at 3,000, with approximately 30 babies arriving each month (Court 1988). One newspaper report claimed that Arlette Hilo alone had sold 1,350 babies to Israeli couples (Yishai 1986).

In early 1988, six Israelis were arrested in Brazil on suspicion of baby trafficking. One of them allegedly bought an infant from a poor Brazilian woman and sold it to an Israeli couple for $10,000.

In April 1988, a Brazilian woman, Rosalida Goncalves, appeared in Israel with a team from Britain's Independent Television Network and tracked down a child she claimed was her daughter Bruna, kidnapped from her and her boyfriend in Brazil two years earlier by a babysitter. The child had been handed over to a child-smuggling ring by a female drug addict who was paid $100. This woman was caught after her photograph appeared in Brazilian newspapers, and she was jailed for three years. She stated that the baby had been transferred to Paraguay. At the same time, an Israeli couple, Simone and Yaakov Turgeman, had adopted their baby daughter Carolyn from "a Brazilian adoption agency." When confronted in the street by Mrs. Goncalves (filmed by the British television crew), the Turgemans refused to part with their two-year-old daughter.

The case was a *cause célèbre* in Israel, involving many ethical, emotional, and scientific issues. Finally, the Supreme Court decided on the basis of blood tests and other testimony that the child should be returned to its biological mother, Mrs. Goncalves, who took the child back to Brazil in July 1988. As a result, hundreds of Israeli couples were terrified that their own Brazilian-born adoptive children might also be at risk. Some thought of leaving Israel; others turned to the Ministry of Social Affairs and the Ministry of Justice and requested blanket *post facto* recognition of their adoption papers in Israel. Those who had hired Arlette Hilo (and another broker, Carlos Pereira) were particularly worried because of fraudulent activity that had recently come to light. These couples had no way of knowing whether their Brazilian adoption documents had been forged or whether their babies had been kidnapped. A curtain of fear and silence fell over all of these couples. To date, no further requests to have babies returned have been received, and Brazilian authorities have not pursued the matter further.

The Carolyn/Bruna case shocked the Israeli public. For the first time, the issues of ICA, supply and demand, and Israeli couples fending for themselves in foreign lands became common knowledge and a shared national problem. The Minister of Labor and Social Affairs planned to establish a nonprofit organization outside the Ministry to provide information on legal avenues of adoption abroad and short-term counseling, to check adoption papers received abroad, and to operate a hotline for couples (Ungar 1988). Beyond these ad hoc activities, however, nothing else developed, and after the furor died down, the Ministry resumed its prior child-focused adoption activities.

Meanwhile, Israeli couples are still seeking to adopt from abroad, including South American countries. Romania became another option for Israelis around 1986 because the process was entirely legal and the babies European. The Romanian authorities required a couple to present official documents from the Israel Adoption Service of the Ministry of Labor and Social Affairs attesting to their qualifications according to Israeli adoption standards. The couple would then fly to Romania to see the adoptive child, who was usually living in an institution. Then they had to wait for the President of Romania himself to sign the papers allowing the child's exit from the country. Despite the relatively low costs involved, many couples were deterred from this option because of the long wait—which was almost unbearable once they had seen the child (Berkowitz 1987).

The Ceausescu regime—particularly the dictator's wife, Elena Ceausescu—banned all permits for adoptions to foreign countries, reversing their previous policy of extracting foreign currency for such permits. Mrs. Ceausescu personally decided that such adoptions were not in line with the dictatorship's long-term goal of increasing birth rates in Romania. Another recent explanation suggests that these children were kept in Romania to be raised for the Securitate police force of Ceausescu. In 1988, dozens of Israeli couples turned to the Israeli Foreign Ministry and the Ministry of Labor and Social Affairs to pressure the Romanian government to release children who had been waiting nearly a year in institutions for exit permits.

After the execution of the Ceausescu rulers in December 1989, three Israeli couples flew to Romania and returned to Israel with their adopted children. Some had waited up to three years for implementation of legal adoption decrees that had been frozen by Elena Ceausescu (Tal-Shir 1990). Clearly, there has been a change in Romanian policy regarding ICA.

In foreign adoption, a child is usually adopted in foreign courts and enters Israel, with its own passport, along with the returning adoptive parents. The Israeli government does not want to secure adoption agreements with other countries, partly because of the embarrassment this would create in formal governmental relationships: officially, governments do not "export" their children to other countries.

RESEARCH FINDINGS ON ICA

Approximately six months before the Carolyn/Bruna situation exploded, this author initiated a study of overseas adoptions under the auspices of the Hebrew University. Cooperation from the adoptive respondents was fairly good. We interviewed 56 couples and single persons all over Israel. Had we initiated the study only six months later, hardly anyone would have cooperated. During our home visits, there was some initial anxiety, but eventually almost all the interviewees became enthusiastic to tell us their stories and to express their almost universal pleasure at the outcomes of their adoptions (Jaffe et al. 1989). This is the only study available on ICA in Israel, and the data are presented here for the first time. Because most of these adoptions were relatively recent and the children were not yet of school age, our research did not include adjustment and other follow-up variables such as those reported by Simon and Altstein (1987). This research is contemplated for a later period, when the anxiety over the Brazilian connection fades away and when the adoptees enter public school.

Method

Because there is no official record of ICAs in Israel, it was extremely difficult to create a list of names and addresses of potential participants in the study. Some parents did not wish to have contact with anyone outside the family, even when promised confidentiality by this researcher. Consequently, we published advertisements in the major Israeli newspapers, in the kibbutz movement magazine, and other media. We asked several nonprofit organizations (including the Association for Promoting Adoption in Israel and the Association for Private Adoption in Israel) to send our explanatory letter to their memberships and to social workers, lawyers, and anyone with any knowledge of Israelis who adopted abroad. After several months, we had gathered a list of 56 families and individuals. We realize that this may not be a representative sample, but because no one knows what the parameters of this universe look like, it's the best available under the circumstances.

The interview schedule developed for this study included factual and subjective data. It was pretested on four families and included information on the adoptive parents, the process, the child, the social and adoption services, and the respondents' recommendations for handling ICAs for Israelis. In cases where more than one child had been adopted by a couple, we filled out a separate form for each child. Although cautious at first, nearly all interviewees gave replies to the questions, including some very sensitive ones. Interviewers traveled to all parts of the country and spent an average of two hours with each family. Following is a presentation of our research data.

Backgrounds of the Adopting Parents

Kibbutz couples made up 43 percent of the adopters; 48 percent were from urban centers, and 9 percent from moshavim (agricultural cooperative villages). The kibbutz movement, which includes only 2.8 percent of all Israeli citizens, is strongly overrepresented in foreign adoptions, primarily because of its high degree of communal concern for its membership, its emphasis on family life and continuity, its access to information and resources, and its combined organizational talent. It is evident that this community took the plight of its childless couples into its own hands and actively helped them find children abroad.

In general, the adoptive parents were highly educated: 70 percent had post–high school education, and 41 percent were university graduates. Only 9.5 percent had only finished grade school. Incomes were also above average or very stable. Of the adoptive fathers, 43 percent were kibbutz members, 32 percent were professionals and independent businessmen, and 25 percent were employees.

Adopters live mostly in Haifa and the north of Israel (36 percent) and Tel Aviv and the coastal plain (30 percent). Fewer lived in Jerusalem (19 percent) and Beersheva and the south (15 percent).

As in earlier years, most adoptive parents (fathers) were of first-generation Ashkenazi (Western) origin (65 percent). Only 23 percent were of Sephardi origin, and 13 percent had been born in Israel. If we distribute the Israeli-born group proportionally among the two other groups, 86 percent of the adopting fathers were Ashkenazim. None of the adopting fathers were non-Jews, but 5.4 percent of the adoptive mothers were non-Jews—most likely from intermarriages, and probably from the kibbutz community.

The average age was 38 for the fathers and 37 for the mothers. These averages are just below the minimum ages of eligibility for adoption of infants in Israel (42 for fathers and 38 for mothers). Thirty percent of these couples were on the waiting list of the Adoption Service, 30 percent had been rejected by the Service, and 40 percent had decided not to apply or be screened at all. (On a five-year waiting list, 37-year-old women would have little chance of ever obtaining an adoptive baby in Israel.)

At the time of adoption, 95 percent of the adopters were married, with the average length of marriage 8 years; 41 percent had been married for an average of 11.5 years. Most of the couples (66 percent) had one other child, and 5 percent had two other children. Many of those with children had apparently adopted previously, because 91 percent of the couples suffered from infertility problems. Also of note is the fact that 5.4 percent of the adopters were single parents.

Regarding the preferences of the adopting parents, 77 percent sought infant children (newborns, if possible), and 14 percent were prepared to adopt children less than one year old. Most got their wish: 73 percent of the adopted children were no older than one month at the time of adoption. Of these, 38 percent were one week old. Only 13 percent were more than two months old. Those who hired local (foreign) brokers were significantly more likely (.05) to obtain the age and sex requested, they spent somewhat less time (up to one month) in the foreign country, and they were significantly (.05) less likely to be required to provide extensive documentation on their qualifications as adoptive parents than couples who worked through professional agencies abroad.

Couples were divided regarding sex preferences: 39 percent had no preference, 43 percent preferred girls, and 18 percent preferred boys. Here, too, the foreign brokers were generally able to deliver.

The Adoption Experience Abroad

Most of the intercountry-adoptive parents (57 percent) had first applied to the Israel Adoption Service but were upset by "the long bureaucratic process with the social workers" (77 percent) or by the long wait (64 percent), which they claimed could take up to eight years. According to their statements, they had already waited a median of 5.5 years. Of this group, 45 percent liked the service, and 35 percent were very unhappy with the way they were treated.

Forty-three percent of the adopters were referred to the foreign-adoptions option by friends and 23 percent by people who had adopted. Eighteen percent had heard about it themselves, and only 9 percent were referred by professional people. Most (75 percent) stressed that support from their close relatives was a critical factor in adopting abroad. Seventy-one percent adopted from Brazil; the others adopted from other countries. Most (32 percent) adopted in 1987, and 23 percent adopted in 1983 or 1984.

Most couples (65 percent) went abroad with medical reports, home evaluations, and income documents—all certified by Israeli lawyers. In the foreign countries, the couples hired local brokers (66 percent), law-yers (68 percent), doctors (79 percent), judges (39 percent), and social workers (29 percent). In 43 percent of the cases, a local broker handled everything. Twenty-three percent involved some cooperation with a lo-cal social service agency, and only 18 percent were handled only by social agencies without a broker.

The median cost of adoption was $10,000 (with a minimum of $2,000 and a maximum of $30,000), including airfare and lodging. The adop-tions themselves cost between $1,000 and $13,000. Despite Israel's strict foreign currency regulations, 45 percent of the adopters took their mon-ey out with them, and 53 percent used foreign accounts. Only 2 percent received government permission to purchase the necessary foreign cur-rency. For 36 percent of the parents, this was their second attempt to adopt abroad, so they had invested significant sums in the effort.

Although 96 percent of the parents had an opportunity to view (and potentially reject) the child, 93 percent did not meet the biological par-ents, nor could they verify any of the information and documents they saw or were given pertaining to the child. Of those who worked exclu-sively through brokers, sixty percent were worried about the legality of their adoptions. The same was true for those who obtained their chil-dren through lawyers. These worries were significantly more common among couples who had adopted in Brazil than in any other Latin Amer-ican country. Apparently illegality was the norm in Brazil: only 50 per-cent of the couples who adopted there were convinced that the proce-dure was legal, and 28 percent were not at all sure.

The Return to Israel

As noted earlier, 96 percent of the children were brought back to Israel with their own foreign passports. Only 52 percent had birth certificates attesting to the adoption, and only 38 percent were registered on their adoptive parents' Israeli I.D. cards. Almost all (91 percent) now have Israeli I.D. numbers of their own, and 25 percent of these have a special prefix or number identifying them as adopted from abroad—which could create problems with the Rabbinate when they decide to marry (Schach-ter 1982).

Most of the children (75 percent) were converted to Judaism. Some couples claimed they could not find a rabbi to do this (16 percent), and some (9 percent) did not agree to the religious conditions and ritual for conversion. Only 4 percent of the parents have not told friends and relatives that the child is adopted, with all that this implies (Kirk 1964; Schachter 1982).

After returning to Israel, 40 percent of the parents sought advice, mostly from professionals (43 percent) or other parents who adopted abroad (30 percent). Most (82 percent) were interested in continued group meetings with other foreign-adoptive parents to share and learn together, and some became members of social action groups to influence policy makers regarding an active ICA policy for Israeli childless couples.

About one-third of the parents predict problems for their children in terms of identity and self-concept because of the interracial, intercountry, and religious features of their adoptions.

All of the parents were happy and satisfied with the adoption outcome: 93 percent said that it had exceeded their best expectations, and 88 percent believed that the child was also "very pleased" with the adoption. A full 91 percent of the parents said they would do it all over again.

Recommendations of Parents Who Adopted Abroad

All of the respondents had comments about what needs to be changed in Israeli adoption work. Nearly 40 percent wanted more "understanding" from the Adoption Service. One-third of the interviewees wanted close cooperation between the Adoption Service and foreign adoption agencies. Nearly 50 percent felt that the eligibility criteria in Israel were unfair and draconian. And 68 percent suggested overhauling the whole system by establishing a service that would centralize all information and agreements regarding foreign agencies.

Nearly all of the interviewees (96 percent) were ready to help other couples to adopt abroad by providing them with advice, concrete information, and emotional support. When asked if they preferred a government service or a private, nonprofit, professional adoption service, 40 percent chose the former and 60 percent the latter. Most (58 percent) of those who favored a private professional service had prior experience with the Adoption Service of the Ministry of Labor and Social Affairs, and most of this group (69 percent) said that they were very unhappy with the bureaucracy they encountered. Similarly, a majority (54 percent) of the couples who had no prior contacts with the Adoption Service preferred establishing a private professional agency in Israel.

PROSPECTS FOR FUTURE DEVELOPMENT

ICA in Israel has now been "discovered" by infertile Israeli couples, the general public, and perhaps, last of all, the social service professionals. The next decade will probably see an increase in foreign adoption of infants by Israelis and the creation of professional advisory, brokerage, and outreach services. Most of all, this service will be legal, public, and serve couples as legitimate clients, rather than making them feel guilty for wanting to adopt an infant instead of an older or handicapped child.

For those social workers who will eventually develop services for ICAs, the emphasis will be on finding babies for Jewish infertile couples as an alternative way of creating families, in addition to the responsibility to find homes for needy children. Rabbi Michael Gold, an adoptive father, has stated the essence of this conceptual change:

Jewish couples are looking for healthy white infants. They are infertile couples, trying to experience the totality of parenthood by raising a child from infancy. . . . Is the purpose of adoption to provide homes for orphaned and unwanted children? Or is the purpose to find children for childless couples? Adoption workers have a responsibility to find homes for needy children, but they also have a responsibility to find children for childless couples. No couple should be made to feel guilty whether they are searching for an older child, a special needs child, or a healthy infant. (Gold 1988: 180–181)

Eventually, this dual-function conceptual change will take root in Israel, and perhaps in Jewish communities in other countries as well. Indicators of change in Israel are the growing formal organization of indigenous nonprofit groups such as Aleph (The Association for Private Adoption in Israel); ELI (The Association for Promotion of Adoption in Israel), Zahavi (The Association of Large Families in Israel) (Danino 1978); Efrat (The Association for Promotion of Birth and Family Life) (1989); and T'micha (The Fertility Communication Center).

In addition to these groups, some social work academics and professionals are seeking to establish a nonprofit ICA service for childless Israeli couples (Jaffe 1989). One of the rationales for a nongovernment organization in this field is the fact that an Israeli government ministry cannot deal with other countries; only a private agency, perhaps licensed by the government, can engage in adoptions work abroad. There is nothing in Israeli law to prevent a nongovernment organization from assisting and advising couples to find children and complete adoptions *abroad*. The eventual goal, however, is to find a way to copy the U.S. model, where the adoption is allowed to take place in the United States after approval is given by the child's native country for the child to leave for purposes of adoption.

Although adoption lobbies in the United States are trying to obtain immediate citizenship for foreign-born adopted children, the current procedure begins when the U.S. Immigration and Naturalization Service allows the foreign-adoptive child to obtain a visa to enter the country as "an immediate relative who is an orphan." The child is then issued a "green card" permitting permanent residence as an alien. After two years of residence, a petition is filed for naturalization and citizenship. Finally, the adoptive couple files a petition for adoption in the appropriate local court (Bolles 1984). Even if a child has been fully adopted abroad and a final decree obtained abroad, most couples also go through the U.S. process.

Fortunately, the Israeli Ministry of Justice already recognizes adoptions legally obtained abroad, thus eliminating the long delay required in the United States to formalize the adoption. Countries such as Korea, however will allow a child to leave after the required documents have been provided (without being adopted there) and enter the adoptive parents' country for subsequent adoption (Americans for International Aid and Adoption 1988). Because the Israeli Adoption Law enables only the Ministry of Labor and Social Welfare social workers to participate in Court hearings, there is currently no possibility for nongovernment social workers to present cases to the Court and request adoption orders. Nor is there any arrangement with immigration authorities (i.e., the Ministry of Interior) for Israeli embassies abroad to issue visas for children to enter the country for the purposes of completing adoption in Israel.

The author has suggested two possible solutions to authorities in Israel. One approach would request the Minister of Labor and Social Affairs to appoint a nongovernment social worker as an adoption officer, thus enabling the worker to appear before the Court, according to the Adoption Law. Another solution involves the nongovernment social worker serving couples already approved by the Adoption Service in Israel, finding babies abroad from legitimate adoption agencies, using home studies and other documents to be prepared or already available from the Adoption Service, but having the Court presentations made by a social worker from the Adoption Service of the Ministry.

The Chief Adoption Officer of the Ministry of Labor and Social Affairs has verbally agreed to the latter procedure, but some of the adoption lobby organizations are adamant in seeking a change in the adoption law, enabling them to have direct access to the Courts and even to seek adoptive children in Israel—in other words, independent nongovernment-organization adoptions.

Whatever the outcome of these negotiations, some change is going to occur. Also, more childless couples will follow the example of the thousands who have recently adopted abroad. Networks are developing rapidly and becoming more organized. Israel is now at a threshold regarding ICAs.

Eventually, future adoption research in Israel will report on the adjustment of children and parents of ICAs and compare studies with those undertaken by Silverman and Feigelman (1983; 1984), McRoy and colleagues (1982), Kim (1977), Simon and Altstein (1987), and other researchers. It is hoped that these studies will also describe significant changes in official attitudes toward childless parents, as well as new social services and systems—both private and public—that must be created to serve this growing client group.

Being Jewish usually means having a family. It is the secret of the survival of Jews as a people and a religion, regardless of its importance to the future demography and security of the State of Israel. There is no way that childlessness will be accepted by Jewish couples anywhere as an acceptable norm. At the present time, for many Israelis, ICA is the answer to their prayers.

REFERENCES

Americans for International Aid and Adoption. (1988). *Adoption Agreement Between A.I.A.A. and Social Welfare Society, Inc. of Korea.* Also, personal correspondence with Nancy M. Fox, Director of A.I.A.A.

Assaf, S. S. (1982). Seeking a Fair Deal. *The Jerusalem Post*, 28 March.

Bar-Am, Aviva. (1986). Too Old At Four. *The Jerusalem Post*, 10 July.

Ben-Israel, Naomi. (1982). *Adopted Children Growing Up in Kibbutz Society.* Jerusalem: Israel Ministry of Labor and Social Affairs.

Berger, Sophia. (1928). *Final Report of the Palestine Orphan Committee.* Jerusalem: The Joint Distribution Committee.

Berkowitz, Ainat. (1987). Adoption of Children from Romania. *Davar*, 13 November. (In Hebrew.)

Bolles, Edmund Blair. (1984). *The Penguin Adoption Handbook.* New York: Penguin Books.

Cohen, Eric. (1972). The Black Panthers in Israeli Society. *Jewish Journal of Sociology* 14(1): 93–109.

Cohen, P. (1967). Israel's Ethnic Problem. *Jewish Journal of Sociology* 9(1): 100–107.

Corinaldi, Michael. (1986). Personal communication from Prof. Corinaldi, expert in Israeli family law, University of Tel Aviv.

Court, Andy. (1988). After Baby Carolyn. *The Jerusalem Post*, 1 July.

Cromer, Gerald. (1976). The Israeli Black Panthers: Fighting for Credibility and a Cause. *Victimology* 1(3): 403–413.

Danino, Abraham. (1978). *The Child-Favored Family: Large Families in Israel.* Haifa: Zahavi Association of Large Families.

Efrat: The Association for Promotion of Birth and Family Life. (1989). *Bulletin of the Efrat Society* 28/29. Jerusalem. (In Hebrew.)

Eisenstadt, Shmuel N. (1950). The Oriental Jews in Israel. *Jewish Social Studies* 12(3): 199–221.

Englard, Yitzchak. (1969). *Adoption in Israel: Implementation of the Law.* Jerusalem: The Hebrew University of Jerusalem.

Falk, Lawrence. (1970). A Comparative Study of Transracial and Inracial Adoptions. *Child Welfare* 49(1): 82–88.

Fanshel, David. (1957). *A Study in Negro Adoption.* New York: Child Welfare League of America.

_____. (1972). *Far From the Reservation.* Metuchen, NJ: Scarecrow Press.

Fricke, Harriet. (1972). Interracial Adoption: The Little Revolution. *Social Work* 10(1): 92–97.

Gazit, Yoram. (1986). Brazilian Woman Remanded by Tel Aviv Court. *The Jerusalem Post*, 16 April.

Glick, Shimon. (1989). Wholesale Suicide. *Bulletin of the Efrat Society* 28/29: 4–5. (In Hebrew.)

Gold, Michael. (1988). *And Hannah Wept: Infertility, Adoption, and the Jewish Couple*. New York: Praeger.

Grow, Lucille, and Shapiro, Deborah. (1974). *Black Children–White Parents*. New York: Child Welfare League of America.

Hoffman, Charles. (1982). Expert Lauds Appeal in Adoption Case. *The Jerusalem Post*, 28 February.

Hoksbergen, Rene. (1984). *Adoption in Holland*. Utrecht: University of Utrecht.

IMSW. (1968). *A Guide to Boarding Homes in Israel*. Jerusalem: Israel Ministry of Social Welfare. (In Hebrew.)

Jacobovits, Immanuel. (1969). In *Responsum on Problems of Adoption In Jewish Law*, edited by M. Steinberg and M. Rose. London: Office of the Chief Rabbi of England.

Jaffe, Eliezer. (1965). Adoption in Israel. *Social Research Quarterly* 12(19): 211–222. (In Hebrew.)

_____. (1982). Adoption Services (in Israel). In *Child Welfare in Israel*. New York: Praeger, 185–212.

_____. (1983). *Israelis in Institutions: Studies in Child Placement Practice and Policy*. New York: Gordon and Breach Science Publishers.

_____. (1986). Economic and Market Determinants in Israeli Adoption Practices. *Journal of Jewish Communal Service* 63(3): 352–359.

_____. (1989). *A Proposal to Establish a Nonprofit Professional Service for International Adoptions in Israel*. Jerusalem: The Hebrew University of Jerusalem.

Jaffe, Eliezer et al. (1989). *Adoption of Children from Abroad*. Jerusalem: The Hebrew University of Jerusalem. (In Hebrew.)

Kadmon, Sima. (1986). A Ray of Hope from Brazil. *Ha'aretz*, 5 September 1986. (In Hebrew.)

Kim, Dong Soo. (1977). How They Fare in American Homes: A Follow-Up Study of Adopted Korean Children in U.S. Homes. *Children Today* 6(1): 2–6, 36.

Kirk, Henry David. (1964). *Shared Fate*. New York: Free Press.

McRoy, Ruth et al. (1982). Self-esteem and Racial Identity in Transracial and Inracial Adoptions. *Social Work* 27(6): 522–526.

Negev, Eilat. (1987). We Called Him Yoav. *Davar*, 28 August. (In Hebrew.)

Nenner, Orna. (1989). Everything on Adoptions. *Segol Magazine*, 29 May: 1–15. (In Hebrew.)

Pilotti, F. J. (1985). Intercountry Adoption: A View From Latin America. *Child Welfare* 64(1): 25–35.

Sapir, Rivka. (1953). Korat Gag—An Evaluation of a Temporary Foster Placement Scheme for Immigrant Children. In *Between Past and Future*, edited by Karl Frankenstein, 147–177. Jerusalem: Szold Foundation.

Schachter, Melech. (1982). Various Aspects of Adoption. *The Journal of Halacha*, 4(2): 93–115.

Silverman, Arnold, and Feigelman, William. (1983). *Chosen Children: New Patterns of Adoptive Relationships*. New York: Praeger.

_____. (1984). The Long-Term Effects of Transracial Adoption. *Social Service Review* 58(3): 588–602.

Simon, Rita J., and Altstein, Howard. (1977). *Transracial Adoption*. New York: Wiley.

―――. (1987). *Transracial Adoptees and Their Families*. New York: Praeger.

State of Israel. (1981). *Adoption of Children Law, 1981*. Jerusalem: Sefer Ha-Chukkim. No. 1028 (28 May): 293.

Tal, Avraham. (1985). What Is The Government Doing in the Child's Room? *Ha'aretz*, 2 August. (In Hebrew.)

Tal-Shir, Anat. (1990). Adoption 1990—The Romanian Children. *Yediot*, 9 January.

Ungar, Carol. (1988). Taking the Blight Out of Adoption. *The Jerusalem Post*, 3 March.

United Nations. (1986). *Resolution of the General Assembly 41/85*. New York: U.N. General Assembly.

―――. (1989). *Draft Resolutions on the Convention on the Rights of the Child*. March.

Weiner, Anita. (1984). *Away from Home: The Roots of Child Placement Policy in Israel*. Tel Aviv: Sifriat Hapoalim. (In Hebrew.)

Woods, F. J., and Lancaster, A. C. (1962). Cultural Factors in Negro Adoptive Parenthood. *Social Work* 7(4): 14–21.

Yishai, Sarit. (1986). A Different Testimony. *Chadashot*, 9 May.

Zipperstein, Steven, and Jaffe, Eliezer. (1980). Antecedents of Jewish Ethnic Relationships in Israel. *Forum*, 42–43, 15–32.

9

Summary and Concluding Remarks

HOWARD ALTSTEIN
RITA J. SIMON

COUNTRY-BY-COUNTRY SUMMARY OF ICA

United States

The history of ICA in the United States may be viewed as part of a continuum that began at the end of World War II with small-scale adoption of orphaned European children. For about 15 years after that, most American couples seeking to adopt did not see foreign-born children as an answer to their childlessness. They preferred instead to use the domestic adoption system with all its foibles. At the end of the 1960s, the availability for adoption of thousands of American nonwhite children (mostly black) drew the attention of many white potential adopters. This type of adoption was known as *transracial adoption,* and it kindled the wrath of many black organizations who strongly opposed permanently placing black children with white adopters. These groups saw this procedure as another, perhaps even more insidious, form of white racism. Positive data notwithstanding, transracial adoption remains to this day a controversial form of child placement to many black organizations.

With opposition to transracial adoption remaining strong, and the general unavailability of infants of any color continuing, many white couples "discovered" that healthy, usually nonwhite, foreign-born infants were available for adoption in their native countries. Not only could a family adopt a healthy infant, but the overall cost of an ICA was often lower than the cost of a domestic one, and it usually took less time. Factors such as these increased American interest in ICA: by the late 1980s, about 10,000 foreign-born children were being adopted annually by

American citizens. An equal number was adopted by Western Europeans. The leading "supplier" of these foreign-born children was (and continues to be) the ROK.

Just as there was (and still is) considerable controversy surrounding transracial adoption, so too are there opposing views on ICA. Some of the same arguments against transracial adoption are heard in opposition to ICA. Just as many black organizations claim that transracial adoption is a manifestation of domestic white racism, many Third-World countries see ICA as a contemporary form of white imperialism, a 1990s version of colonialism. These countries are under considerable internal pressure to reduce—if not eliminate—the "export" of their children to the West. Some Western child welfare experts support this call to curtail ICA, suggesting instead that the West should support programs and policies in Third-World countries that would develop a social climate that would allow orphans to remain in their native lands.

In actuality, Western support for social programs in developing countries may not be necessary to effect a change in these countries' policies toward ICA. Domestic political pressures and improving economic conditions in many Third-World countries, particularly Korea, are allowing more money to be appropriated to family and children's projects. These events will influence the course of ICA from these countries. A logical consequence, therefore, would be a natural ebbing in the numbers of children available to foreign adopters.

Studies of intercountry adoptees in the United States suggest that children who are adopted as infants make positive adjustments to their new environments. Parents are eager to have these children, and the children perceive themselves as fully integrated family members. American parents make considerable efforts to maintain multiethnic environments in their homes. When problems arise they are usually almost completely a function of trauma the children experienced in their native countries prior to adoption.

Canada

In both Canada and the United States, social work has historically been the main provider of services in the child welfare field, particularly with regard to foster care and adoption. In both societies, up until only a few years ago, the ranks of these professional deliverers of service have reflected the values, standards, and demographics of the majority (white) population. Social work's clients have for the most part traditionally been the (nonwhite) underclass, minority groups, and new immigrants.

In no more glaring a fashion is the clash of class differences demonstrated than in Christopher Bagley's contribution to this volume, "Adoption of Native Children in Canada: A Policy Analysis and a Research

Report" (Chapter 3). His discussion of Canada's aboriginal populations—specifically his analysis of the devastation of Native Canadian families and the widespread removal of their children to white environments—is both impressive and frightening. In these environments, a great many Native Canadian adoptees have suffered severe emotional and psychological problems, many stemming directly from the fact that they were ethnically and culturally isolated in white surroundings.

According to Bagley, the leading culprit in the Native Canadian travesty is the profession of social work, which through ethnocentric lenses removed thousands of aboriginal children from their nuclear families for reasons of (culturally defined) "neglect." According to Bagley, social work has minimized vital "nonwhite" strengths of these nuclear and extended families. No one can deny that this almost wholesale removal of aboriginal children occurred. In all likelihood, its intent was not consciously malevolent, but its results were devastating. Overall, the children of Native Americans have fared no better.

Bagley presents compelling evidence of the destruction of the Native Canadian family, and argues that living conditions of Canada's Native populations are sometimes lower than those in Third-World countries. He cites infant and adult mortality rates resembling those in Indonesia and Nigeria, high unemployment rates, and so on. The removal of aboriginal children from their families for reasons of so-called neglect (to be adopted in a significant number of cases by white Canadian families) has operationalized in the minds of Native populations the "cultural imperialism" of the dominant white population.

The fact that most Native Canadian communities do indeed possess epidemiologic characteristics usually attributed to Third-World nations clearly makes the adoption of these children by whites akin to ICA. The difference in the Canadian case is that both birth parents of the adopted Native Canadians have usually been alive—an enormous exception.

Although social workers (in particular, protective service workers) have in the past enforced what can legitimately be termed racist child welfare policies (especially in relation to native populations), current social work practice strongly deemphasizes the removal of any child from its cultural environment. Removal is now sanctioned only in extreme circumstances. On the contrary, considerable emphasis in social work practice today is placed on supporting indigenous environments so that the removal of any child from his or her family does not occur.

In the United States, the Indian Child Welfare Act of 1978 (PL95-608) makes it almost impossible for whites to adopt Native American children. The law's intent is to support Native American cultural institutions, particularly the family. Similar Canadian legislation would go far toward protecting the civil rights of Canada's Native populations, especially Native children.

Norway

Norway, Denmark, Israel, and (to a lesser extent) Holland share several important characteristics. Each has a relatively small population and few native-born infants available for adoption. Adoptive couples in these countries also share one overriding characteristic: the only source of healthy infants in any real numbers lay outside their countries' own borders. In most cases, to adopt means to adopt a foreign-born child. If this option is precluded, childlessness is the result.

ICA into Norway began in the early 1970s on an individual basis and developed over time into an agency-based operation. Today, there are two Norwegian adoption agencies specializing in ICA, and all ICAs must be channeled through one of these agencies. This pattern of ICA, from an individual to an organizational basis, is similar to the German experience as described by Martin Textor.

Saetersdal and Dalen review some of the existing research on Norwegian ICA and conclude that, although there were some initial adjustment problems with intercountry adoptees (particularly with Indian- and Vietnamese-born children), they tended to diminish over time. Problems that did remain were in the area of language—not its acquisition or use, but the interaction between language development and conceptual learning. The latter difficulties were seen most sharply in educational environments.

Based on their data, Saetersdal and Dalen suggest that there may be an "intercountry-adopted personality" (not to be confused with the "adopted child syndrome" discussed in the opening chapter of this work). For Saetersdal and Dalen, the "intercountry adoption personality" is seen in adoptees who outwardly appear well-adjusted and quite attached to their adopted families, perhaps even too attached. These children are in fact anxious and insecure about their positions in Norwegian society. As adolescents, they keep a low profile, are afraid to take risks, and, although they have many friends, few are considered close. As with other situations described in this investigation, whether these traits are related to the adoption itself or are the result of preadoption experiences is difficult to ascertain. The authors suggest that, as adults, these children run the risk of becoming marginal to Norwegian society.

Germany

ICAs make up about 25 percent of all West German adoptions, and the experiences of intercountry adoptees thus far appear uneventful. In fact, the great majority of foreign-born adoptees in Germany are making excellent adjustments both within their adoptive families and to their adopted country. For example, on critical indices such as self-concept measures and "disruption" rates, these children's acclimation to their environments seems highly satisfactory.

Martin Textor's "International Adoption in West Germany: A Private Affair" (Chapter 5) raises highly important policy and ethical issues regarding ICA into Germany. Of particular concern to Textor is the basic issue of the "moral correctness" of ICA, an issue raised by other authors in this volume. The query is worded along the following lines: Rather than fulfilling the desires of Western couples for parenthood with the Third World's abandoned and orphaned children, would the West's energies be more honestly and appropriately spent by encouraging family and children programs and policies supporting the efforts of developing governments to keep their parentless children within their own societies? Programs aimed at increasing day care facilities and increasing family planning and economic opportunities for women (to name but a few) could significantly reduce the numbers of children available to the West for ICA. Irrespective of where the West places its priorities, the question of whether to allow ICA to continue at its current rate or in its current form is now being actively debated in Third-World countries. The resolution of this discussion will strongly influence this type of adoption in the 1990s.

Another concern of Textor's is the fact that about half of all ICAs into Germany are privately arranged. Many of these adoptions appear to border on the illegal—with money being exchanged between birth mothers and prospective adopters, incomplete filing of necessary documents, and so on. Textor presents the positions of those calling for greater state control of this type of adoption.

Denmark

Beginning with a short history of ICAs into Denmark (10,000 since 1970, half involving children from the ROK), Mette Rorbech presents a comprehensive analysis of this form of child placement in her small northern European country. Denmark differs from other Scandinavian states in one fundamental way: whereas neighboring Sweden and Norway register all intercountry adoptees as "immigrants," in Denmark they are registered as Danish nationals from the moment they arrive. This may have some impact on how these children view themselves as adults.

With an impressive national sample of 384 intercountry adoptees between the ages of 18 and 25, Rorbech examines a number of variables germane to these children's integration into Danish society. Noting that about two-thirds of her sample arrived in Denmark after age three, Rorbech observes that practically all of them had various levels of native language development—a characteristic not dissimilar from intercountry adoptees into Norway. Although her overall conclusion is that ICA into

Denmark has been quite successful, Rorbech discusses several areas where difficulties have arisen, particularly in education and employment. For example, 20 percent of the intercountry adoptees have not gone beyond the ninth or tenth form (grade). Of this group, half were unemployed at the time of the study, and the other half were under-employed. Both, therefore, seem to be at risk. As a consequence of this shortened period of education, a larger percentage than average no longer lived with their parents. Additionally, 20 to 25 percent of these adoptees indicated that they rarely saw their adoptive families.

In terms of national identity, 70 percent did not consider themselves a "kind of an immigrant," and 90 percent felt "mostly Danish." Again similar to their Norwegian counterparts, there was some confusion in their reaction to continued nonadoptee immigration from their birth and other countries. For example, two-thirds would like to see the flow of refugees into Denmark controlled.

Holland

Hoksbergen's contribution on the Netherlands (Chapter 7) is both a presentation of research findings on recent ICA studies and a discussion of policy considerations. His is the clearest call for a redirection of Western efforts away from providing Third-World children to childless Western couples. While presenting convincing data demonstrating positive adjustment to Dutch society by intercountry adoptees, Hoksbergen strongly urges the West in general and Holland in particular to aid social and economic programs aimed at correcting the conditions in developing nations that contribute to family disorganization. Successful implementation of these programs would both strengthen family ties in developing nations and reduce, if not eliminate, foreign adoption of their children. Hoksbergen and others see the latter as a positive development. These programs and policies are similar to those in Germany described by Martin Textor. Although Hoksbergen states that some large adoption agencies in Holland have already developed just such programs, much more needs to be accomplished.

Hoksbergen also raises an adoption issue currently receiving considerable attention in the United States—whether to provide postadoption counseling and other services to adoptive families. By inference, the question of the adopted child syndrome (discussed in the opening chapter of this book) is also mentioned. Hoksbergen states that, not only are adoptive families four to five times more likely than nonadoptive families to request postadoption psychological assistance, but six percent of all foreign-born adoptees, at one time or another, have been removed from their adoptive families and placed into residential treatment facilities. For 25 percent of these children, residential care was a temporary placement. The question of whether preadoption experiences in birth countries were responsible for these adoption disruptions, or whether they were caused by a failure to satisfactorily adjust to adoptive environments is raised. Age at time of adoption is discussed as a crucial predictor of success.

Israel

Although Eliezer Jaffe's "Foreign Adoptions in Israel: Private Paths to Parenthood" (Chapter 8) offers interesting demographics on an ICA study he recently conducted, his chapter focuses primarily on the history of (intercountry) adoption into the British Mandate of Palestine and present-day Israel. He also traces the development of Israeli adoption policy.

In Israel, as in Holland, many adoptees are foreign-born. Like other countries discussed in this volume, it is also a country where the probability of adopting a native-born infant is infinitesimal. In 1988, only 115 native nonrelative children were adopted by Israeli couples. At the time Jaffe's article was written, not only were there about 3,000 Israeli couples awaiting adoptable children (a staggering figure given Israel's small population), but the ministry responsible for adoption services in Israel had practically abandoned these couples, leaving them to fend for themselves. These couples' only realistic option for a healthy infant is to explore the ICA marketplace.

The combination of a severe shortage of adoptable Israeli infants and a lack of involvement on the part of the appropriate ministry forces most potential Israeli adopters to attempt privately arranged ICAs. Although this method appears to be the only realistic way for these couples to deal with their childlessness, the situation is quite precarious because Israeli law does not recognize private and independent adoptions made through any means other than government agencies.

The fact that Israeli law forbids private adoptions forces many couples to use less-than-legal methods. In some cases, these methods make international headlines. Jaffe describes the circumstances surrounding the ICA of Brazilian-born children by Israeli families. It appears that many infants adopted in Brazil by Israeli families were not legally free for adoption, but had either been bought or stolen from their birth parent(s) by intermediaries.

CONCLUDING REMARKS

The seven societies covered in this volume report different experiences, but some generalizations can be made, the broadest one concerning the age of adopted children. Older adoptees—even those of the same racial, ethnic, and religious backgrounds as their adoptive parents—pose more problems than younger ones. (By "older," we mean over one year at the time of placement.) Each of the authors reports directly from his or her own data (or via secondary sources) that older children make for more problematic placements. Their emotional and social adjustments are more difficult, their learning problems more complicated, and their integration into families harder to achieve. These findings have also been reported in studies of in-racial and in-cultural adoptions, but they are exacerbated when the older child comes from a different racial and ethnic background. And they are even further exacerbated if the child experienced trauma in his or her birth culture, as many of these children did—being deserted by one or both parents, living in war zones or in areas of terrorist activity, or observing their mothers engage in prostitution. Age emerges as the major obstacle to successful adoptive adjustment.

The heterogeneity or homogeneity of the society into which a child is adopted makes a difference in the success of an ICA. Saetersdal and Dalen argue that Norway is too homogeneous a society to adequately socialize Asian, African, or any other non-Caucasian children. To a lesser extent, Rorbech makes a similar observation about Denmark. Foreign-born adoptees in these countries stand out too sharply, and their physical differences induce insecurity, fear, and denial on their part which in turn result in poor school performance and poor overall adjustment.

Bagley's chapter on Native children in Canada provides the most negative account of adoption. Native children adopted by non-Natives have poor self-esteem, manifest serious suicidal ideas, and engage in deliberate acts of self-harm. Identity problems, including confusion and denial, are much more prevalent among Native adoptees than among other adoptees. Bagley strongly urges keeping parentless Native children within their own communities and helping those communities organize indigenous systems of child welfare and adoption.

Hoksbergen is one of the leaders among adoption researchers who advocates long-distance sponsorship as an alternative to ICA. He expresses ambivalence about transporting children out of their native cultures into Western societies. He advocates instead policies that would keep children in the homelands of their birth parents, but with institutional supports to provide them with educational opportunities, economic security, and healthy emotional ties. Hoksbergen's views on establishing systems whereby children are supported and maintained in their birth countries has allies in West Germany and other parts of Europe. Textor, for example, observes that motivations for ICA in West Germany are more altruistic (stemming more from a sense of "noblesse oblige") than they are in the United States, where the desire to parent a child is the uppermost consideration.

The major findings that emerge from these case studies are the variations that exist across societies. One should not generalize from the experiences of any one society. Although the age of a child may be important in each society, how that variable interacts with the motivations of adoptive families, the homogeneity or heterogeneity of the adoptive society, and the attitudes of the adoptive society to the ethnic and racial backgrounds of the adoptive children produces scenarios sufficiently different to make it difficult to predict how successful ICAs are likely to be as an overall strategy for helping homeless, parentless children in Third-World countries.

As we enter the 1990s, a major question emerges: Are we witnessing the beginning of the end of wide-scale ICA? Recent figures and statements from supplying countries seem to support the notion that ICA is waning. Whether it will permanently disappear remains to be seen. As noted at the beginning of this book, orphans are an inevitable result of national and international conflicts. Romanian orphans in 1990 are an example of a momentary addition to the world's pool of children available for adoption by foreigners. But as a long-term, world-wide phenomenon whereby nonwhite children from poor nations are transferred to families in rich, white nations, ICA appears to be declining. It is not coming to an end because of any Western initiatives. On the contrary, it is being eliminated in part because of nationalistic feelings in "supplying" countries combined with improved economic conditions in those countries.

The adage that one person's gain is another person's loss is reflected in these developments. If "Third-World countries" is substituted for "one person" and "childless Western couples" for "another person," we have what is developing into the current outlook for ICA in the 1990s. Childless Western couples seeking foreign-born children will all share a common denominator—bleak chances of ever becoming parents.

SELECTED BIBLIOGRAPHY

Bagley, Christopher. *The Dutch Plural Society: A Comparative Study in Race Relations.* Oxford: Oxford University Press, 1973.

Bagley, Christopher, and Young, L. "The Identity, Adjustment and Achievement of Transracially Adopted Children." In Verma, Gajedra and Bagley, Christopher (Eds.), *Race, Education and Identity* (pp. 192–219). London: Macmillan, 1979.

Ben-Israel, Naomi. *Adopted Children Growing Up in Kibbutz Society.* Jerusalem: Israel Ministry of Labor and Social Affairs, 1982.

Dalen, Monica, and Saetersdal, Barbro. *Intercountry Adopted Children in Norway: Socio-cultural Factors, Identity and Adjustment.* Oslo: Norwegian Institute of Special Education, 1987.

Fanshel, David. *Far From the Reservation: The Transracial Adoption of American Indian Children.* Metuchen, NJ: Scarecrow Press, 1972.

Gardell, I. *A Swedish Study on Intercountry Adoption.* Stockholm: Liber Tryck, 1980.

Gill, Owen, and Jackson, Barbara. *Adoption and Race.* London: St. Martin's Press, 1983.

Gold, Michael. *And Hannah Wept: Infertility, Adoption, and the Jewish Couple.* New York: Praeger, 1982.

Hoksbergen, R. A. C., and Bunjes, L. A. C. "Thirty Years of Adoption Practice in the Netherlands." In Hoksbergen, R. A. C. and Gokhale, S. D. (Eds.), *Policy and Legislation in 14 Countries.* Lisse, Berwijn: Swets & Zeitlinger, 1986.

Hoksbergen, R. A. C., Bunjes, L., Baarda, B., and Nota, J. (Eds.). *Adoptie van Kinderen Uit Verre Landen* (Adoption of Children from Far Countries). Deventer: van Loghum Slaterus, 1979, 1982.

Jaffe, Eliezer. Economic Determinants in Israeli Adoption Practices. *Journal of Jewish Communal Service,* 62(2): 352–359, 1986.

Kadushin, Alfred, and Martin, Judith A. *Child Welfare Services,* 4th ed. New York: Macmillan.

Kirk, David H. *Adoptive Kinship: A Modern Institution in Need of Reform.* Washington: Ben Simon, 1985.

———. *Shared Fate.* New York: Free Press, 1964.

McRoy, Ruth, and Zurcher, Louis. *Transracial and Inracial Adoptees: The Adolescent Years.* Springfield, IL: Charles C Thomas, 1983.

Morse, B. "Native Indian and Metis Children in Canada: Victims of the Child
    Welfare System." In Verma, Gajendra and Bagley, Christopher (Eds.), *Race
    Relations and Cultural Differences*. London: Croom-Helm, 1983.
Pilotti, Frank J. Intercountry Adoption: A View From Latin America. *Child Welfare*
    64(1): 25–35, 1985.
Sachdev, Paul. *Adoption: Current Issues and Trends*. Toronto: Butterworths, 1984.
Simon, Rita James, and Altstein, Howard. *Transracial Adoption*. New York: Wiley,
    1977.
———. *Transracial Adoption: A Follow-up*. Lexington, MA: D. C. Heath, 1981.
———. *Transracial Adoptees and Their Families*. New York: Praeger, 1987.
United Nations. *Draft Declaration on Social and Legal Principles Relating to the Protec-
    tion and Welfare of Children, with Special Reference to Foster Placement and
    Adoption Nationally and Internationally*. New York: United Nations General
    Assembly Document A/40/998-6 Dec. 1985.
United Nations. *Resolution of the General Assembly 41/85*. New York: U.N. General
    Assembly, 1986.
Young, L., and Bagley, Christopher. "Self-esteem, Self-concept and the Develop-
    ment of Black Identity: A Theoretical Overview." In Verma, G. and Bagley,
    C. (Eds.), *Self-Concept, Achievement and Multicultural Education* (pp. 41–59).
    London: Macmillan, 1982.

INDEX

ABOUT THE CONTRIBUTORS

HOWARD ALTSTEIN is Dean and Professor in the School of Social Work at the University of Maryland. His major research interests are transracial and intercountry adoption. He has co-authored (with Rita Simon) three books on transracial adoption: *Transracial Adoption* (1977), *Transracial Adoption: A Follow-Up* (1981), and *Transracial Adoptees and Their Families* (1987).

CHRISTOPHER BAGLEY is a Professor in the School of Social Welfare, University of Calgary, Calgary, Alberta, Canada. He has written many books and articles on racial identity and achievement among transracially adopted children, including *Race, Education and Identity* (1979).

MONICA DALEN is Professor of Special Education at the Norwegian Post-Graduate College of Special Education in Hosle, Norway.

RENE A. C. HOKSBERGEN is Director of the Adoption Center, Faculty of Social Sciences, University of Utrecht, The Netherlands. Since 1984, he has been Proprietor of the first chair in adoption.

ELIEZER D. JAFFE is a Professor in the School of Social Work at The Hebrew University of Jerusalem, Israel. He has done extensive research in the fields of child welfare and public assistance and is actively involved in formulating adoption policy in Israel.

METTE RORBECH is a researcher with the Danish Institute of Social Research in Copenhagen, Denmark.

BARBRO SAETERSDAL is Professor of Special Education at the Norwegian Post-Graduate College of Special Education in Hosle, Norway.

RITA J. SIMON is a sociologist and University Professor in the School of Public Affairs at the American University, Washington, D.C. In addition to her work on transracial adoption, she has written *The Jury System in America*, *Public Opinion and the Immigrant*, *Women and Crime*, and *The Defense of Insanity*.

MARTIN R. TEXTOR is at the State Institute of Early Education and Family Research in Munich, West Germany. He has written on family issues, marriage and divorce, drug abuse, and adoption.